THE REPAIRING

We have a wonderful set of DVD's to compliment this book at www.AfricaDestiny.com. You can follow Keidi at www.Keidi.biz.

Look for the upcoming documentary film coming in June 2017.
Go to www.TheRepairing.com for more information.
Be sure to sign up for our mailing list.

E-mail me (Keidi@libradio.net) for those who want to have a workshop, personal consultation or other interaction on the spectrum of subjects covered in THE REPAIRING. The telephone number to reach my office directly is 323.902.2919.

Photo is courtesy of Choice Imagery, Baltimore
(www.ChoiceImagery.com)

Contents

THE REPAIRING: Making Reparations Practical

What if Reparations were such a practical idea that we deliberately took the lead and did it for ourselves?

What if we discovered ourselves today at the leading edge of one of the most significant changes in world history to occur in many centuries?

Would you do everything within your power to create the capstone to hundreds of years of our people's tremendous self-sacrifice so that our children and future generations would inherit the most powerful empire that history has ever known?

Introduction

"You have seen how a man was made a slave; you shall see how a slave was made a man." - Frederick Douglass

---

Seizing the Reparations Initiative NOW!

Like a deer caught in the mesmerizing headlights of an approaching truck, there you are on the highway and your gaze if fixated on something rapidly approaching. This is something that you have never seen before, although you know deep in the recesses of your mind that "there is nothing new under the sun." So, your mind scrambles to make sense of this thing that is approaching which seems to be getting more massive with each passing second. You see its approach and at a certain point, your ears have confirmed that what is bearing down upon you is increasing from what was barely a perceptual sound just moments before. Your physical sense of this mass increases as you start to feel the ground rumble under your feet; the increasing diffusion of these sensory perceptions combine to draw you into a trance. Mesmerized you stand there frozen as your senses become ever more excited with this mass which is headed directly at you.

My friend, you have a big problem which you will need to deal with and your time for indecision has expired. Something that has never happened to you before is impending: you are about to be run over by something that can best be the equivalent of a speeding truck which has passed the point that its braking system would spare your catastrophe. You are in the pathway of a historical disaster that you've never experienced and for which you've never been properly instructed by those who know from their own direct experience what is about to happen. You have run out of time and the culture and civilization within which you have become accustomed to living are no longer capable of sustaining your existence or that of your children. What I am attempting to draw attention to has been called "a clash of civilizations," and what you don't know is that so much of what you *have* become accustomed to is now an integral part of your inability to survive the catastrophe which is at hand.

Because this has happened before, this "remaking of world order," and those that have either experienced it firsthand or have examined it forensically toward the aim of preventing it from happening to their kind, they have written about this phenomenon, conducted numerous seminars on the central topics which dissect the nature of the problem, and they have verified that their proposed solutions are viable through extensive field research. This problem of group survival within a global clash for survival is compounded by several key factors which include: demographics, culture, focused awareness, economics, education, family, security, leadership, and healthy living – all of which have unfortunately become disadvantageous for our group interests. African Americans (who for the bulk of this book will be referred to as Afri-Amers) have become that "deer caught in the headlights of an approaching truck." Within this larger report, I will identify an overwhelming number of data points which verify this fact.

We have seen things building to this point of crisis evolving all around us for more than a century. We have examined this in great depth to the point that many viable options to remove ourselves and our children from this danger have come into our understanding. For the deer to exit the roadway and save itself from disaster, the solution may be as simple as to merely take a few brisk leaps in one direction or another; choosing that right direction for the deer leaves it a 50/50 chance of complete success if acted upon within time. For human societal development, things are quite a bit more complicated yet there is still a 50/50 chance that we will implement the right choices within our window of opportunity and thus save ourselves from cultural collapse and race suicide.

I am a long-time journalist, investigative reporter, I've engaged in the biological sciences for most of my life, and as well, I'm deeply educated and involved in the numerous interrelated disciplines of what is referred to as *scientific futurism*. As such, I have spent nearly my whole life looking closely at the evidence of how things work, what verifiable data can be assembled, how others have sought to solve certain existential problems, and how to produce scientific formulas for controlling the outcome of those things which might come under our scrutiny. There are of course, limitations to the capacity of "the scientific method," and it is at the fringes of these limitations where I have found the most compelling space for exploration.

By constantly pushing the boundaries of my understanding, from deep within the incredibly broad spectrum of scientific futurist inquiry across some 15 fields of human engagement, I have come to some very profound and engaging beliefs and understandings about the limits of both individual and societal capability. The more I explore the more minute nuances of solutions-based-engagement, the more I feel driven by a compelling optimism. I have become resolute in my conviction that *abundance* is the primary order of the universe that we inhabit. Tapping that abundance as much as my spirit can allow has become for me, an empowering process that further feeds the drive to explore this pathway with ever more passion.

And so it is that I fully commit the whole of my scientific and experiential genius toward the primary aim of this book, *The Repairing*. It is my most sincere commitment to include within the pages of this book virtually all the avenues by which we shall rescue this noble race for whom this book is being dedicated – African people around the world, some 1.5 billion strong at this stage – and this directly affects this mass of 45.7 million of African heritage who inhabit this nation within which I am domiciled, the United States of America. Further still, this work is intended to be a life raft for millions of Africans from across the global Diaspora, who can be found in large numbers in Brazil, the Caribbean, North, Central and South America, Europe, and elsewhere.

Within this master blueprint for current and future revitalization, we can assure that our prosperity will expand with few limitations. We can create more balanced and harmonic relations within family and community, help our people overcome habits that have led too many of us into chronic illness and premature death. Our plan will further our sense of pride and direct investment in the fate of our African continental homeland, causing our Pan African engagement to increase immensely, thereby gifting all black children with every possibility that their future society will be even more prosperous than that into which they were born. Another of our achievements will be ushering in an era wherein the entire planetary civilization can once again become beneficiary of the wise, empathetic and sustainable leadership which has already been proven "when Black Men ruled the world."

During the course of this book, I will show numerous examples and a mound of data-driven evidence that such responsible *social engineering* does work to great benefit for those who do engage the process. It has worked for us in past eras of oppression and deprivation. We can document rapid and sustainable forward progress in nations like China, Singapore, and most recently Ethiopia and Rwanda. You as an individual, along with your family and community, will see the great benefits of the master blueprint, and this will fill you with a tremendous sense of your competence and capacity to make meaningful change in the world. For those of us who are deeply spiritual in the way we move through our life and times, there can be no greater satisfaction than becoming solidly aware that you are measurably doing *the greatest good* in your life per your tradition of faithful engagement. By every mental, physical and spiritual means necessary, we are a noble people and we aim to prove so now and for all time hereafter.

Becoming Whole Again

As I break down the meaning of the title of this book, "The Repairing," there are several thoughts here. The prefix "re-" denotes a return to a previous state of wholeness; "pair" indicates that some duality is joined together; the suffix "-ing" indicates a progressing state, and the word "repair" is bound to the concept of Reparations. Thus, the whole conceptual meaning of "The Repairing" bridges these and thus serves a broad conceptual framework for the transforming mission toward which we are engaged.

Our *pairing* envisions joining the African family which was scattered over the globe during the holocaust of enslavement, **The Maafa** (Kiswahili for: disaster, calamity, adversity or misfortune), into a single unified (paired) group with this critical mission of reinstating our essential *wholeness*. Our pressing task of correcting the trauma of the devastation of being conquered and taken as prisoners of war, ripped from our homelands, transported into an unknown fate which has persisted for as many as 20 generations, brutalized, exploited and depleted of over 500 years of our laborious wealth – this has become the great mission of our time. Like our use of this terminology of "The Maafa" to refer to this historical catastrophe, in other parts of the world, such as the U.K. and East Africa, many have come to use the term **Maangamizi** to refer to the same process (*Maangamizi*: destruction, annihilation, catastrophe, doom, holocaust).

History, circumstance, and the progress of humanity has brought us to the point that our deliberate efforts can restore a great sense of self-sufficiency, self-determination, unity and dignity for every one of our members, some 1.5 billion strong scattered around the globe. Where our laborers were forced to build up colonial wealth throughout the western hemisphere and beyond, today we are witnessing a great *paradigm shift* wherein the development of immense wealth from our sustained labors is benefitting the long-term, sustainable inheritance of our own younger generations.

This current history, the massive transformation of the global economy, and other factors such as our great demographic advantage, are all coming together toward placing our people on the world leadership stage after having been dethroned as or among the world's most advanced societies during earlier eras of human civilization. This return to highly impacting global leadership could not come at any more critical time than the present. Certain excesses of leadership from other ethnic groups have placed all of humanity and multiple species at the very plausible danger of suffering from one or more *extinction level events*.

Saving Earth from a human-made catastrophe should be among the primary motivations for genuine, holistic African leadership to come to full empowerment. These disasters could come from the continued degradation of the natural environment, nuclear warfare, intentional creation of deadly biological warfare agents, geoengineering (intentional weather modification), cyber warfare along with the highly questionable pursuit of artificial intelligence and robotic warfare.

Part of our sacred mission toward becoming whole again is to correct the greatest lies in history regarding our narrative, the role of spirituality in civilization evolution, balance between the masculine and feminine forces within Nature, as well as deconstructing the caste-based hierarchical system which too often pits groups and people against one another based upon such factors as skin color, height, gender, wealth, education, religion, nationality, age and other arbitrary factors.

To truly be whole again, our great task is to free ourselves and subsequently free humanity from "spiritual and intellectual enslavement" by imposters, pretenders to civilization, imperialists, anti-humanists and homicidal maniacs – the biggest liars, thieves, and murderers to have come to dominate the world in the last 2000 years. This daunting set of tasks should serve as a powerful driving motivation for ours and future generations. That we have been born now, arriving at such a major crossroads in human civilization development, should be regarded as a great and mighty challenge. We should be proud to be members of this generation called upon to complete such a magnificent task for all humanity.

Our Purpose and Our Passion

So, I write to you with a high degree of passion for the months that it will take to complete this task of authoring a master blueprint for advancing the race. I need a great amount of cooperation and collaboration; most certainly, what is being proposed within *The Repairing* is far beyond the capacity of an individual or even a small vanguard to fulfill. I want YOU to take as great a leadership role in this transformation as your sober and creative imagination can envision. Your rewards will be many including increased prosperity for you and your family, security and peace in your neighborhood, greater access to the world through travel, learning and engaging with others of our global family, and assuring that the numerous investments which you already are making yield a much greater *return on investment* than what you have become accustomed to having returned to you for spending habits. You are a winner – I know that and you know that. Now it is up to us to work together so that the entire world will know that for generations to come.

The risk to us as individuals as well as a group can be rightly compared to the example of the deer caught in the headlights of which I spoke earlier. This is indeed a world of tremendous abundance but the strong evidence can be shown to verify that unless we have the right plan, we will continue to be left behind and caught up on the wrong side of a growing wealth divide in the world. Some powerful people are acting as if there could never be enough to feed our children and theirs, and therefore they are prepared to act as ruthlessly as possible to assure that their children will survive and thrive, especially when competing for what they perceive as limited resources and their demographic failings.

The resistance to our self-determined revitalization is ever more brutal, and we have got to stop pretending that it isn't so. We had always warned that there would come a time when our "backs were against the wall" and that we would have to strike out firmly to secure our survival in such a fatalistic hostile situation. Such a moment of decisiveness has arrived and ours is the very generation to prove that we are worthy of inheriting and passing on a sustainable future for our posterity.

Throughout this book, we will make our plans as precise and clear as possible. As much as can be reasonably accomplished, we will show minute details of steps necessary to move us toward our stated aims. I will do my best to convince you to do your detailed research and confirmation that these methods have been proven to work. We will strive to reduce all margins for error and to obliterate indecisiveness so that our actions and expectations can be as seamless as possible. The stakes are much too high when we are considering matters of group survival amidst a global "clash of civilizations." We are aware that multiple civilizations throughout history have appeared on the stage of history only to find themselves no longer viable and thus disappeared from the world – and we must guarantee that this will not happen to us for thousands of years to come. We have already proven to be great and powerful survivors; our legacy of capture into enslavement has already proven the power of our will to survive and thrive. Now we must sober up and apply that willpower toward a new globally integrated society. We cannot again allow integration to crush our ambitions toward self-preservation. Our success must, therefore, become guaranteed!

From the time that you have started to read this text, your subconscious and conscious mind will become more excited over the possibilities within this empowering paradigm shift. You note a heightened awareness of the bounty of resources all around you. Relationships that you have cultivated over your life now begin to take on a new sense of urgency as you continue to imagine how many ways that you can be an important part of this great revitalizing of our people.

Common conversations within which you engage begin to take on more serious intent. You realize even more just how precious your time is and how valuable your leadership is to the vitality of family and community. When you look in the mirror at the start of the day, you find a renewed commitment to do something, as much as possible, each day, which will be meaningful to our self-initiated Reparations. You start to discipline yourself about personal habits, empower your creative capacity with an ongoing study of methods of self-development, seek out new alliances that are complementary to your intentionality, and stride boldly through every daily encounter so that those around you will see your confidence and seriousness. You have returned to your *champion consciousness* at a time when history required that great champions need to arise and take up leadership stations in life.

I cannot overemphasize this point that we have run out of time for indecision. Due to such widespread inattention, distraction, and avoidance of primary responsibility, which has plagued our people for nearly four birth generations within the American society, we are just generations from ethnic cleansing and race suicide. I make these statements with the utmost of sincerity as I have examined this data and confirmed it with numerous experts for more than 25 years. A fate was determined for us, people of African ancestry living within the U.S., as early as the mid-1930s and further confirmed by written documentation from every decade since. As much as we would like to avoid awareness of the direness of our problem, there are powerful and sinister individuals and organizations who want it all for themselves and who perceive that Africans are the least capable of competing against them for the prosperity of ours and our children's generational prosperity.

Because we have dug such a deep cultural hole within which we are being manipulated, exploited, and mutilated, the time for extracting ourselves from this killing zone cannot be delayed even for a day or for another hour. The sooner that we act, the more of our beloved race can be spared the humiliation of being erased from history or confined to the margins of the irrelevance of the meaning of their existence. We are good and noble people and we deserve a place in the future development of humanity just as much as any member of any other ethnic group. Yet, mere words alone will not confirm our future status – we MUST act now or continue to suffer and die.

Everything is *not* lost; all is not dire; we do have much about which to be excited. The mere process of connecting 1.5 billion people of African heritage in a large, global and functional body to compete for the future, itself will be one of the greatest accomplishments in the world in the last 600 years. Engaging this task of restoring ourselves to a state of wealth that we as Africans enjoyed within ancient Egypt, Mali, Songhai, and other powerful empirical nations will extend a tremendous sense of pride and self-esteem to each of our members.

Our babies are born bright, precocious, and a delight to every member of family and community. We need not diminish their life prospects by failing to provide for their nurturing to successful adulthood adequately. We can build for these children and their living grandparents such a brilliant culture and global society that the other enlightened peoples of the world will once again look upon the African with esteem and great appreciation for the status which we have carved out for ourselves in the ever-ongoing competition for prestige, security and national capacity.

There is every reason on Earth for Africans to be optimistic, well-informed as to our capacities, and excited to engage a continuity of tasks which confirm our aspirations to Greatness.

We are indeed a winner, and we won't let nobody hold us back, so we should indeed just "keep on pushin'."

Chapter 1 – Extracting Ourselves from the Pit

"We owe ourselves internal Reparations. We don't have to ask anybody for it. We don't have to beg anybody for it. We don't have to plead to anybody to give it to us. We simply must do two things: we've got to love ourselves more and love our race more; and then we will look inside and do for our self."

- Ken Bridges, Co-Founder of Matah Network

Let me begin our extended conversation with an important confession, one which only those with whom I am the closest are aware of: I have become intolerant of a broad spectrum of dialogs which are centered around Africentricity (interchangeably referred to often as Afrocentric thought, black studies, etc.), black progress and what to do about the fate of Americans of African ancestry. I am no beginner in these conversations. My experiences as a journalist for 49 years, as a member of countless Afrocentric study groups, activist organizations, I'm an internationally-featured lecturer, and have attended dozens of such community forums every year since the early 1990's – these experiences have exposed me to every facet of such dialog to very high degrees. This set of experiences is also underwritten by my broadcast career wherein I've created a catalog of over 5000 archived recordings on virtually every topic with thousands of accredited intellectuals of our generation. I've heard it all and I find myself increasingly bored or frustrated with what I am hearing.

Understandably, not all of what I am hearing is provoking this great frustration. Specific dialogs without appropriate calls to action are particularly troublesome for me. I hear them on talk radio, read them within books, blogs, social media postings, as well as hear the same from too many of the callers who are to be heard during mine or other broadcasters' feedback with their audience. When I say "appropriate calls to action," what I mean are realistic proposals based upon available or accessible resources that are guided by foundational principles that address the heart of what is the problem or challenge at hand.

I have nearly stopped going to lectures because so many are redundant. I have always loved lectures, workshops, and focused community gatherings, partly because I have a great fondness for the community who comes together at such functions. Yet, as an author of so many published solution-oriented positions on so many topics, these lectures don't move me anymore. Too often, it appears to me as if the gatherings are self-serving missives, whereby people who are convinced that their limited knowledge and understanding is the end-all, be-all, merely get together to confirm what they already know. I have come to conclude that too many of those who are presenting are stuck in a box and rather than work to expand the understanding of their audience, merely pander to the audience's self-gratifying tendency to want to hear that they already know what is needed to know.

There is one thing about these public dialogs that is especially disturbing for me. I am particularly fed up with presentations that are based on, or riddled with inaccurate facts. So much of my work over these years has been scientific, and, for those of us who appreciate such, the scientific process demands reliable and replicable data input, analysis, facts and calculation. From the most obscure voices to those at the top of the leadership pyramid, the presentation of what is passed off as "facts" or "evidence" has become shameful within this broader *Black Consciousness movement*. The presenter too often skews facts of history, economics, culture, political reality, demographic trends and other key areas that directly impact our future. This appears to reinforce the perception by both presenter and audience that we already know everything that needs to be known to meet our challenges. Then the question yet remains as to why we then seem to be so inadequate at solving these challenges.

So many of the conversations we witness are driven by hyper *religiosity* and superstition. Like so many of our group born within the western societies, I've come to know religion I was raised within a Christian community, but through my adult explorations, I've spent many years studying other religions, spirituality, faith-centered community organizing, and culture. I regard spiritual expression and the sharing of faith to be among the great positives within the community toward which this work is being addressed. Yet, expressions of religiosity have too often become detached from reality.

Even among many of those who profess to have freed themselves from the constrictions of religious fundamentalism, often what is then represented as a "new reality" is still founded upon pseudo-religious mythology, superstition, and the blending of fable with real history. This also applies to certain of these "New Age" expressions of esoteric mysticism. While I do regard such spiritual expression as a critically important component of social organization and individual expression, there are certainly times when hyper-religiosity interferes with the processes by which we will solve problems.

We are witnessing endless rounds of reactionary finger-pointing at *chimeras* (frightening but mythological fire-breathing dragons) as the source of our shortcomings. There seems to be a convenient boogeyman waiting around every corner to absorb the blame for our individual or group shortcomings. Be it "The Man," "the government," white people, Christianity, Jews, the "Illuminati," feminists, corporations, the media, the police, or a large cast of external entities, it has become all too popular and convenient for loud voices within our community to direct us away from our indigenous *response-ability*, self-reliance and capacity for doing better. Certain of these "race hustlers" are quick to steer us instead into remaining perpetual *victims* to any convenient external sources that have demonstrated past obstacles to our progress.

When we look to members of our community for cooperation, collaboration, and the creativity that we can bring to bear to solve longstanding challenges, too often, what we are met with is widespread malaise, frustration and depression. This is the end consequence of the constant drone of voices perpetuating the victim mentality. Victimization is the *opposite* of what calls us to our greatest human capacity, creativity and a long history of great accomplishment would again achieve. True indeed, sustained poverty, injustice, insufficient development, poor education and a constant stream of negative media imaging can push members of the targeted group into a depressing social and psychological state. Yet, it isn't as if we don't have access to resources that could turn this pessimism around and create momentum for progressive engagement by the group and its members. Despite this widespread malaise, frustration and depression, we would have a great reason for optimism if we could do a better job of aligning to our strengths, talents and resources.

Another of my great frustrations when listening to calls for change is that too often, people are offering up overly-simplistic explanations of complex issues. In the recent past, I published an essay listing the top problems affecting African Americans. The first problem to have made that list was that too many of us don't even understand the complexity of "The Problem." Societies these days are complex, dynamic aggregations of numerous interrelated systems. I have produced extensive research over the years, pointing to this intricately interwoven nature of complex societies.

Our economics, culture, education, health, labor policies, family, community, demographics, transnational relations, and other key factors all directly correspond one to another. As such, explanations or proposed solutions that do not incorporate diverse processes into an integrated strategy for problem-solving are nearly always doomed to failure from the outset. Additionally, as society advances more into technology-centered industrial development, mechanisms of societal function will get even more complex. Our comprehension must expand ever more rapidly alongside this technical progress of society, especially since we Africans are engaging this global contest from a distinct deficit.

Too often, people are blaming "straw men" for causing all or most of our sufferings. By "straw men," I mean invisible, unreachable entities that are all but impossible to isolate and compete against; this can include past events or whole epics of history as well. There is a strong tendency within our accepted leadership to constantly reach for a perceived *common enemy* around which to focus reactionary anger. This is a long-utilized and well-known technique of social manipulation toward the creation of and control over a "herd mentality." It has proven to work on a vast scale throughout society and thus is still widely used today by unscrupulous politicians, fascist governments, demagogues, political parties, and media pundits. Yet, when examined closely for the factual value of such mind-controlling manipulation, the foundation of Truth that can set us free is too-often missing.

I have honestly come to despise the convenient rationalization of "White Supremacy" as a ubiquitous process, dominating all aspects of culture and society. I wrote a book years ago, called **MOVING BEYOND RACE-ISM: NEW STRATEGIES FOR A NEW MILLENNIUM**, wherein I proposed that what we often refer to as "Racism/White Supremacy" is but a subset of a set of social hierarchies that have come to dominate society. These *caste-based hierarchies* include colorism, gender, religion, wealth, educational level, and physicality. Thus, I perceive this thing called "White Supremacy" as a form of "colorism" combined with degrees of other caste hierarchies. As well, using the precise meaning of the words white and supreme linked together, I long ago came to conclude that so much of that which Whites have advanced in the world is not necessarily supreme over what non-Whites have created. I've made this comparison within a broad spectrum of human achievement and civil interactivity.

Thus, from this position, which I came to by the early 1990s, using language which upholds concepts centered around notions of "White Supremacy" nearly always binds us to the very forces from which we supposedly seek to liberate ourselves. I am convinced that "White Supremacists" do exist as individuals (sometimes gathered together for group reinforcement), yet their desperate cry for self-esteem seems to be the very *proof* that they subconsciously suspect that they are not superior to that against which they strive to compete.

It appears that the people who are most in need of highly-functioning knowledge and wisdom are increasingly abandoning literacy, and this is one of the great tragedies of our generation. As a baby boomer, I was born into a generation that built upon the great gains in the functional literacy of the generations that came before ours. Ours could have greater access to libraries, electronically stored information, the

Internet, documentary films, and bookstores with expansive collections of the wisdom of all ages. Yet, during my lifetime, I have seen our advances toward science and literacy reversing within our ethnic grouping within the U.S. Many adults point fingers at youth as problematic regarding failing literacy. I assure any who would take my analysis seriously that the youth inherited this problem just as they have so many other failings of modern society and culture.

We must demonstrate to young people that books are treasure chests full of value with experiences, ideas, logic, values, traditions, and fine details of world history that can be utilized in this time to liberate our tremendous potential. When a society abandons literacy in a widespread manner that we are witnessing all around us, that society has committed itself to degeneration and decay; don't blame this on our youth.

Our supposed "experts" are too often as woefully unprepared as are the people that they propose to serve. I have encountered so many of these individuals and have consistently been disappointed in their lack of appreciation for and comprehension of the complexity of the issues which challenge our generation. We would like to believe that our political, institutional, and community leaders would represent the "best and brightest" of us all. The sad fact is that it has become obvious that this is not the case. Too many have been elevated to positions of authority based on charm and charisma, nepotism, a tendency toward "sucking up to power," back-door deal-making (ahem..., yes, this is proven to include sex-cults) or due to a grip on leadership that is commonly held among secret-oath-takers.

Within certain streams of the conversations that I am frequently witnessing to, the "scarcity principle" dominates over any counterbalancing notion of abundance in the world. In other words, from observing these discussions, one might conclude that: the sky is perpetually falling or that our people "don't got nothin', do nothin'" or know nothin'." Most of the time, when I hear this, if I am in a position to respond, I immediately assume the contrary position.

In an ever-changing world, where abundance yet remains Nature's overriding quality, it serves us best to be better informed than such a pessimistic outlook would presume. Relative to any other large population of Blacks within any nation, Afri-Amers are wealthier per capita, have amassed an incredible range of viable skills, are broadly creative and talented, as well as have a broad spectrum of organizations within which we are valued members; many of these organizations are our own creation. It just seems that, toward the aim of consolidating sorely-needed structures for advancing group self-interest, we are not yet adequately organized. With the toolsets that are available within the larger society which can help to produce exponential growth for organizations savvy enough to apply them, I have become convinced that substantial progress can rapidly occur. We must merely create a much better widespread organization.

Although precisely-organized processes drive progress within any given society, our "team" doesn't readily utilize them towards the specific aim of self-interested problem solving and group advancement. This book intends to identify these processes, available resources, newly-appearing and disruptive trends, as well as to spark that creative innovation that *does* flow through our demographic. We will at all points within this report refer to formulas that are utilized by other self-developing groups, including one very precise script for the process called "social engineering" that was laid out by a university professor more than 80 years ago.

There have been no small numbers of social scientists who have examined our group, our distinct history, our strongest qualities, as well as our long stream of failures and setbacks. This is why maintaining a high level of literacy is so very key to group advance. As models, formulas, strategic pathways, tactical steps and prior examples for sustainable development are to be found in so many libraries, and it shames our group to witness the near-collapse of literacy due to distraction from a constant stream of "electronic variances," a concept based upon temporal distraction which was explored in my 1996 book **MIND CONTROL**.

It is increasingly all too apparent that many of our people are having a hard time separating reality from imagination, or to the contrary, successfully integrating *creative* imagination into reality. We display many behaviors and habits which, in the long run, produce outcomes wherein we are weaker, less engaged in productive organizing, more easily distracted, angry and reactive. By using our creative intelligence more responsibly, these degenerative pathways can be reversed, and a new culture of success propagated within our communities.

There are so many things that we have come to hold dear and valuable over the long course of our *Maafa* journey of enslavement, such as religious zealotry, dietary madness, excessive political liberalism, failure to accept our natural physical features, pop-culture trendiness, sexual license and worse. These new behaviors have introduced extremely toxic and destructive elements into our collective culture. The religion we celebrate undermines our spirituality. "Soul Food" creates widespread chronic disease among those who most consume it. Clinging to Democratic Party liberalism has made our political demographics almost completely irrelevant. Our group spends billions of dollars annually toward dubious efforts not to be recognizable as people of African genetic heritage with coarse hair, broad noses, dark skin, thick lips and fine hips. These maladaptive behaviors persist.

So many of our race chase one media-promoted consumer obsession after another, constantly in search of elusive self-esteem and confidence. As well, buying into myths of black sexual prowess, originally pinned upon us to undermine our humanity, has increasingly risen to destroy the very fabric of relationships, family, community and nationhood. These and other patterns of reactive *conditioned behavior* have coalesced to make weak people out of those whose history, when correctly examined, would have us evolving otherwise.

There is just so much more to add to this list of social woes that have created this tragic pit from which we seek to extract ourselves. We must admit to a terrible crisis of intergenerational misunderstanding, distrust and lack of cooperation. This generation gap is not just between generations labeled as "the Greatest Generation," "Baby Boomers," Generation X," or "Millennials" – we can also identify gaps of continuity between generations which struggled to defeat Jim Crow, migrated to industrialize America's cities, struggled to great sacrifice to secure civil, economic and judicial rights, fought to overcome urban decay and police militarization against our youth, as well as fought to educate ourselves into higher income and wealth that would uplift the extended family and community.

Today, too few of us are aware that "there is a river" which ties these generations of struggle together. Today, too many believe that theirs is the single greatest battle that we have ever fought. Today, most of us are unaware of grave dangers that face us now and in the near future.

So many people within our group, as well as within the larger society, are sick all the time, and it appears that we have yet to develop an appropriate plan for getting whole again. At the time of this writing, the nation, and our ethnic group is in the grip of a mass of disturbance over the disproportionate rate of police homicides against our youth. Fueling this blazing fire is the regular presentation of video evidence confirming the abuses to which we have long suffered but too often lacked convincing proof other than the integrity of our testimony. Corporate-controlled mass media, ever eager to exploit an attention-grabbing headline story, pushes these incidents in our face with relish as they also fuel an opposing point of view with equal fervor.

During this same time, I have pointed out that if it were truly a matter of survival based upon life-threatening data, we would be focusing far, far more attention on the number of homicides committed by the medical-pharmaceutical industries whose annual toll of "death-by-doctor" towers over police homicides by an overwhelming ratio of 900-to-1; these figures include Americans of all ethnicities. Separating black *iatrogenic* deaths from the rest of the population, this amounts to an estimated 170,000 who die each year from inappropriate contact with medical industries.

What makes this even more frustrating is that our contact with killer medicine is largely driven by our group's tendencies toward poor diet, lack of exercise, exposure to toxic products, addiction to legal drugs, medical illiteracy and quiet compliance with medical industries. We have become moved to *voluntarily* cue up for a killer medical cartel complex that irresponsibly snuffs out an estimated 3269 of our members weekly, while U.S. law enforcement agencies will kill about 9 Blacks each week during this same year. Somehow these statistics have convinced me that our priorities are out of balance when it comes to matters of life-threatening dangers.

I trust that you might as well conclude that, to too great an extent, we are overly driven and motivated by media hype and propaganda as well as consumer marketing. A programmed mentality is spreading like a raging virus among our members, weakening our resolve to resist exploitation and distracting us from those things that should be allotted highest priority for the group's sustainable development.

One cannot underestimate the power of psychological operations that have been developed to direct the responses of the target groups. We have among our members no small numbers who seemingly understand the need to resist psychological manipulation. Still, our best evidence of understanding is the mass of behavior that we can identify. As such, as a member of the group, I must confess that we have become weakened and vulnerable to constant streams of mind-controlling communications, assaulting our members from every conceivable direction. Because many of us have taken the time to study this brainwashing, we must marshal our creative intelligence toward achieving a more beneficial outcome using specially-designed cultural communications, social media and all "electronic variances" which would come under our control.

In this sustained and constant state of cultural weakness, we have become superficial and irrelevant to vital mechanisms of societal advancement. Blacks were brought to America and other nations against their will because we were regarded as an ideal source of "cheap and inexhaustible labor." When threats from unequal birthrates first began to be considered by American demographers in the 1930s, there arose a new priority to replace us as such a low-cost labor force eventually. During WWII, as the nation mobilized for total war, our highly-valued labor became one of the absolute keys to America's industrial might. As such, this is how America rose to economic, military and political dominance in the decades that followed the end of that war.

New priorities arose in more recent decades, and this nation's scions of industry realized that they could outsource the high-cost labor to less expensive parts of the planet. Left behind, the urban black population now devolved into what these industrialists and their social scientists increasingly referred to as "redundant labor" and "useless leaders." We failed at raising from amongst our midst a leadership cadre that truly understood these trends and was prepared to create an appropriate pathway to guide our people away from the edge of this economic, political and social abyss. We have thus increasingly found ourselves irrelevant and mentally depressed because we are so unappreciated within America. This trend is still worsening as each decade passes, especially since our demographic and fertility advantage has begun to diminish within the broad face of America's ethnic tapestry.

Writing this introductory chapter so far is exhausting. Yet, this exercise is necessary because there is a very important point that I am striving to set up: We are in desperate need of real and tangible change. The group has a right to exist and members of the group should feel an obligation to be responsible for the group's survival and sustainable advancement. We have grown to become all too unappreciative of ourselves and our great potential to return to being powerful change-agents for our self-interests along with the progress of the nations within which we find ourselves. We are damned if we cannot appreciate our immense set of experiences, creative tendencies, inventiveness, talents, acquired skills and physical abilities that should all combine to make us a powerful, competitive group.

Our population numbers, most recently stated as upwards of 45.7 million within the United States, to which is included some 2 million talented and high-achieving continental Africans residing within this country, would rank us as the 32nd largest nation on Earth, placing us about the equivalent population size of Spain, Colombia, Kenya, Ukraine or Argentina. Throughout this report, I will use several of these equivalencies to put into perspective the great potential that should be expected of us once we "get our act together."

We thus commence to repairing ourselves

As Eldridge Cleaver famously said, "You're either part of the solution or part of the problem."

We *must* focus our vast spectrum of resources towards the strategic vision of creating a global transformation that becomes our living legacy. We should revive development models from within the periods of greatest accomplishment within the history of our Noble Race. Our youth should not only know the biographies of these great leaders but should also be expected by all to become even higher accomplishing than those who came before them whose actions gifted this race with immense pride through achievement.

Each child should be encouraged to stand before the community and recite their own personal council of *ancestral advisors*. I have used this inspiring process for decades. My council includes Harriet Tubman, Sojourner Truth, Frederick Douglass, Booker T. Washington, Marcus Garvey, Ida Wells-Barnet, George Washington Carver, Madame C.J. Walker, Mary Mcleod Bethune, Malcolm X, Martin L. King Jr., in addition to my talented parents and the one grandfather I've known. There are just so very many historical figures who are on record as highly-accomplishing ancestors, along with living elders who have risen from our unique historical experience to inspire our people to ever-greater achievement.

We have available, to our great advantage, a magnificent and inspiring history. We have awe-inspiring talents and innovative minds among us. Our present circumstance compels us to develop an equally brilliant *master blueprint* for individual and group elevation and sustainable development. As well, we are a global people. Beyond the borders of the United States, emanating from every direction around the world, especially from our African homeland, we are consistently demonstrating high levels of accomplishment, resource abundance, demographic advantage, rich cultural legacy, and the enduring spirit of fortitude when faced with immense challenges. We already have everything we need as a people. We have now come to the point where we recognize our need to commit to and commence with numerous processes for repairing ourselves and our condition.

There is another very important point to make here, which will be reinforced throughout the book. The process of *Reparations* as most people perceive it would be an accomplishment; once engaged, it is to be completed and signed off as done. For our purposes, *The Repairing* is an ongoing, organic process that will have no precise completion but will continue to build upon its successes, replenishing its momentum through each generation. This is analogous to the often-cited idea that "Life is not about the destination, it is about the journey," – Reparations is regarded as an accomplishment while *The Repairing* is our journey of transformation which must never cease. As such, while many could become frustrated that Reparations has gained so little traction among culpable nations and international organizations like the United Nations, to the contrary, *The Repairing* is an ascending pathway which we should be engaging every day of our lives, always with the idea that we are continually scaling it up to where it has a permanent and transforming global impact.

Your mind, body, and soul, committed to this *massive transforming purpose,* become both agents and evidence of this movement. **THE REPAIRING** becomes the guiding pathway for our "journey of a thousand miles" upon which we keep stepping, stepping, stepping in rhythm – headed toward our distant goal.

Chapter 2 – The Nine Foundations for Reparations

"I am not tragically colored. There is no great sorrow dammed up in my soul, nor lurking behind my eyes... Even in the helter-skelter skirmish that is my life, I have seen that the world is to the strong regardless of a little pigmentation, more or less. No, I do not weep at the world—I am too busy sharpening my oyster knife."

– Zora Neale Hurston

Contrary to many from my generation who have enjoined the struggle for Reparations, I have very little expectation that America's legislatures, politicians, corporations or other responsible entities will take our century-old demand for reparatory compensation seriously. The tragic fact is that most Afri-Amers similarly don't take this demand seriously enough even to study the detailed nuances of what would entail a Reparations remedy. I will avoid citing the broad spectrum of ill-informed responses that are frequently expressed when the topic of Reparations is raised. Let us herein examine these nine key areas for corrective actions that have been advanced by those who have long championed this cause. We are obligated to repair the debilitating damage that has been done. Inattention to this repair negatively impacts the status of our group across our past and within the present. We must reverse the debilitation that is handicapping our future.

I strive to consistently acknowledge and appreciate those who have organized for Reparations over the past century, many of them actively organizing long before I was even alerted to the topic myself. There have been numerous organizations, individuals, authors, attorneys, politicians, religious leaders, journalists, community activists and grassroots organizers who have raised the demand for Reparations in the past and continue to do so today. While I don't allocate herein the space to name those whose work has inspired and influenced me as I have grown into the Reparations movement, there are some of these activists with whom I have become close over the past few decades. To these friends, colleagues, elders and ancestral spirits who have championed this cause, I trust that this work meets your approval. I will do my best to incorporate your guidance into my comprehension of this need to get to the resolution of achieving Reparations for our people.

The nine areas for the focus of Reparations which we will discuss in more detail, could each easily take up an entire volume for publication, yet I will strive to be as concise as possible in describing these areas. Throughout the entire book, these will serve as the foundations by which we will create practical avenues for correction and advancement. These nine areas for Reparations encompass: 1) Compensation for Stolen Labor; 2) Land Recovery; 3) Family and Community; 4) Economic Development; 5) Education; 6) Revising our Historical Perspective; 7) Transnational Relations; 8) Repairing our Health Status; 9) Crime and Justice.

Throughout this book, each of these broad categories will be further broken down into numerous subcategories and tangential themes for further narrow-focus. As stated previously, in the limited space of this book and the time allocated for its publication, I can only be so comprehensive. Numerous volumes have been previously published which can provide greater insights into specific areas of injury. Undoubtedly, many more studies will follow which address these same critical areas of group self-interest and community development. Our greatest priorities herein are to excite you the reader, issue very specific calls-to-action, and to generate momentum through specific tactical steps that contribute to sustainable growth and development in the direction of our stated goals.

Another key point about these nine foundations is that they are listed in the order in which they appeared in my recollections and should not be prioritized in any manner which is exclusive of the others. So often people have claimed that economics, education, health, security or otherwise are each more important than the others. This isolation is a tragic and consistently non-productive error. What we absolutely must generate is a *cumulative solution,* whereby all of our initiatives reinforce each other across a spectrum of corrective actions. Better economics without education will have us remaining irrational consumers. Better education without health will drain our people of intergenerational transfer of wealth. Access to more land without developing the labor to bring it into productivity will empower the working class of others with whom we are often in competition. Revising our historical perspective while ignoring our transnational, global presence, will only deepen our isolation and vulnerability.

Our methods must be comprehensive. They need to entail an understanding of synergistic relationships spanning all of these nine foundations. Orchestration of our efforts must properly allocate resources across this spectrum to achieve a masterful and grand blueprint for group elevation. The stakes for the future are much too high for us to continue a long streak of historical failures.

Let us look closer at these nine challenges that compel our commitment toward accomplishing *The Repairing*.

1) Compensation for Stolen Labor

How could we possibly go about the task of calculating the immeasurable cost of the stolen labor and the immeasurable grievances committed against tens of millions of persons enslaved, brutalized, robbed, lynched, unjustly incarcerated, displaced and otherwise abused by the centuries-long suffering of our African ancestors brought to *just this land* of America from the early 17th Century onward? While it is nearly an impossible debt to assess comprehensively, we can establish a set of protocols that will allow us to construct a formula with which we can produce a *reasonable* figure for this portion of Reparations debt due. A few years back, I worked to determine this figure. At that time, I concluded then that Reparations due for the unpaid labor of these enslaved Afri-Amers amounted to $14.6 trillion at a minimum. I have since focused deeper on various particulars of this unpaid labor formula and accordingly, as you will see shortly, have significantly upgraded the bill due to satisfy compensation for this historic transfer of wealth.

Considerations which figured into the updated formula that I've created include:

- We have recent examples of citizens wronged by government agencies, law enforcement, or the judiciary, who were compensated for each year of abuse, suffering and incarceration that followed unjust jailing. Some of these published accounts show compensation rates for being locked away to amount to a reasonable average of about $30,000 per year, yet recognizing that this is just for unjustified *confinement*, not extending to torture, abuse and forced labor without compensation. For our formula, this figure will stand.

- Calculating the total number of Africans who were enslaved in America during the period of chattel slavery was a difficult task. We can find projections that 10 to 12 million Africans were kidnapped and deposited in the western hemisphere, some 650,000 of whom made it to the Colonies, which formed the U.S. from as early as 1640. At the time that the USA declared independence, 1776, the population of enslaved Africans was estimated at 500,000 but by 1860, the U.S. Census estimated that they had grown to nearly 4 million. A cumulative total of enslaved Blacks in this nation is harder to research but a reasonable deduction, based on generational lifespan, might put our estimate at 12 to 15 million or more, the *median* of which we shall use at 13.5 million.

- What was the average life expectancy of an enslaved person in the U.S.? Largely due to high infant mortality and early death due to exhaustion and violence, life expectancy for enslaved Blacks in the U.S. was only 30 years, 17% shorter than the general population. Thus, to generate this formula for total labor Reparations due, since slavery was generally a life-long condition, compensation for every year of life is central to our calculation of the unpaid debt due to the individual, whose lifetime compensation in today's dollars would have been at the very least $900,000. Today, those with associate college degrees are estimated to earn $1.1 million in their lifetime while those with advanced degrees can expect to earn an average of $1.8 million. Understandably, our calculations err on the conservative side, especially when we consider that enslaved persons were expected to work from sun up to sundown, six days a week with minimal breaks during the workday, likely exceeding 60 hours of labor weekly during their prime laborious years.

- How many legally emancipated Freedmen were kidnapped and forced into slavery with the tacit support of government agencies? It is a fact that thousands of Blacks were snatched off the streets and transported into slaving territories. Snatching Freedmen was increasingly problematic after the federal government passed the **Fugitive Slave Act of 1793**. This was called the "Reverse Underground Railroad," and it was prevalent in cities such as New York and Philadelphia. It was reported that over a hundred such kidnappings of men, women and children occurred in Philadelphia within just one two-year period. Children were particularly victims of such kidnappings. The U.S. Supreme Court's infamous **Dred Scott decision of 1857** further reinforced the federal government's collusion with institutionalized slavery.

- The single greatest input of the Reparations Due bill is unpaid interest on the lifetime compensation that was rightly-due to enslaved persons who were never paid for their labor. Because this yet remains an unpaid debt, the wealth generated from this uncompensated labor was never passed on to subsequent generations. Beyond mere unpaid labor, modern courts would additionally award for pain and suffering brought about because of such cruel inhumanity – unfortunately, that is a figure that we cannot adequately factor into our equation. Assuming a moderate interest rate of 5% on an unpaid debt, accumulating merely from the end of the era of enslavement, this will produce a stupendous outcome. If we use today's dollar equivalence, just one person, enslaved and unpaid for 30 years at an annual compensation of $30,000 (in today's dollars), would also have earned compound interest (just as the very same type of debt obligations that you and I are held to). Thus, today that unpaid $900,000, accumulating at a modest interest rate of 5% from 1860 to date, would have accumulated an unpaid debt balance of $1.818 billion per person. This calculation is a conservative estimation of Reparations debt due to the descendants of each one of those who were violated. Seeing that each of our families have at least one ancestor who was enslaved, this labor and interest compensation should make Afri-Amer households the wealthiest ethnicity in the nation. But our wealth was steered into the coffers of others.

- How much money was made in profits from the centuries-long trafficking in humans as commodities? Between 1800 and the beginning of the end of the enslavement period in 1860, the auction price of an enslaved human increased on average from $1300 to $3000. All along the slave industry chain, there were profits to be made. Profiteering in human trafficking included trading captured prisoners on the African continent and reselling them at the departure points for the Trans-Atlantic voyage, as well as including the seaports, shippers, insurers, auction houses, moneylenders as well as those who manufactured boats and equipment which all supported the human trafficking. There are also to be considered the railroads, construction industries, fabrics manufacturers, sugarcane industries and other wholesale industrial sectors whose profit margins were dependent upon this base of uncompensated labor.

- Using a complex formula which incorporates a cumulative estimate of 13.5 million enslaved Blacks in the U.S. since the nation's independence; a fair-labor annual compensation in modern dollars of $30,000 per year; an average of 30 years of life spent enslaved; 5% compounding interest on $900,000 in unpaid debt which has now accumulated for 156 years since emancipation began in 1860; as well as the profits made by those who profited as stakeholders in the inhuman trafficking – my *determinately-conservative* calculation of the Reparations-due bill for enslaving Africans within the U.S. between 1776 and 1860 equals an astounding **24.57 trillion dollars**.

Which institutions benefited from the slave trade?

This stunning figure of $24.57 trillion debt due for uncompensated slave labor, and again I reiterate that this is unquestionably a very conservative calculation, must be considered in the context that such *value* is not merely hypothetical. As we consider how the profits extracted from stolen labor recycled throughout the global economy, this debt might be compounded many times over. This money has dispersed to all corners of the complex U.S. economic system, to governments (federal, state and municipal), wealthy families, corporations, private businesses, banking industries, insurance, transportation, agriculture, armaments, railroads, fabrics, as well as colleges and universities along with the media – slavery was one of the most fundamental cornerstones of America's rise to the pinnacle of global wealth and power. As well, the monies extracted from the unholy institution underwrote Europe's place in the history of the global economy, especially in the deep economic ties between the U.S., Britain, France, Spain, Portugal and other enslaving colonial powers.

Corporations that have persisted to date whose foundations have been identified as part of this unholy institution include some of the biggest names in American and international industry. These include (but most certainly are not limited to): Lehman Brothers, Aetna, Inc., JPMorgan Chase, New York Life, Wachovia Corporation/Wells Fargo, NM Rothschild & Sons Bank, Norfolk Southern, E.W. Scripps & Gannett, FleetBoston, CSX, the Canadian National Railway Company, Brown Brothers Harriman, Brooks Brothers, Barclays Bank, AIG and others. Predictably, these companies have their economic tendrils thrust into virtually every facet of the broader modern economy. These are just some of the institutions whose coffers contain our Reparations monies.

Toward empowering our own hand, it would serve our group self-interests to develop some means of a public outing of these companies' disgraceful legacy in capitalizing off the great misery of our ancestors who were enslaved. Putting together well-defined sanctions would be suitable for the aim of creating the right climate for compensation. Many of these companies provide products and services which are not even vital to our economic well-being. While others might be more needed for our continued development, still we can transform our relationship with these companies to be more complimentary with our pathway toward self-determination.

Another aspect of my perspective on dealing with the culpability of these merchants of human suffering is to disengage, divest, seek other partners, or create parallel institutions to eliminate their further profiting from exploiting our members. This strategic shift is the essence of the larger reportage, vision and tactical implementation for this book's effort.

Paradigm Shift – Creating black wealth from black labor

In the spring of 2014 (6254 KMT), in preparation for a 3-minute presentation at a youth leadership development conference at Morehouse College in Atlanta, I created an outline entitled *Paradigm Shift*. The central focus of the document is reasserting the power of black labor as a long-valued economic resource. In the two years that followed that document, I have returned frequently to this theme of black labor valuation as well as expanding on this Paradigm Shift as a powerful wave that can move us firmly and rapidly in the direction of self-determination and sustainable development.

Let me share this brief outline herein again:

PARADIGM SHIFT

1. **Definition – Paradigm**: a theory or a group of ideas about how something should be done, made, or thought about. Paradigm Shift is a dramatic change in the paradigm of a scientific community or a significant change in the paradigm of any discipline or group

2. Malcolm X said in the noted speech **Message to the Grass Roots**, "Of all of our studies, history is most qualified to reward our efforts." One hundred years ago, and beyond, the value of black labor built the most powerful agriculture-based economy that modern history has recorded spanning North and South America along with the Caribbean.

3. Our **agricultural genius** brought rice farming to the U.S., who used our expertise to become, at one point, the world's leading rice exporter.

Additionally, the genius of just one black botanist and inventor, George Washington Carver, saved endangered southern agriculture when he introduced the science of crop rotation, America's first scientific approach to sustainable ecology.

4. A hundred years ago, Blacks controlled nearly **six times the amount of farmland than they do today**. Historically, ancient African agricultural mastery served as the foundation for the rise of human civilization. It was the economic value of black agricultural and industrial labor that allowed the U.S. to rise to become the wealthiest nation on Earth. Land for development is traditionally the basis of the wealth of nations.

5. After World War One, **Blacks migrated away** from terrorism, which plagued us in the nation's agricultural south, leaving for industrial centers such as New York, Philadelphia, Washington, Detroit, Chicago, Kansas City, Baltimore, Pittsburg, and others. During WWII, it was the total mobilization of this black labor force which allowed this nation to become the economic superpower that rose to dominate the world.

6. Beginning in the 1980s, there has been a **paradigm shift in American capitalism** and, toward the pursuit of profits, corporations increasingly betrayed the urban industrial workforce and shifted manufacturing to areas of the world with low-cost, high-value labor. As well, they allowed the increase of cheap immigrant labor into this country largely to displace black labor, which was now costlier.

7. For large numbers of **black laborers left behind** as industry deserted the cities, a new illicit economy rose to supply the sustenance voided by these now-deserting factories, which had served us for generations. Accompanying this now-overwhelming cash flow drawn from drug-fueled escapism, came ultra-violence, superstition, religious fantasy, and the valuation of superficiality over substance – We started "faking the funk."

8. Most young people have **little understanding of the macro-economics** that drive whole societies. Black youth have been referred to as "redundant labor" and "useless eaters" within the highest levels of national power. We cannot risk another generation falling from its former place as the most valuable labor resource in America. We now have insights, resources, skills, and opportunities to reverse this degenerating course and recover the power of valued black labor.

9. 12 of the **35 fastest growing economies** in the world today are African or black Caribbean nations. In just the agricultural sector, it is expected that Sub-Sahara African agribusiness will triple in yearly production over the next 15 years to provide $660 billion of new annual revenue for the global economy. In other sectors, similar growth is being forecast. How much of those trillions of new global dollars do we plan to acquire?

10. Now we see the reason to **pool our money, invest in rural properties, build facilities** on our land with our own trained workforce, and create industries from farming to high tech sectors. That is when we will be the primary directors of our economic fate and then this nation and the world will once again recognize the awesome power of Back Labor and Black Wealth.

I left the Morehouse College campus that weekend quite disheartened by what I witnessed at the leadership conference and most of what was said by those who shared the podium. Still, I have remained convinced that this focus on labor productivity, land, agribusiness, and self-determining development is valuable, much-needed and practicable toward our sustainable growth and development. When we accurately assess the spectrum of resources available in abundance from within and among our group – resources that have proven over the long run to add lasting institutional value – it is our creative and engaging labor productivity that stands out as our greatest asset. We can now tap this labor resource for the spectacular Paradigm Shift immediately ahead.

2) Land Recovery & Development

We do exist as a People, distinctly identifiable as such, and thus should be accorded all the rights, responsibilities, and valuation as such. As a people, we must also own and control sufficient real estate to produce for our group's members those things that are needed for our sustenance and survival. Land, along with labor, is the basis of economics, wealth, society and civilization. Land belonging to individuals of our group, to families, community-serving organizations and our business enterprises, is thus a very critical component of our existence as well as a measurement of our ability to adapt and survive.

Unfortunately, when it comes to land ownership and development, things have not been going well for Afri-Amers over the past century. Compared to land ownership and tenure in the aftermath of the Reconstruction period, where we made significant gains in land acquisition and development, we are currently doing very poorly. Examining land tenure records from 1912 in comparison to what is under our control today, some 85% of our collective land under control has been lost in the past century. This single metric alone is enough to predict doom for our group's economic status over the remainder of the 21st Century and beyond. We have got to become aware of the factors which led to this great loss of land and how this single factor continues to produce more significant challenges as the problem of land deprivation persists.

One of the greatest factors which influenced not only land loss but also much of our cultural transformation was the Great Migration away from the lands of the South where racial segregation, Reconstruction economics, and strong fertility all forced us to acquire and develop agricultural and industrial real estate for more than a half-century after emancipation. Due to multiple factors, such as racist terrorism, unfair trade conditions, limited opportunity for education, entrenched poverty, and the lingering ghosts of the brutal past, a huge wave of migration from southern farmlands into northern, mid-west and western cities skyrocketed after the First World War disrupted society.

From 1916 until as late as 1970, more than 6 million people of African ancestry left the rural south and embarked upon journeys that ended in the northern cities, Chicago, Detroit and Cleveland in the Midwest, and as far as California and other western states. Cities such as New York, Los Angeles, Philadelphia, Baltimore, Pittsburg, Detroit, St. Louis, Gary and many others became primary destinations whose black populations swelled because of migration driven by the huge demand for unskilled industrial labor. While this trend served our masses within this nation for decades, the impact of abandoning so much agricultural land has now proven to have created a great deficit to the group.

We can compare U.S. Census surveys for Afri-Amer farmland ownership as it changed between the years 1910 and 1997. The data shows that Afri-Amer land ownership declined from a peak of 15 million acres in 1910 to 2.4 million acres in 1997 – A dramatic decline of 84% in less than 90 years. Other estimates have projected that Blacks owned as much as 16 to 19 million acres of rural land, to include non-farmed properties. Today, we are generally estimated to be about 13% of the national population, yet Afri-Amers own less than 1% of the nation's privately-owned rural land. As of this writing, black-owned rural property, most of which is owned by non-farmers, is still being lost at a dramatic rate of up to 50,000 acres a month. [1]

Today overall numbers still show that the highest numbers of Blacks within the U.S. occupy Southern states such as South Carolina, Georgia, Alabama, Mississippi, and Louisiana. Yet, for more than half of the 20th Century, our northern and westward migrations produced for us decades of urban demographic domination in many cities. Northern municipalities such as New York City, Cook County (Chicago), Los Angeles, Philadelphia, Baltimore, Detroit, Flint, and Columbus all amassed large concentrations of black residents. Southern urban centers of significant black populations included Memphis, Washington, Dallas, Birmingham, Atlanta, Montgomery, Jackson, New Orleans, Baton Rouge and Norfolk.

---

[1] What is African-American Land Ownership? By Miessha Thomas, Jerry Pennick and Heather Gray, Federation of Southern Cooperatives Land Assistance Fund, 2004

In many of these municipalities, black population numbers and geographical concentration generated decades of political dominance, producing black mayors, council members, police and fire chiefs, county commissioners, state, and national elected officials. This all culminated in a great degree of influence and prominence within a spectrum of political and social arenas. Such demographic representation created a sort of "Golden Age" for black urban life which resulted in a period of unprecedented advance for our political engagement, education, income and wealth, as well as advance in access to community services.

For many, it would have appeared that we had made it in America and would be forever unleashed from the societal shackles which had bound us during and after enslavement. There even arose in more recent years talk of "erasing the color line." Despite the election in 2008 of an African American president, there has remained little justification to dismiss racial identity as a factor in determining status and power within the U.S.

Many black communities lived as if this bounteous period would last forever. Because of rising prosperity, more and more of our members adopted cultural behaviors that mimicked those of Euro-Americans. One of the more tragic new patterns which rose within our community was the consolidation of a wealth hierarchy accompanied by a failure to cultivate value and worth among the have-nots of our race. We stopped caring about each other the way that we had been forced to be supportive under the constrictions of exclusionary Jim Crow conditions. Even though increasing income and opportunity was coming to members of our race, gaps in income and wealth became more apparent and the rapid expansion of a desperate urban underclass rose like a cancerous malignancy from deep within our communities.

This toxic reality was partially propagated by external forces that resented how black concentrations had come to dominate real estate in closest proximity to the centers of metropolitan economic power. Having to witness our hungry and seething faces daily as they commuted in from the suburbs to capture their paychecks became too much for many of these suburbanites, who might have thought that they had escaped their insecurity around large concentrations of Blacks.

A remarkable confession occurred in March 2016 from U.S. Transportation Secretary Anthony Foxx during a presentation at the *Center for American Progress*. He admitted to his audience that in the first 20 years of the federal interstate highway system construction, 475,000 families and well over a million Americans had been displaced by the construction of the highways and that the majority of them were "low-income people of color in urban cores." [2] His revelation exposed how multiple federally-directed urban infrastructure projects have in the past and to date contributed to isolation, inequality and poverty.

Urban renewal and the breaking up of communities not only continues but seems to have increased the pace of displacement of black urban populations who held significant sway over metropolitan affairs for much of the past century. Under various descriptions, such as "urban renewal," "revitalization," "empowerment zones," and "gentrification," this process moves steadily forward changing neighborhoods from majority-black populations into mixed ethnicity, increasingly dominated by young urban professionals, a disproportion of them Whites.

This new urban revitalization phenomenon follows a half-century of "white flight" from the cities to the suburbs and the concurrent deindustrialization of America's urban cores. As white people fled the cities for the suburbs, at first industry also relocated to where its dominant workforce was more conveniently found. Later, these industries began relocating to low-cost labor markets overseas and America largely shifted to a service-oriented economy dominated by financial services. As such, the urban core has now become the place to be for young professionals seeking a career in a new economy.

Unbearable traffic jams moving the working population back and forth between the core economic centers and suburban housing ultimately led to an increased rate of gentrification. In many cities, black communities became vulnerable to a spectrum of challenges which devalued the real estate, disrupted the continuity of political power, shut down schools, and incarcerated large numbers of resident youth, all of

---

[2] Top Infrastructure Official Explains How America Used Highways to Destroy Black Neighborhoods, by ALAN PYKE MAR 31, 2016 / ThinkProgress.org

which increasingly serves to force long-time residents away from neighborhoods which produced an economic boom for their grandparents' generation.

The now-dominant financial services economy served up a particularly nasty set of home lending policies that moved many working-class Blacks out to suburban "Bantustans" through predatory lending that served to not only remove stable-income-households from urban cores but also disproportionately saddled this new group of urban-to-suburban migrants with housing costs that would ultimately prove unmanageable.

These contrary trends of urban revitalization versus suburban Bantustans culminated in a wealth transfer that, during the worst of the financial crisis from 2007-2012, resulted in the transfer of an estimated $260 billion in real estate equity from "minority" families in the U.S. to an omnipotent banking hierarchy. America's mainstream financial industries had created a spectrum of exotic instruments into which it poured all manners of lending arrangements. This resulted in the greatest seizure of wealth from our people since the times of enslavement and Jim Crow. Making this grand theft even more bitter, the national government, through the Federal Reserve, lent this same banking hierarchy *trillions of dollars* in bail-out money at near-zero interest, yet only a tiny and ineffective trickle of federal support ended up helping black families to save their homes. Even for many of those who managed to stay in their home loans, they had been drained of their *perceived* home equity wealth.

As I write, there is another major land-loss challenge facing the largely African-descended population of the Carolina Sea Islands, the Gullah/Geechee people. The Gullah people represent the most distinct surviving cultural groups of Blacks within the U.S. Their ancestral lands have been held and shared in an informal system which made them accessible to all members of the extended family; a system which they call "Heir's Property." Of recent, corporate developers have been using legal loopholes to pick away at this land and bulldozing their traditional inheritance. These investors plan to replace Gullah family lands with golf courses, resorts and condominiums. This may be the single most critical current challenge to all Blacks in the U.S. regarding maintaining real estate integrity.

Within this book, we will often return to this topic of the value of our real estate tenure for the group's self-interest. We will explore practical solutions such as our eight years of experience assisting the development of rural Kujichagulia Villages. As well, we must develop workable proposals for innovation zones within the urban cores wherein we still can create a window of opportunity to secure a strong presence within the nation's largest metropolitan areas. My studies have followed the closure of over 400 school campuses in predominantly black urban areas since 2009 in just seven cities: Chicago, New York, Detroit, Baltimore, Washington, Philadelphia, and Kansas City. These facilities are being sold off at a mere fraction of their true real estate value. There should be nothing to stop us from creating the type of urban real estate development strategies that would capture such properties and repurpose them as innovation zones wherein our young urban professions could reside as they begin post-college careers. The only thing which has been lacking is proper planning, investment and development.

Although so much of what I have described thus far reflects a painful history for which too many of us have succumbed to a perpetual victim mentality, this book is being composed from the perspective of *abundance*. There are great resources, talents, viable skills, human capacities, technological advantages, and transnational opportunities to sustain a high level of confidence within people of African ancestry in this nation and elsewhere around the world.

For me, the central question is *not* whether the glass is half full or half empty. We must promote the perspective that our vessel is filling at an ever more rapid rate. We must make sure that this metaphorical glass is firmly within our grasp, lest we lose our focus, drop and break it. As well, we must be very clear about the source of clean, potable water that is being poured into our glass. There is indeed a great reason to be optimistic and excited about the road ahead.

3) Family and Community

The very fabric of culture, society and even civilization is bound to the enduring strength of family and community. During the centuries-long experience of enslavement, which we have come to call *the Maafa*, numerous assaults on the black family have produced devastation. Even attempting to list the myriad offenses, too many of which have become self-inflicting, presents itself as quite an overwhelming task.

These injuries would include: kidnapping of fathers, mothers and children; splitting up families during slave auctions and sales; forced breeding; extensive rape, molestation and sexual mutilation; forced segregation; separating mothers from their newborn children; creating economic conditions that undermine the stability of two-parent households; driving family members into exile through lynching and terrorism; unceasing anti-black propaganda; forced conversion to religions of our colonizers; social welfare policies that undermined family unity; the promotion of dangerous and unnatural birth control; race-specific eugenics and forced sterilization; urban renewal policies that broke up ethnic communities; gentrification and ethnic cleansing; co-opting black leadership; promoting sexually irresponsible and degenerate behaviors among our childbearing age population; encouraging consumption of products and services which undermine our reproductive health through ethnic-specific target marketing; unfair lending practices that undermine home and business real estate ownership; the prison-industrial complex's impact on parent-child relations; as well as a broad spectrum of economic policies that deprive our families from transferring wealth forward for the benefit of future generations.

The sum of these offenses has presented the current black generation with crippled family and community. Parts of nearly all this nation's largest cities have produced ghetto enclaves wherein the youth are functioning socially at a level just above that of savage beasts. Still, because these injuries to the integrity of family and community can be identified, reasonable solutions centered around cultural development can be strategically organized.

Reading through that extended list of offenses against our people probably made you feel somewhat depressed or overwhelmed; imagining and writing it certainly had a similar impact on me. Yet I prefer to get excited about immediate possibilities for joining with creative, committed and like-minded people whose aim is to produce action-oriented policies, programs, cooperatives and structures that solve problems.

It is vitally necessary when we are set upon resolving deep and persisting problems that we approach this task with an optimized attitude. We must always be well-prepared to initiate corrective procedures, and that we are sufficiently excited to sprint into action. We should be even more excited to collaborate with others who are similarly inspired.

Revitalizing the family and community is not only *doable*, but we should anticipate it to be rewarding and transforming in its outcome. We should be eager to commence the precise planning that will accomplish this mission.

4) Economic Development

Simple and precise definitions to serve as foundation for our corrective Reparations programs and policies should be very helpful. **Economics** is defined as: 1) the branch of scientific knowledge which supports production, consumption, and transfer of wealth; and 2) the *condition* of a group or region as it regards material prosperity. Economics entails scientific study of human behavior, particularly as it relates to choices that utilize resources most effectively. Economics is supported by theories, principles and models that deal with market processes. Contrary to widespread belief, economics is not necessarily bound to the advance of market-driven capitalism and the pursuit of profits. Indeed, the right type of economics creates sustainability which most certainly also supports the generation of profits. As important as any other aspect, and this correlates well with our specific African history and cultural values, sustainable economics supports the fair distribution of wealth among the group in a manner which benefits the maximum number of it's members.

Until these higher needs of our group members are reliably met, and until the process of transferring wealth forward into an expansive future is accomplished, then our economics will not be expected to support our own sustainable development. Separate from the economics of America, we as people of African heritage are in great need of a broad based economic upgrade. No one cannot best lead from the back of the pack. We need to organize toward being the most productive national group that our immense talents might allow.

These days, we as a distinct ethnic community within the United States only *produce* about 1 of every 7 dollars that we spend as consumers. This observation is derived from the much touted "black consumer power", projected to be as much as $1.3 trillion for the current year (what we spend), compared to the income generated by black-owned businesses, some 2.584 million of which, on average, only generate about $60,000 each annually, thus presenting a collective *producer* outcome which my best estimates determine to be no more than $182 billion this year. This disproportionate ratio explains why we don't see the dollar circulate within the black business community for very long; we simply don't produce enough of what we require as consumers to fulfill our needs and capture our spending. The good news is that we are creative, resourceful, widely-skilled and live within one of the most industrious nations in world history. Therefore, solving the challenge of economic dependency is not beyond our current capacity.

Throughout the course of *The Repairing* we will frequently return to topics of economics with specific themes, programs and proposals to make practical what has too often remained hypothetical, theoretical, rhetorical or mere bombast.

5) Education

Near the end of a month-long February 2014 LIBRadio broadcast series on African global history, we capped the month by identifying a 6-part formula upon which great empires have risen throughout history. This breakthrough revelation of this formula will form a critical basis for *The Repairing* which is the subject of this book. One can readily find extensive research regarding the importance of these components which comprise what we call the "Six Pillars of Empire." I've never seen these functions assembled into such a concise bundle. They are:

1. Demographics
2. Resource extraction and manufacturing to finished goods
3. Intrastate trade
4. Transnational trade
5. Security and expansion of territory
6. Education of youth to power

This presentation of the Six Pillars of Empire to you the reader is itself a function of educating and informing. While this formula emphasizes the "education of *youth* to power," we acknowledge that education is best when it continually informs and educates all members of the group throughout their lifetime. Education takes place within a broad spectrum of sources throughout one's contact with society. Formal education within home schooling, pre-school, elementary, middle and high school, community colleges, universities and distant learning environments have all become well-defined models for bringing young people into their adult status with the needed skills to be able to negotiate all aspects of social, political and economic engagement.

Historically Black Colleges and Universities (HBCU's) have presented themselves as a critically vital set of institutions since the time of emancipation from slavery. From within their ranks great leadership has emerged in every field of societal engagement. For most of our history, these institutions represented great pride, self-esteem and value within the best ambitions of the entire community. When one studies the role of HBCU's in the evolution of Afri-Amer society over the past century-and-a-half, there is great reason to see their immense value.

Yet, despite this noble history, today black colleges and universities are increasingly caught up in crises of survival and relevance. Where they were beneficiary of the segregation policies that affected black communities for most of our history, they seemed not to have adapted to desegregation well enough to ensure their long-term viability and survival. There have been 11 HBCU's which closed their doors up to 2013 and another 3 are reportedly close to collapse today. These institutions are plagued by issues of funding, enrollment, poor administration and such, but their primary problem is that the communities that would support them have largely come to view them as irrelevant. I strongly contend that if any of these institutions were somehow picked up and relocated to Sub-Saharan African nations, they would be highly appreciated, vital and strongly supported. As we get to solutions to the problems of educating our youth to inherit, develop and maintain power, we will return to the idea that these HBCU institutions should best fulfill needs of rapidly expanding Sub-Sahara African growth and development.

The debt burden born by far too many graduates has risen to a national crisis in America and this undoubtedly is an even greater burden on Blacks. There is a myriad of trends which are compounding this crisis, much which has been brought on by factors such as diminishing household income, dissolution of the family, the concentration of wealth and income, profiteering by the private banking industries, and lack of political will on the part of government. Making matters far worse is that this debt burden, which can persist for decades after graduation, accompanies a time when the nation no longer produces enough of the right kind of employment for these graduates. Too many of these young and middle-aged graduates are being cast into an employment market where they must compete against people who have been experienced in careers for many years but have been forced to look for new jobs. Thus, many of these recent grads end up looking for any opportunity, including retail services, seeking occupation in areas completely unrelated to the specific education which they had pursued. These days, many corporations are using the college degree as an employment qualifier; their interest is that the student had the persistence to capture a degree and hence is qualified to be hired.

Perhaps the most tragic means by which we can determine the status of education of our youth can be measured in high dropout rate of many students (in both secondary school and college) as well as the pace at which urban school closings are taking place. My own research of school closings since 2009 in 7 U.S. cities, New York, Baltimore, Washington D.C., Detroit, Chicago, Philadelphia and Kansas City, puts the number of these closings at more than 400. This school-closing crisis is not limited to these cities that I have examined; it is a national crisis and is a part of the gentrification trend that has become another plague affecting black urban policies.

Obviously, due to these and other challenges to the integrity of education for our youth, a new set of policies must be brought to the forefront. Thus, this is a key area for *The Repairing* which is immediately at hand.

6) Revising our Historical Perspective

Throughout this report, we will frequently refer to the critical importance of *culture* as the most significant transforming agent within society. Culture is: our spiritual expression, linguistic communication, our expressed values, common traditions, logical thought processes as well as our perspective of history. Far too many Afri-Amer individuals and institutions are teaching from the perspective that our history and national emergence begins with embarkation from the slave ships. By adopting the perspective that we are a people created and shaped in large part by the racist history of our oppression, we paint ourselves into a corner whereby we are cut off from a tremendous base of critically needed resources from our global history, current state of international affairs, as well as a future where transnational, Pan African collaboration will be a key determinant of our group's global success.

As well, we too often buy into false narratives of the "history" taught to us by those who have overtly and covertly stated their need to restrict our self-determining ambitions. We have been taught religious mythologies as actual factual history. Too many of us have failed to question just how much of this religious myth, fable and allegory is tangible, usable history. We are too often taught that the advance of civilization began with Greeks, Romans or Asians, with no regard to the long and glorious history of African empirical dominance.

The spectrum of historical narratives that must be corrected to restore cultural integrity, pride and functional wisdom to our people is sufficient to challenge our race for a century to come. There is an old proverb, believed to be attributed to Kenyan sources, which states that "until the Lion leans to write, the tale of the hunt will always reflect the glories of the hunter." Today, I am proud to announce for all who are not aware that the Lion has learned to write. The Lion has learned to make films, create poetry and sing powerful lyrics which set our historical perspective in proper order. We have the Internet, digital media and an ever-expansive set of communications technologies which can compel our story to be heard and understood not only by our members but for all the world's inhabitants, too many of whom have accepted a terribly false narrative which is the consequence of unrelenting propaganda from our historic oppressors.

7) Transnational Relations

We are living in an ever-more connected global environment and those organizations or groups which do the best at integrating themselves into this new world of *transnational relations* can be expected to be the highest performing groups in the world of today and tomorrow. None of us can deny that the sustainable development of ethnic groups such as Europeans or Chinese is greatly enhanced by their multinational status and cooperative efforts. Books such as Joel Kotkin's, **TRIBES: HOW RACE, RELIGION AND IDENTITY DETERMINE SUCCESS IN THE NEW GLOBAL ECONOMY**, clearly point out the spectrum of empowering advantages which such transnational ethnic groups enjoy. For such successful groups, shared culture, economic collaboration, shared development financing, mutual security, and a continuous push to maximize empathetic contact between their members around the world – these all combine to make for the most powerful global empires of today and the world of tomorrow.

Yet there exists a long record of broken relations among African peoples as they have been dispersed around the world since the horrors of the Maafa, the enslavement process which captured our bodies and shattered our cultural integrity; this has shown itself to be crippling and devastating. Despite the fact that most of us came to the Americas from West African kingdoms, we were broken up into various linguistic groups by enslavers from Britain, France, Spain, Portugal, Holland, Belgium and others. Today there are an estimated 1.22 billion people residing on the African continent, constituting 1 of every 6 people on the planet. By 2050 this continental population is expected to increase to nearly 2.5 billion, equating to slightly more than 1 of every 4 people on Earth. Africa has the world's youngest nations when the percentage of youth is considered compared to the elderly. Sub-Saharan Africa has the fastest rate of growth of the middle class of any region of the world and is thus projected to be one of the greatest consumer markets of the mid-21st Century and beyond.

Outside the African continent there are many countries with black majority populations or significant numbers of Blacks with which we should be developing collaborative relations. The largest 11 of these nations were listed within an online website in December 2015 (and many of these numbers are in need of update) [3]:

1. Brazil (85.78 million Blacks)
2. United States (45.7 million Blacks)
3. Columbia (9.45 million Blacks)
4. Haiti (8.70 million Blacks)
5. Dominican Republic (7.99 million Blacks)
6. France (5 million Blacks)
7. Jamaica (2.73 million Blacks)
8. Venezuela (2.64 million Blacks)
9. United Kingdom (2.02 million Blacks)
10. Cuba (1.13 million Blacks)
11. Trinidad and Tobago (1.05 million Blacks)

The potential of a current global population of African-descended people exceeding 1.5 billion portends a demographic potential that, once raised to functional unity, competes directly against China, India, the EU and USA *combined*, or the global Islamic population. During the course of this study and strategic planning for *The Repairing*, we will clearly

---

[3] 11 Countries with Highest Black Population Outside Africa, by Milica Radenkovic, InsiderMonkey.com

demonstrate how this global demographic will be key to building a powerful and sustainable *African Global Order.*

8) Repairing our Health Status

To repeat an important message that we shared earlier and which will no doubt be repeated throughout this book, when it comes to transforming our grand vision into a sustainable reality, an entire spectrum of focused advancements must take place. As such, we cannot and will not overlook the critical area of health as one of the foundations of group elevation. When one looks through the spectrum of health status indicators which allow us precise assessment of individual and group health, Afri-Amers rate poorly across the board. Members of our group are disproportionately plagued by higher-than-average rates of overweight, obesity, cardiovascular disease, cancer, diabetes, dialysis-dependent kidney disease, mental illness, infant and maternal mortality, metabolic disorders, hypertension, chronic inflammatory diseases, reproductive diseases, autoimmune disorders, asthma, as well as all manners of drug-dependencies and alcoholism. Americans are themselves sicker than residents of most developed nations and Afri-Amers are consistently among the most disease-plagued of the nation; vying for certain Native American groups for the worst statistics of all.

Because of this poor health status, the group, along with families and individuals within the group, is burdened with healthcare expenses that have sucked much of the viability out of a thriving future existence. From cradle to the grave, when statisticians in the healthcare fields look at Afri-Amers, they consistently point to us as the sickest within the nation. In previous books I have sited these statistics regarding morbidity and mortality among our members and it is indeed a very sad case.

Within Afri-Amer academia there is an obvious chasm between scholars who advocate for our advancement in various fields of group transformation. Far too often, the topic of our health is ignored and omitted by those purporting to lead us. Further, in many cases, those who are our health advocates are paid by profit-motivated healthcare businesses to encourage us to engage in remedial behaviors which frequently make matters even worse. We are constantly being encouraged to "get tested" for a range of disorders using testing methods which are more problematic than they are worth; these to include (but not limited to) diagnostic tests for HIV, PSA (prostate specific antigen), mammograms, sexually transmitted diseases, cholesterol and colonoscopy. We are further constantly cajoled into taking pharmaceutical medications for a spectrum of conditions which show up on these diagnostics, sometimes for years on end, without any remedy of the disorder for which drugs are prescribed, only to have additional symptoms appear from the impact of long term drug medication, for which another set of drugs is often suggested.

According to recent published reports, America has the most expensive national healthcare system in history and the highest spending-per-capita on healthcare of any other nation, averaging right around $10,000 per person and increasing at an annual rate of 6%. For Afri-Amers this is expected to exceed a $400 billion annual sickness burden. Making matters worse, successful outcome and patient satisfaction for this nation's hyper-expensive medical system rates poorly when compared against other countries. The World Health Organization's annual ranking of national healthcare systems has lowered satisfactory ranking by America's healthcare consumers from 31st to 37th in recent years.

At the time that I am writing this chapter, for most of the past two years the black community has been up in arms over the terrible incidences of police homicides against our community, especially the killing of unarmed young black males and females. You've undoubtedly seen the numerous videos documenting this carnage, heard endless debate on news talk stations and television news on the topic, and witnessed the uprising of hundreds of thousands of protesters across the nation under the banner of "Black Lives Matter." There is no doubt whatsoever that there is a shocking number of law enforcement homicides that take place in the United States and the public should be outraged; it is expected that police in the U.S. will kill around 1200 Americans of all ethnicities this year, over 400 of which are expected to be black people.

Yet, there is not so much alarm when an estimated 1,069,000 Americans of all ethnicities will succumb to *iatrogenic death* (Death-by-Doctor) this year, of which 170,000 Blacks will be included. When compared to police homicides, iatrogenic episodes will kill at a ratio of 900-to-1 for all Americans, or a ratio of 425-to-1 for Blacks. If *all* Black Lives Matter, then we might need to redirect much more of our reactive outrage to this devastating statistic of the impact of bad medical practices that are prematurely ending the lives of many of our family members, our elderly, our peers and community members. My perception is that people really cannot grasp the profound impact of just so much death and injury at the hands of the American healthcare system even when given these findings in the most direct and comprehensible manner. I have strived for decades to explain the function of this massive medical killing-machine to people, who soon thereafter return to this very system when they sense that they have developed some manner of disease or disorder.

As we examine the research which indicates the future for this outrageously expensive, runaway healthcare process, there is even worse on the horizon. New and experimental vaccines are being rushed to market, despite unproven safety and efficacy of these and already-existing injections. The American child is the most vaccinated child in history as well as the most cancer-diagnosed child in history. Some of the medical research that is currently in development borders on pure evil as the federal government just this week (August 2, 2016) approved federal funding for research which pursues *genetic-crossing* between human stem cells and animal species toward the aim of growing organs within pigs, cows, sheep and rats that can be transplanted into humans. This is just one example of a research community gone stark-raving mad!

Solving this massive and debilitating healthcare crisis for our people might seem as simple to some of us as getting the mass of our people back to the natural order of things. As this is a field within which I have a lifetime of experience, I am completely convinced that we do know *what to do and how to do it*, but our persistent problem is convincing those who would be beneficiaries of our preventative health strategies to modify their behaviors toward successful disease prevention, non-drug healing solutions and protecting our members from the ravages of corporate profiteering. As with the other areas of *The Repairing*, we cannot fail at this critical mission to revitalize our health status within this nation to the best of our current capacities.

I would be negligent to not discuss the multiple crises of health which affect our African continental motherland. Within the U.S., United Kingdom, France and other western countries, incidences of *communicable diseases* have declined significantly as a cause of death and serious injury due to a spectrum of improvements in hygiene across the board; this while the impact of *non-communicable diseases* such as cancer, heart disease, obesity-related metabolic disorders, diabetes and dementia are all rising in incidence. Across Africa, problems of communicable disease are still quite problematic and most certainly must be dealt with as more Sub-Saharan African nations advance within the status of *Middle-Income Countries*.

Indisputable facts have shown that widespread hysteria over HIV/AIDS in Africa was greatly overblown and fortunately we have a huge bank of data to prove that it has *not* devastated nations as was being projected 2 and 3 decades ago; similarly, Haiti was spared the dire consequences of rampant HIV infection that was the basis of anti-black propaganda of that era. The real problems with communicable diseases in Africa have virtually nothing to do with our sexual lifestyles, fertility rates or failure to use condoms.

Malaria, which is the result of a parasitic infection, remains the top disease impacting Africa. The World Health Organization reported more than 188 million cases across the continent for 2015, resulting in an estimated 394,200 deaths. During the period between 2000 and 2015, the incidence rate of malaria in Africa fell by 42%, and mortality declined there by 66%, which is notable. Yet that decline compared to the decline in mortality due to malaria worldwide by 72% in the Americas, 65% in the Western Pacific, and 64% in the Eastern Mediterranean Region.

As reported in my recent book **EBOLA, AMERICA AND THE NEW SCRAMBLE FOR AFRICA**, the U.S. and other western nations have their goals set on capturing and retaining the African population, which is expected to double in the next 35 years, as a lucrative market for their pharmaceutical products; that was one of the outcomes to have followed the August 2014 US-Africa Summit of leaders, hosted by Obama in Washington. News stories are frequent which talk about the great toll that malaria has on Africa. I was listening just this morning to a radio broadcast talking about efforts to build a program called "Seasonal Malaria Chemoprevention:

> In Western and Central Africa a new technique to combat malaria is rapidly gaining traction across the Sahel. Health officials in 11 countries are now giving children antimalarial drugs during the rainy season in this semi-arid region and seeing a dramatic drop in the number of malaria cases.
>
> The technique is called Seasonal Malaria Chemoprevention. Over four months, health workers give four doses of anti-malaria drugs to children under age 5. And it's been incredibly successful. Studies have shown that this health intervention can reduce the number of malaria cases in some parts of Africa by as much as 75 percent. [4]

Just as with many other drugs, chemotherapies currently in use for malaria do come with notorious side effects which can include: nausea, vomiting, abdominal pain, diarrhea, convulsions, heartburn, skin eruptions, rapid heartbeat, loss of bladder control, increased sensitivity to sunlight, large hive-like swelling on the body's soft tissues (including eyelids, lips, tongue, throat and sex organs), muscle spasms, sever mental changes and many more severe and minor complications. What would be the outcome if these western medical strategies became the new norm and nearly all of Africa's inhabitants became dependent on taking these chemotherapies on a constant basis? Such an outcome is unacceptable.

Fortunately, there are wonderful herbal alternatives for preventing the impact of malaria parasitic infection. A long-known herb used in Chinese medicine, *Artemesia annua* (also known as sweet wormwood, sweet annie, sweet sagewort, and annual mugwort – pinyin or qīnghāo in

---

[4] The Rainy Season Strategy To Stop Malaria, by Jason Beaubien, Nov. 16, 2016, from NPR.org

Chinese [5]) is perhaps the most promising natural solution to alleviating the severe impact of malaria on populations within Africa and around the world. While the western medical world, supported by the World Health Organization, have been resistant to using the herb as a primary anti-malarial treatment and would prefer to use it in combination with their pharmaceuticals, we do have evidence of its effectiveness as reported in controlled studies. The good news is that Artemsia annua can be grown within African countries and just a weekly dose of the bitter black tea made from the plant's leaves has shown to be effective as an anti-malarial treatment. *Slate Magazine* shared this good news as it reported on WHO resistance to this low-cost program:

> The tea comes from sweet wormwood (Artemisia annua), the Chinese plant that is a source for the world's most powerful anti-malarial treatments, which combine artemisinin derivatives with an older class of drugs. It can also be grown in wetter parts of Africa, and a year's supply costs no more than a few dollars. Although the tea itself has traditionally been used in treatment, not prevention, in China, a randomized controlled trial on this farm showed that workers who drank it regularly reduced their risk of suffering from multiple episodes of malaria by one-third. For a group of people who were once waylaid by this mosquito-borne disease four or more times per year, the tea is a godsend.
>
> Which is why you may be surprised to learn that the World Health Organization and a majority of malaria researchers are adamantly opposed to it. [6]

There are numerous other herbal solutions to endemic African diseases which have been known within indigenous healing systems for centuries. Many current western medicines are based on such herbal compounds that have been extracted and concentrated for commercial exploitation. As we move our own global agribusiness strategies forward, the production of organically-grown medicinal herbs such as wormwood,

---

[5] Botanical Society of Britain and Ireland, BSBI List 2007

[6] The WHO vs. the Tea Doctor: For once, an herbal remedy actually works. Why are malaria experts against it?, By Brendan Borrell, Slate April 2013

neem, gum Arabic, bitter aloe, rooibos, centella, Madagascan periwinkle, honeybush, devil's claw, bitter melon, umckaloabo (African geranium) and others can serve as foundation for profitable means of averting disease with safe herbal protocols. [7] Another wonderful side benefit of such a program will be to capture a significant income stream within the anticipated $660 billion in new annual revenue in African agribusiness expected to be in place by 2030.

9) Crime and Justice

America has a huge problem with crime, justice, violence and incarceration. If incarceration in the U.S. could be considered a bad case of the flu, then for Afri-Amers the analogy would be to that of a case of raging pneumonia. An article published in the *Huffington Post* highlighted this catastrophe by comparing imprisonment within the nation of India, with about 1.2 billion people, to the U.S., with a quarter of that population. Yet, the U.S. incarceration *of just Blacks* was higher "than the total prison populations in India, Argentina, Canada, Lebanon, Japan, Germany, Finland, Israel and England combined." [8]

The PEW Charitable Trusts published a report entitled *One in 31: The Long Reach of American Corrections*, within which it revealed the growth of "the population of the American corrections system [which had swollen] to more than 7.3 million, or 1 in every 31 U.S. adults...", slightly less than 3 percent of the national population. [9] From that report we can now determine that today 1 in 11 adult Blacks are under the control of correctional facilities, a stunning 9.2 percent of our population. For Hispanics this rate of corrections was 3.7 percent and for Whites 2.2 percent.

---

[7] Traditional Medicines in Africa: An Appraisal of Ten Potent African Medicinal Plants, by M. Fawzi Mahomoodally, from Evidence-Based Complementary and Alternative Medicine, Volume 2013, Article ID 617459

[8] The Black Male Incarceration Problem Is Real and It's Catastrophic, by Antonio Moore, Apr. 19, 2015 / The Huffington Post

[9] One in 31: The Long Reach of American Corrections, March 02, 2009 / The PEW Charitable Trusts

Currently, the population of Blacks within the U.S. corrections system is believed to be slightly less than 1 million. As the average economic output of an American worker is around $70,000 annually, then the economic drain to our community alone from the lack of productive contribution to the nation's industrial base would equate to tens of billions of dollars in lost labor potential. Then again, there is the residual impact of a lifetime of wage compensation that is diminished by the tag of being a convicted felon. The clear majority of men and women incarcerated are there for economic crimes, mostly non-violent drug offenses. Driving factors behind this situation are the separate-and-unequal status of wealth and income within the nation, the poor status of urban vocational training, the dearth of living-wage-earning jobs in the inner cities and the subsequent proliferation of an illicit economy.

Since the end of the era of struggle for civil rights, there has risen a pernicious and discriminatory "Drug War" in the U.S. which has been shown in many ways to be a conflict that targests urban youth of color. Blacks are disproportionately arrested and convicted for drug offenses even though Whites use and sell more drugs than do Blacks. Collaboration between legislatures, the judiciary, law enforcement, municipal prosecutors and mass media has allowed this *phony drug war* to grow far beyond its practical utility to the national interests of the nation. For the Afri-Amer community, this depth of social, economic and judicial stress is catastrophic, especially as the ill-effects reverberate into all critical aspects of the social cohesiveness of the group.

State-sanctioned murders of black leadership have gone unpunished for decades. We now have accumulated much evidence regarding the assassinations of Malcolm X, Rev. Martin L. King Jr., Medgar Evers, Fred Hampton and others which directly implicates the role of government agencies as collaborators, organizers and even perpetrators of these killings. Yet, those in large part or wholly responsible for these murders were not brought to justice. Political killings have also occurred around the world and the crimes against those such as Patrice Lumumba, Murtala Muhammed, Walter Rodney and others could also be considered as American justice unfulfilled.

Quite obviously, the crisis of police homicides against Blacks has persisted within the national consciousness as it has remained an intolerable blight upon the black community. Although there has been a never-ending continuance of such police killings of unarmed black youth for our entire history within this country, the appearance of videotaped witness widely circulated across the news and social media has again brought this crisis to a boiling point. Currently the movement known as Black Lives Matter has galvanized support across the major metropolitan areas of the nation, drawing in hundreds of thousands of outraged protestors from even beyond the black community. Resistance to these humiliations are engaging tens of thousands of conscientious participants from other ethnic groups, particularly among the younger generation. Pressure from continued conflict between our community members, male *and* female of all ages, and law enforcement, continues to build and is so close to a national emergency that many municipalities are now outfitting their police forces with capabilities for violent suppression which were once thought to be the exclusive capability of the nation's military forces.

Americans have long had a deep passion toward gun ownership from the very founding of the nation. Generations of hunters supported this cultural tradition and that remains a primary justification for bearing arms, despite the proliferation of full-service supermarkets which can supply all of the meat for human consumption that would ever be desired. There has also persisted an attitude that a part of "manhood" is to be able to kill, even if not for food sustenance.

This gun culture history has borne out over thousands of documented encounters between domestic militias, as well as the compelling rite of manhood to serve in the nation's armed forces. While, indeed, the need for national security is a priority, with American history there appears to be greater motivation towards domination than merely to protect home, business and direct national interests. Simply put, most of the world is convinced that Americans just like to kill. This is evidenced in the history of the conquest of the nation, annihilation of the people of the First Nations that previously occupied this land, the brutal excesses of enslavement and its aftermath, to include the Jim Crow apartheid era with its thousands of incidences of lynching. This killing record also includes government participation in murders of progressive leadership, which usually included some measure of nongovernmental collaboration, along with some measure of organized crime elements.

One of the most despicable and undeniable histories we can examine is the long account of encounters between Blacks and this nation's inequitable justice system. This shows up as disproportionate rates of incarceration, poor representation by attorneys appointed to defend the accused, exclusion of Blacks from being seated on juries, racist-affiliated judges and other court officials, disproportionate sentencing, the inequities in the way that the so-called "drug war" has particularly impacted black families, and the mass of anti-black propaganda that permeates media coverage of crime and justice.

Author Michelle Alexander made these trends all too apparent in her excellent book **The New Jim Crow: Mass Incarceration in the Age of Colorblindness**. The book pulls the blinders off the reader, the community, the lack of progress under the Obama administration and the nation. She used her legal scholarship to argue that "we have not ended racial caste in America; we merely redesigned it." Her work points out the degree to which "the U.S. criminal justice system functions as a contemporary system of racial control…" and produces the necessary evidence to prove her points. Using Alexander's superb research as one of many key studies of our relationship to the criminal justice system, we can find multiple points for which focused analysis and crafting of solutions can be implemented.

Summarizing the 9 Foundations for Reparations

Focusing on composing this extensive chapter of the book has not been easy or always pleasant. I've long resisted lamentation on topics of our group's painful past, shortcomings, continued sufferings and debilitating deficits. When engaged in discussion on such topics, I am generally quick to take a position of abundance and emphasizing the great possibilities which are presented before us. Still, for this book on *The Repairing*, we need to have a realistic starting point. Hence, these 9 Foundations for Reparations serves as a baseline from which numerous tactical steps must commence.

I want this book to be one to inspire us all, especially the young, to work in collaboration toward creating a better and sustainable future for all of our group members. We want to utilize the best-available tools, social media, transnational partnerships and lifestyle patterns toward the aim of developing an overwhelming and all-encompassing *culture of success*. There truly is great reason for us to be optimistic. I will offer as many references as possible throughout the book to highlight past and current models for success toward resolving each of these 9 key areas. More importantly, I will do my best to tie each of these Reparations strategies to the others so that we can truly get to a comprehensive integration of the bridges which span these 9 foundations. It is only through cumulative solutions that we will create the sort of massive Paradigm Shift that will confirm that *The Repairing* is manifesting in real time. We possess the resourcefulness to do great things. We can do this.

Chapter 3 – Visions of a New Day

"Where there is no vision, there is no hope."
– George Washington Carver

"If you keep on thinking the way you're thinking, you'll keep on getting what you're getting." – Rev. Meri Ka Ra

Key and central to the achievements which are mapped out in *The Repairing* is the capacity to envision a distinct destination, even to minute details of what will be transformed, and to excite this vision across the entire spectrum of our community. From the youngest to the eldest among us, even to include the unborn and those who have become ancestors, we intend through this book to clarify just how great is the potential to generate a new operational paradigm. This *visioning* process has long been shown to be a great way of reprogramming both the individual and the collective mind. The communications tools available in today's world of commercial marketing, "perceptions management," social engineering and social media are multiplying and can be coordinated toward our aim of propagating our specific cultural values.

This task of displacing the widespread pessimism, anger, psychological trauma, and diminished self-esteem which have become prevalent, is undoubtedly a great challenge. We won't understand and act upon the nuances of *sustainable power* unless and until we comprehend the great spectrum of opportunities that this moment in history has presented to us. Living in a highly-technological and socially complex nation such as the United States and other such advanced developed nations, we can be overwhelmed as individuals by the sheer mass of complex responsibilities and capabilities that make up nations, provincial governments, municipalities and self-sustaining communities.

One of our most important tasks immediately at hand is the proliferation of a *Massive Transformative Purpose (MTP)* to serve as a national and transnational motive for our people. What doesn't help our mission ahead is the great degree of pessimism, which has cumulatively overtaken too many of our group's members. Consequently, overcoming this widespread negativity is something that needs to be accomplished at the very beginning of our program to free up the creative and self-motivating capacities of the people. Throughout this book, we will frequently refer to a specific formula that has been discovered for social engineering toward the aim of repairing our masses. Using the specific methods within this formula, we can isolate those avenues by which pessimism is fed and reverse-engineer an optimistic, can-do mentality within our collective who, after that, should approach each problem or challenge as yet another solvable issue wherein we can demonstrate the innovative spirit that we have come to bear witness as our greatest asset.

A "scarcity mentality" has become all too pervasive within our ethnicity. In contrary to the logic and practicality which would feed our drive toward success, this debilitating scarcity mindset persists through deeply emotional and psychological injury. Much of this is due to the depth and persistence of historical and cultural trauma, which periodically arises to interrupt our focus on development. Yet, to persist with viewing our world as that of scarcity flies in the face of the best available facts at hand. Afri-Amers constitute the best-educated nation of Blacks on the planet. We have the highest ranking among the 1.5 billion people of African ancestry on this planet concerning *purchasing power parity* and household wealth. Members of our group have been trained and proven highly-accomplishing in managing all aspects of a complex industrial society. Our skilled expertise ranges from chemical, mechanical and architectural engineering to city management, building major infrastructure, mastering media and mass communications, administering space-based technology industries, and commanding the most complex national military system that history has ever presented. In a world of immeasurable abundance, there should be no sane person who could reasonably deny the overwhelming amount of evidence which confirms that Afri-Amers have been blessed with many talents as a people.

Most adults have learned through their life experiences that short-term sacrifices make for long term gains. We know that we can sacrifice buying some transient consumer items, put that money away in savings and enjoy compounded benefits for that effort later. We can avoid wasting our leisure time by consuming television and other non-productive efforts, put that time into a book study, learning a new craft, exercise or developing our culinary skills – all of which will result in a greater sense of empowerment and pride in our productive efforts. There is a part of the human brain, the *prefrontal cortex*, which is tasked with calculating the impact of immediate events as they will manifest over time; it helps us to envision over-the-horizon outcomes of what we are experiencing today. For too many people, environmental stressors have diminished the actual functioning of the prefrontal cortex, resulting in a "live for today" mentality whereby our actions are not deliberately contributing to distant goals which will facilitate sustainable transformation.

Toward the aim of being able to plan and develop for a sustainable future accurately, the challenge of cultivating *scientific futurism* as a discipline within the intellectual class serving the group is a primary and critical task. Scientific futurism differs from astrological charting, numerology, palm reading, crystal ball gazing and "casting bones." methods by which people seek to determine what might become their fate. This focus of our attention on science is not to cast aspersions upon those who practice these esoteric crafts. Yet, for managing nation-building, we need to advance highly functioning capability in more logic-based means of forecasting the future. Scientific futurism includes the disciplines of demographics, science and technology trends, economic patterns, geology and planetary resources, sociology and culture, politics, environment and climate change, the humanities, alternative futures analysis, health and biology, as well as trends in education. Scientific futurism requires the intellectual organizing of data patterns across this spectrum of disciplines toward the aim of creating processes for traversing the future. We will return to this subject of scientific futurism in great depth in a later chapter of the book as we move into the strategic and tactical steps necessary for the successful implementation of *The Repairing*.

One of my chief criticisms of how Afri-Amer leadership has developed is their lack of insight into what I have often called "the 800-pound gorilla in the room": Pan African development. This inattention will serve as a major theme throughout this book, the idea that Pan African solidarity, transnational collaboration, and tapping the strengths of a global African population which today stands at 1.5 billion will all best serve the facility of Blacks within any given nation to consolidate their wealth-producing potential along with their sustainability. I do not hesitate to confess that as I listen to advocates for Black Power, security, economic advance and group-serving issues, too often I find that the fatal flaw of their plan is that they fail to equate the 1,454,300,000 (1.453 billion) other people of African ancestry *not* living in America who inhabit this planet. Among this additional global population, there is every aspect of human potential to be expressed. Extending our small percentage to this larger group with successful plans for cooperation and collaboration on a massive scale would transform the entire planet. The fact is, for every 3 Blacks living in the United States, there are potentially 97 Blacks in other countries who should be serving as our natural allies. To continue to overlook, ignore or be unaware of this Pan African potential practically dooms our group within this country or other similar nations where we are a demographic minority is tragic and raises the ultimate specter of "race suicide." We will return to this theme much later. To briefly summarize this position, we can rapidly "fill our glass" by tapping the great resources of our global ethnic family and that is a great reason for optimism.

Over the years, my studies have been greatly assisted by the amount of time I spent analyzing the largest study of Blacks with the U.S. which has ever been revealed. In 1944 the book **AN AMERICAN DILEMMA: THE NEGRO PROBLEM AND MODERN DEMOCRACY** was published by Harper & Brothers Publishing. This massive 1400-page study was the consequence of an intensive research project funded by the Carnegie Foundation, authored by the (later Nobel Prize-winning) Swedish economist Gunnar Myrdal. It was presented to President Franklyn Roosevelt during the Second World War when there was a great concern that there could be groups within the nation who could be radicalized by America's enemies to become a "fifth column" and cause internal security issues. While this massive study contained many profound and useful insights about the nature of our people up to and beyond the 1940s, it did allow certain insights which will be utilized in this strategic study as well.

One of many keys to our mission of generating sustainable momentum will be our comprehension and utilization of the principle of "cumulative causation." Under this principle, any efforts to build up one segment of our group affairs, such as economics, without supportive development in other areas as education, health, political structuring, etc., essentially is doomed to fail. We did not get into our present dire straits merely because of one area of debilitation; we are challenged by a spectrum of issues that have accumulated, and thus it is required that we bring our initiatives toward social engineering to a broad spectrum of policy advances which uplift the greatest number of our people. Focus on the 9 Foundations for Reparations can serve as a proper base to spread our policies across this spectrum within strategies which will mutually reinforce each category along with associated initiatives.

Our strategic solutions will require the coordination of a complex set of actions that are analogous to coordinating a large-scale military operation wherein command and control, communications and technology, land-air-sea based movement of assets, supply lines, healthcare and support for families must all be part of the ultimate success of that military campaign. Ours is similarly a complex operation and at present, we presumably do not have an academy capable of coordinating and managing such complex systems in place. I am firmly convinced that filling in this gap of leadership is not beyond our future capabilities.

This type of social engineering campaign must mobilize every segment of our group. It must do right for every age group, to include specific programs that serve the needs of elders, the children as well as everyone in between. For every segment of the larger group which can be identified, there must be delineated specific policies, programs, calls to action and resources allocated to engage each group member within overlapping circles of collaborative engagement. As we will shortly confirm, as a distinct group of people, Afri-Amers have an immense base of natural resources that will serve this grand scheme for group elevation and sustainable development. We have the demographic numbers, acquired skills, industrial experience, historical models of successful engagement, technical resources and financial base to generate any number of powerful agencies that can shatter any notion of our historical weakness and dependency.

Adapting to the changing world around us while preserving cultural traditions, values, and sustainable communities will be a great challenge to our status quo. Part of our efforts will be in response to future trends, disruptive phenomena in the world, the impact of *exponential technological development*, and galvanizing the will of our people. As we look back to the explosive growth and impact of the Garvey-led UNIA-ACL, we see a brilliant model of large scale, group-serving initiatives that led to rapid improvement for all segments of our Noble Race that cooperated with this dynamic organization. Some of the fundamental values which became common within that period need to be brought forward to serve us now. They include the notion of a race-first ethnic stance, Pan Africanism, highly-motivating shared visions, generating a spirit of short-term sacrifice for long-term gains, appreciation of our self-worth as a Noble Race, as well as acknowledging our long history of empires. What served members of the UNIA-ACL so magnificently a century ago is available to serve us today and indefinitely into the future. As Marcus Garvey frequently espoused: "The only protection against INJUSTICE in man is POWER; Physical, financial and scientific." The purpose of this book is to build practicable plans to implement such instruction.

There is one important component that has never been properly addressed during the long history of our people's journey through this period since we were led into this land enslaved and in captivity. We do have a critical need for a National Black Plebiscite. For the overwhelming majority of us, there was no deliberate decision to cut ourselves off from our African national identity. Our becoming citizen to the very state which enslaved and brutalized our ancestors was not through any willful participation on the part of our forbearers. Our indigenous names were stripped from us through violence and terrorism as was our native tongue and spiritual systems of expression. We were "emancipated" through a process that still denied the overwhelming majority of our families' true sovereign independence and the ability to govern ourselves. To this date, there has been no National Black Plebiscite which could be used as an objective base upon which to build sustainable sovereign development. Too many times, when we showed this natural tendency to govern ourselves, develop a self-serving economy and raise an autonomous leadership, we were confronted by violence, terror, assassination and vicious treatment by those who would have us portend that they are our protectors.

Ours is a *vision of a new day*. Within this vision, our glass is not merely half full but is *filling* at a steady pace with the most pristine waters that will nurture our evolution. We envision every segment of our large and diverse community displaying its innate creativity, engaged and excited about the pathway upon which we rapidly tread. Over our heads shines a brilliant *Massive Transformative Purpose* which prompts all our group members to reach deep within their souls to create and produce for the absolute benefit of our collective and future generations. Each of us sees all others of our Noble Race as partners, collaborators, in synchronization with one another, excited by the pathway immediately ahead and charged with the spirit which consolidated so very many of our past accomplishments and victories.

Thus, we commence with this sacred task immediately before us, that of *The Repairing*. We are fired up and infused with confidence in our ability to address these tasks with an absolute conviction toward success. We were born for this moment in world history, and our Great Ancestors made tremendous sacrifices for countless generations, always with the vision that we would arise to this task at this moment in time. Let *The Repairing* begin.

Chapter 4 – Assets and Liabilities

"As long as the colored man look to white folks to put the crown on what he say... as long as he looks to white folks for approval... then he ain't never gonna find out who he is and what he's about." – August Wilson, Jr.

In doing what I do as a journalist, talk show host, community organizer and health consultant, I have strived to continue perfecting the art of deliberate listening. I work hard to not only hear and listen but to extract precision and truth from that which has captured my attention. As such, I must admit that I am far more disappointed than satisfied with the mass of self-criticism I hear coming from my African-centered compatriots.

How terrible and frustrating it is to hear members of our group lament in terms of our destitution, lacking in morals and perpetual victims of imagined deifications – a people who are lacking everything necessary to make us great competitors for sustainable wealth and a dignified future. Even a frustrating number of our so-called "leaders" are frequently obsessing over this imagined scarcity: "Black folks don't got nothin', don't do nothin', ain't got no morals, and ain't capable of competing for anything of substance." You've no doubt heard some form of this pessimistic lamenting more often than you would like to remember. As a long-time talk show host, as well as having attended over a quarter of a century of black community empowerment lectures, I can assure you that I have heard this lamenting more times than I would ever want to remember. I don't believe it.

I have come to call this stream of negative assessments of our status as Blacks in the world today as "The Litany." Merriam-Webster's dictionary gives us two definitions for this term Litany: 1) a prayer in a Christian church service in which the people at the service respond to lines spoken by the person who is leading the service; and 2) a long list of complaints, problems, etc.

As I hear The Litany coming forth from the mouths of those who go on and on about the spectrum of black folks' shortcomings, more and more it sounds as if they are praying to the *god of our perpetual misery*, for which they seem to anticipate a call-and-response from their audience signing onto their scarcity-biased analysis of our situation. I hope it seems obvious that I'm not in agreement with such a dismal outlook.

I have come to the habit of countering The Litany with as much positive assessment of our status, or its potential, as my creative analysis can allow. To counter what I perceive as fatalistic pessimism, I contend that "Black Folks Do..." Note the following positive assessments:

- Our people have a vast treasury of skills, capacities, assets and talents;
- We have created a glorious historical record of accomplishment throughout the entirety of human civilization;
- Our people consistently demonstrate deep spiritual and moral values as well as being generous and empathetic;
- We have accumulated a large base of businesses, material assets, wealth-producing industries, real estate, and other hard assets;
- We are courageous, committed and consistently sacrifice for the benefits of family, community and other members of the group;
- We are some of the most creative artists in the world of today and of historical record;
- Globally we have the great advantage of sustainable positive demographics that will drive the whole evolution of planetary civilization for centuries to come;
- African-peopled nations, on the continent and beyond, have dominion over concentrations of natural resources which rival or exceed those under control of other ethnic groups;
- Our physical skills, athletic ability and natural beauty as great or greater than any other competing groups and we are proven to be great team players;

- We have direct access to some of the wisest and most conscientious Elders of any group or ethnicity;
- Our children are bright, precocious, talented and disciplined, especially when families and communities are stable and supportive;
- We have a long record of strong relationships within family and community, which have proven to withstand tremendous stresses and pressures from external aggression but still couldn't break our will to build for the success of generations to come.

For this effort to bring forth self-determining Reparations, it is imperative that we correctly assess the resources available to the group and that our plan incorporates calls-to-action which engage our members toward sustainable development. There are numerous elements to coordinate, to include religious organizations, non-governmental agencies, grassroots constituencies, businesses owned, run or managed by group members, members of unions, guilds and trade organizations; HBCU's and other educational facilities, agribusiness and farmers' markets, industrial production, foreign embassies and consulates, print, broadcast and Internet media outlets, public sector agencies that conduct specific programs that build community, extended family structures, women's and men's associations, financial institutions, banks and credit unions, think tanks and academic associations, sports clubs and athletic unions, some 2 million continental-born African Diaspora members living among us, arts and entertainment societies, vast libraries of accumulated knowledge and wisdom, real estate (both urban and rural), technical facilities such as recording studios and video sound stages, meeting halls and community centers, as well as incorporating deep, rich and transforming cultures that can guide our individual and group behaviors.

We have within the 45.7 million Blacks whom we identify as Afri-Amers the entire range of acquired skills to do virtually *anything* that humans are currently capable of doing. As well, if there might be anything for which we further lack, we can turn to the other 1,452,000,000 Africans dispersed all over the planet to draw upon this huge global demographic for valuable assistance.

Black Folks are *not* poor; we are *not* weak and powerless. We are NOT perpetual victims of this *chimera* called "White Supremacy." We merely lack the type of comprehensive planning which engages the broadest spectrum of immense talents, skills, resources and assets in an undefeatable Master Blueprint. On the contrary, it may be that our people have just so much wealth and resource within our immediate grasp that we are maybe just overwhelmed by our rich capacity.

Being constantly aware of just how blessedly rich we have become must be an early central task of our efforts. All talk of scarcity, repetitive reciting of The Litany, and the frequency of pessimistic proclamations can and must be obliterated with an accurate accounting of our many, many, many blessings. We have what we need, and we should all be immensely proud and self-confident with our renewed comprehension of just what it is that we currently possess.

We are also in great need of comprehending liabilities as a group and as individuals within the group. We have numerous challenges that need to be addressed, to include:

- We suffer from the widespread adoption of a foreign culture that does not support and embrace our long history of civilization and spiritual traditions. Ours is, to too great an extent, a culture imposed upon us by our historic oppressors (both Arab and European) that was created to keep us subservient and under control. Within this culture, we have displaced our language, our very names, spiritual systems, traditions, an accurate perspective of history, moral values, and indigenous logic. This imposed/adopted culture has even interrupted the way that we bring our children into the world and raise them from birth through to adulthood.

- Our economic dependence upon the same mercantile system which captured our bodies and stole the productive value of our labor centuries ago has today crippled our ability to build intergenerational wealth and prosperity for ourselves. We've negotiated a very poor deal in trading our valuable labor for an unsustainable consumer culture; this is evidenced by the fact that of every 7 dollars that U.S. Blacks spend as consumers, our businesses currently only produce 1 dollar.

- Education and literacy, something which previous generations of our people within this society had such great value for, have become devalued in recent decades resulting in reversing of progress for the generations which followed our historical struggles for social, economic, judicial and educational freedom. The failure of literacy within too many of our fellows within this nation points to the devolution (de-evolution) of our group in all key aspects of social organization.
- A major liability for the great majority of our people within this country is a great disconnect with the very fact that we are African people on this planet. This deficit is pervasive throughout all of the major social institutions serving the group as it affects leadership, religion, political organizations, academic institutions, black media, community leadership, economic organization and our demographic potential. When members of our group see someone of an Asian American community, they immediately identify them as Chinese, Korean, Japanese, etc., with the expectation that this person of such ethnic identity will act in accord with others of their nationality wherever they are to be found. Yet, we most often don't accord ourselves the same advantage of global identity and the advantage which should follow. According to my long term projections of demographics for Afri-Amers, we will be forced to accept and function within a global African identity within another 50 to 60 years or else we will face ethnic (race) suicide within the U.S., a prospect of which the great scholar W.E.B. DuBois warned us a century ago.

- Blacks in the U.S. have a tremendous and crippling debt burden that has cast an ominous shadow over our future development. We have been coerced by mass marketing to squander precious and often-scarce resources on mindless consumerism. In November and December 2015, embracing seasonal holiday spending, Blacks in the U.S. increased the pace of their average yearly household expenditures by an estimated 49.7 billion dollars. This amounts to one-third of the annual GDP (purchasing power parity) of the African nation of Ethiopia, a country that has committed its resources to the point that it has now risen to be the 2nd fastest rate of GDP growth of all nations on the planet. When we consider what long term rewards that we might expect from two months of holiday shopping madness compared to the sustainable progress of great nations, we might come to see that ours has been a shameful, wasteful and foolish investment in holiday traditions that emerge from what is essentially a foreign culture. [My calculation of November-December 2019 holiday spending topped 67 billion dollars for Afri-Amers.]

- Perhaps our greatest liability has resulted from the disruption of traditional family patterns and the pitiful state of relations between Afri-Amer women and men. Within the larger nation, the breakup of traditional marriage-based partnerships, two-parent households and extended family structures have all suffered. Yet, when it comes to analyzing the state of the black family, things go from awful to worse. Despite a seemingly never-ending stream of forums and conversations intended to address this dilemma and to construct bridges to overcome this divide, with each passing decade, things seem to keep getting worse. The problem has continued to grow for some three birth generations now, and it has become a major factor contributing to the negative birth rate that increasingly burdens our group with the prospect of impending demographic collapse.

- Our people are too easily distracted by anti-Black propaganda, disinformation, irrelevant social trivia, fixation on celebrities, and subject to provocation by clandestine forces. We have been too quick to latch onto unproven theories about power and society, hysterical over Internet hoaxes, superstitious, and hyper-religious. There is a pervasive weakness in our individual and collective intellect that becomes all too apparent when one gages opinions within our masses by listening closely to responses shared within talk radio and community forums. Trends and fads work their way into our common behaviors and distract too many of our members from the critical long term policies which will support sustainable growth and development. Our accepted leadership itself feeds our constant need for emotionalism, distraction and blame fixation. To too great an extent, we have become intellectually lazy and quick to latch upon the easiest-available justification for non-competitiveness.

- Lastly, as stated elsewhere in this report and to which we will return in much greater detail, one of our greatest liabilities is that we do not own enough urban or rural real estate to facilitate our independent, sustainable and sovereign development. We have been told continuously by credible voices the critical importance of controlling land. In his milestone speech, Message to the Grassroots, delivered by Malcolm X in 1963, he informs the audience that "Land is the basis of all independence. Land is the basis of freedom, justice, and equality." At our present state, and following the current established trend, our land tenure status within the U.S. is bad and getting worse every decade.

So, herein I have presented an extensive listing of our group assets and liabilities in as concise a manner as possible within the limited space allotted within this chapter. Perhaps I should have listed the liabilities first, as I feel as if I slipped back into *The Litany* during the latter part of this chapter. After Chapter Two's focus on the problems which **THE REPAIRING** is to address, I was eager to start this following chapter with a reversal of the pessimistic outlook which emerged from that assessment.

Life is both positive and negative; we constantly seek to find an inspiring balance between the forces of challenge and resolution. Our stated intention with this publication is to engage positive and sustainable development, to seize upon all advantages available toward our visionary mission, and to engage every bit of the creative human capacity which is found within our large mass of 45.7 million Afri-Amers, in league with the others of the 1.5 billion of African heritage with whom we share this generation on the planet.

Liabilities must be acknowledged, understood, and appreciated for how they've come to direct our livelihood. Liabilities present us with definable problems and challenges which compel us to function responsively and with deliberation. Because we know beyond dispute that we are a deeply resourceful, creative, empathetic and blessed people, we can tolerate no question of our abilities to meet these and any future challenges which confront our progress. As one of our greatest musical poets of recent generations Curtis Mayfield sang in his inspiring and timeless hit song:

We’re a Winner…
No more tears do we cry
And we have finally dried our eyes
And we're movin' on up
(Movin' on up)
Lord have mercy, we're movin' on up

Chapter 5 – Replicable Models and Historical Precedence

"Of all our studies, history is best qualified to reward our research. And when you see that you've got problems, all you have to do is examine the historic method used all over the world by others who have problems similar to yours. And once you see how they got theirs straight, then you know how you can get yours straight."
– Malcolm X, Message to the Grassroots

I will confess and am proud to do so, that I am addicted to the study of history. I love the history of empires, cultures, technology, biographies, war, social movements, and an entire spectrum of little-known chapters of the long narrative of the evolution of humankind. Thus, the insight shared to us by Malcolm X that "history is best qualified to reward our research," which was based upon a similar statement from Elijah Muhammad, strikes right at my heart and serves as a significant foundation for a life-long mission. It is this long and compelling engagement with historical analysis which I put forward as one of the primary *qualifiers* for my stepping forward to engage this strategic plan I am calling *The Repairing*. By gaining access to the entirety of history and being able to pull from this knowledge bank, we can find countless past episodes that parallel the challenges we face today; from history, we can extract practical strategies and tactics which resulted in a positive outcome for the groups involved.

Let's look at a spectrum of historical models which can be utilized for our mission of *practical* Reparations for our people. It should be our expectation that each of these models offers some replicable patterns, insights, or methods which are appropriate for our time, our mission and our unique circumstance toward the aim of creating a paradigm shift within which our people can build a sustainable future. While each of these models would be worthy of an entire volume of study, I will try my best to summarize key points in the most concise manner possible.

The advance of great ancient African empires

Any accurate and in-depth analysis of world history cannot overlook or ignore the appearance of several African continental empires, which left a long and important impact on the evolution of human civilization. Great empires that emerged, including ancient Egypt (Kemet, Ta Meri), Zimbabwe, Kongo, Axum, Carthage, Songhai, Mali, Ghana, and Ethiopia/Abyssinia, are outstanding examples of some 15 powerful African empires which have been identified and examined in great depth. From these empirical centers, some of which rise to prominence at the very beginning of human civilization, we have examples of great achievement in every field of human accomplishment, including invention, mathematics, archeology, chemistry, biology, technology, leadership governance, the arts, wealth production, agriculture, astronomy and astrophysics, and much more. We have numerous examples of tremendous wealth being produced within these empires, particularly outstanding examples of which include the treasures of numerous Nile Valley Pharaohs as well as the single wealthiest man identified in world history, the great Mansa Musa, Sultan of the Mali Empire.

Numerous black historians have worked diligently over centuries to help us to recover our comprehension of the extent of African historical greatness, their names too numerous to list here, yet we owe these scholars an immense debt of gratitude for their individual and collective efforts to recover this glorious history. Each of these empires can be scoured for specific strategies and tactics which resulted in their rise to the pinnacles of power and human achievement. I have previously written about the *Six Pillars of Empire* which undergird each of these and other world civilizations. I will return frequently and in much greater depth to the subject of these Six Pillars, which include: 1) strong demographics, 2) producing industry from raw materials, 3) creating internal commerce, 4) producing surplus for external trade, 5) securing and expanding the group's territory, and 6) educating youth to power. Each of these 15 empires established in African history rose upon these six pillars and as such, provide us replicable models as well as a sense of confidence which is enjoyed when we inform ourselves with such historical truths. The deep study of the evolution of these empirical civilizations is a requirement for all who would aspire to lead our people toward the future status which we seek.

Post-enslavement Reconstruction era

Within our long historical journey through world history is the comparatively brief period of enslavement. A spectrum of traumatic horrors was imposed upon our ancestors during this tragic period, which we have come to call the *Maafa (the Great Suffering)*. In the aftermath of emancipation from American slavery, from 1865 until 1898, there was the era known in U.S. history as The Reconstruction. Amidst the national effort to restore the Union, the formerly enslaved African population, along with its already-emancipated brotherhood, was enumerated by the U.S. Census in 1870 at over 4.88 million of the nation's population of 38.5 million. This was an increase of 9.9% over the previous decade although charges of a significant *undercount* of Blacks were leveled against the Superintendent of the Census Francis A. Walker; this charge of deliberate undercounting of Blacks in the U.S. has continued even to recent decades.

In the southern states, which had been devastated by their unsuccessful rebellion, some 4 million Freedmen (newly freed Africans) were forced to forge a new reality for themselves and, in many instances, moved to reconstruct whole new communities. Within these efforts, Blacks proved that they were not a helpless population as they tackled widespread illiteracy by creating new avenues for education, which eventually served as a primary model for public education for the nation. During Reconstruction, they struck new deals for the utilization of black labor, too many of which were still so grossly inequitable that they were hardly a step beyond chattel slavery.

Our Reconstruction-era ancestors acquired and developed land at a phenomenal rate, with estimates of as much as 15 to 19 million acres of land coming under the control of our members (as much as 6 times the amount of farmland that we own today). Under the "protection" of the 13th, 14th, and 15th Amendments to the Constitution, Blacks began to vote, organize for political power, use public accommodations and create businesses on a great scale. During this period, we saw the creation of vocational training schools and numerous other institutions of higher education with dozens of HBCU's being raised across the nation within which to encourage our youth to self-reliance and empowerment. Black banks, benevolence societies and insurance companies sprang into existence. We raised a vast network of religious institutions to serve our specific means of worship and to further function as neighborhood centers which provided a foundation for as many as 14 distinct needs of the community.

During the Reconstruction era, several back-to-Africa movements took hold among our people and served up participants to repatriate to African destinations such as Liberia and Sierra Leone. As well, African-centered scholarship began to take hold within various academies and credible accounts of our repressed history began to appear within our group-serving print media and publishing houses, along with other circles of education and enlightenment.

The overriding spirit of this nearly 35 years of intense push forward by Freedmen in league with their emancipated brethren during the Reconstruction era was truly historic. It most certainly qualifies as a periodic model for which specific patterns of our organization could be replicated and from which parallel initiatives might be patterned. Despite a host of deprivations, setbacks, abuses and acts of terror, our people pushed forward across a broad front encompassing nearly every aspect of sovereign development. At the heart of all our Reconstruction-era endeavors was a spirit that compelled our people to overcome the vast set of traumas that had been inflicted during enslavement. Despite the lingering wall of racial segregation, we remained confident in our ability to create better, stronger communities within which to raise our children.

The end of Reconstruction is marked by a series of political setbacks, the 1896 Supreme Court ruling in the case of Plessy V. Ferguson (which furthered "separate but equal" racial segregation), and the key event of the Wilmington Insurrection of 1898. This was the incident that saw the violent destruction of the city council in Wilmington, North Carolina, whereby a racially-mixed cooperative government, duly-elected by the city's black majority, was violently overthrown through racist terrorism. In contradiction to the post-Civil War protection of the federal government of constitutional rights of the Freedmen in so many public affairs, the government of President William McKinley refused to lend protection to the citizens of Wilmington. During the violent episode, let by white militia supporters of the Democratic Party, it is estimated that from 14 to 60 people were killed, the overwhelming majority of them were Blacks. This insurrection closes the door on the period of Reconstruction and ushers in the period of American apartheid known as Jim Crow.

Race First – Marcus Garvey and the UNIA

In the aftermath of the end of Reconstruction, during the worst deprivations of the Jim Crow era, there arose within the souls of Blacks inhabiting various nations of the Americas a movement that was so dynamic and fast-spreading that it still stands as one of the most glorious moments in our post-Maafa history. Birthed from within a powerful vision from this brilliant Jamaican-born printer and journalist, Marcus Garvey galvanized an organization that became the largest membership of the century for black self-development, racial pride and economic organization. From the time of Garvey's entry into the United States in 1915 until Garvey's deportation from the U.S. in 1925, the UNIA-ACL galvanized a mass of Africans in the Americas, Europe and across the African continent, that at its peak counted as many as 5 million members or more.

During the brief but fiery rise of the UNIA-ACL, the Harlem borough of New York City ascended to such wealth and prominence that it made Harlem the center of urban progress for Blacks around the world. The noted period of artistic and cultural achievement known as *the Harlem Renaissance* was birthed from this era of Black Racial Pride and accomplishment which built upon the vision of Garvey's organization.

In my book, **THE ROAD TO POWER: SEVEN STEPS TO AN AFRICAN GLOBAL ORDER**, I used the foundation, philosophy, and mission of the UNIA-ACL as the first of these seven steps to power. I will use a few select paragraphs from that chapter as an excellent source for this focus on the best available models for us to emulate for *The Repairing*.

Destiny delivered into this mix an almost miraculous burst of hope in the form of a talented race leader. Migrating to America from the British-colonized Caribbean island of Jamaica comes a remarkable young visionary named Marcus Garvey. After arrival, within an initial period of three years of intense organizing, Garvey brought this dehumanized "colored people" to a position of widespread influence. Within the hearts and minds of recipients of his message was birthed a highly-energized enthusiasm for all things complimentary to black esteem. Garvey's tremendous appeal with his people sprang from his ability to passionately articulate a grand vision of African destiny and the great legacy of the black race. Garvey preached:

> But when we come to consider the history of man, was not the Negro a power, was he not great once? Yes, honest students of history can recall the day when Egypt, Ethiopia and Timbuctoo towered in their civilizations, towered above Europe, towered above Asia. When Europe was inhabited by a race of cannibals, a race of savages, naked men, heathens and pagans, Africa was peopled with a race of cultured black men, who were masters in art, science, and literature; men who were cultured and refined; men, who, it was said, were like the gods. Even the great poets of old sang in beautiful sonnets of the delight it afforded the gods to be in companionship with the Ethiopians.
>
> Why, then, should we lose hope? Black men, you were once great; you shall be great again. Lose not courage, lose not faith, go forward. The thing to do is to get organized; keep separated and you will be exploited, you will be robbed, you will be killed. Get organized, and you will compel the world to respect you. If the world fails to give you consideration, because you are black men, because you are Negroes, four hundred millions of you

> shall, through organization, shake the pillars of the universe and bring down creation... [10]

Between 1918 and 1921, Garvey and his fellow organizers built the Universal Negro Improvement Association (UNIA) to become the largest black-progress organization in modern history. By 1924 the UNIA had grown to the point of purchasing ocean liners, the then-equivalent of today's jet aircraft—an amazing accomplishment. "Race First," for Garvey, was the ideological linchpin. Garvey saw this movement as necessary toward protecting the security and material interests of Blacks in all corners of the globe. As he had observed firsthand, all around the world, Africans suffered a similar fate, that of repression at the hands of more organized races:

> "When we, as members of the Universal Negro Improvement Association, talk about a government of our own in Africa, a flag of our own and a national anthem of our own, some Negroes laugh at us, but we only have pity for them, as they know not what they do. When Uncle Sam lynches her black boys with her uniform on their back, and John Bull calls her ex-soldiers aliens who helped her in the Ashanti and Zulu wars to take big slices of Africa, then it is high time for some dull, apathetic Negroes to think in terms of nationhood.
>
> ...we are determined to solve our own problem, by redeeming our Motherland Africa from the hands of alien exploiters and found there a Government, a nation of our own, strong enough to lend protection to the members of our race scattered all over the world, and compel the respect of the nations and races of the earth.

The first chapter in **THE ROAD TO POWER** was quite extensive and is highly recommended reading for the sake of this specific research report on *The Repairing*. The summary of that chapter contained the following two very important missives:

---

[10] THE PHILOSOPHY AND OPINIONS OF MARCUS GARVEY by Amy Jacques Garvey, The Majority Press1986, pg. 77

One cannot help but become profoundly encouraged and emboldened upon internalizing these ideologies from the great Marcus Mosiah Garvey. We must keep in consideration that he was operating at a time when the resources available to him and his community were very limited. He functioned largely without means of electronic communication: the radio, movies, television (which had not yet been invented), the telephone, etc. He was organizing at a time when Blacks were not only undereducated and locked out of the upper levels of the economy and employment, but as the industrialized world was rapidly moving towards a crippling economic depression.

What magical talisman did Marcus Garvey possess that allowed him to overcome these perceived limitations and accomplish the seemingly impossible in such an incredibly short period? Garvey possessed a clear vision of what his people's destiny was; he was consumed with a *burning desire* to see his vision become an actuality; his self-discipline was such that he could overcome virtually every obstacle and get done the task at hand. Also, he developed the means of communicating his vision into the psyche of his audience so effectively that the recipient would immediately begin to make self-sacrifices in furtherance of the interests of the larger group.

Black towns

The history of "Black Towns," autonomous, self-segregated and self-governing incorporated communities, provides us with impressive examples of the historical drive by people of African ancestry to determine their own economic reality and govern their collective fate. Beginning as early as the 1820s, from upper Canada to America's northern states, all-black communities sprang up as an offshoot of the abolitionist movement. In Ohio, "Wilberforce was created to resettle black refugees expelled from Cincinnati." [11] Estimates on the number of Black Towns that were created over the next century range from as few as 50 to as high as 200, including the U.S., Canada and Mexico.

[11] Black Towns, Encyclopedia of African-American Culture and History, 2006, Thomson Gale

Agriculture served as the basis of economic sustenance for many of these municipalities, although, as they matured, local economies expanded to include a spectrum of businesses, crafts, light manufacturing, trades, and consumer merchandising along with newspapers whose pages included advertisements for others to immigrate into these newly-founded black communities.

The first American Black Town is regarded to be New Philadelphia, Illinois, founded in 1835 by an ex-Kentucky slave named "Free Frank" McWhorter. In the 1860s, additional towns such as Shankleville and Kendleton sprang up in Texas. Most of these communities were created as part of a westward migration of Blacks leaving the South as the short-lived Reconstruction protection of the federal government failed to protect Blacks from southern oppression and terror. Across the west, in Oklahoma, Kansas, Colorado, California and elsewhere, largely agricultural communities of freedom-seeking Africans sought their destiny within newly forming all-black municipalities.

As the federal government breached the boundaries of territories which had been placed under control of First Nation Peoples (so-called Native American or Indian) from the time of the Land Run of 1889, Old South Afri-Amers migrated westward in a massive wave. Many of the formerly enslaved eventually ended up taking residence within the newly-opened Oklahoma Territory. There they incorporated 23 all-black communities, 13 of which are still in existence with the most famous being Boley, Oklahoma.

Boley was settled in 1903 by Africans who had formerly been enslaved by the Creek Indians. Known as the Creek Freedmen, they set up several independent townships. After the Fort Smith & Western Railroad opened a railway station in the area, Boley was incorporated in 1905 and named for an official of the railroad. It was one of the wealthiest Black Towns in the U.S., with nationally-chartered banks, its own electric company, home to two colleges, a Masonic Lodge regarded as "the tallest building between Okmulgee and Oklahoma City," when it was built in 1912, and boasted a population of over 4000 residents by then. Booker T. Washington, the most powerful national black leader of the generation, visited Boley in 1905 and was so impressed that he frequently spoke of the Oklahoma Black Town as an example of black self-development. Because Boley's prosperity was so closely linked to the railroad, the Depression years were not good for the municipality, and it began to decline to the point of declaring bankruptcy in 1939. Although the town of Boley still exists today, although its population was listed at only 1,184 residents in the 2010 census.

The examples of Black Towns as a direct response to immense stress upon the black population during the long period of our suffering within this nation stand as models of what determined willpower in defiance of prolonged oppression can bring about. As we will later discuss our own experience of creating Kujichagulia Villages, the practicality of us building intentional communities is one whose time has returned.

Black Wall Street

We have been discussing various historic models within which people of African ancestry have created dynamic, expansive, self-determining institutions and self-governing towns, kingdoms, and even empires. Within the Greenwood Avenue section of Tulsa, Oklahoma, beginning before 1907, when Oklahoma became a state, there arose one of the most dynamic and celebrated communities that Blacks have known in the western hemisphere. This racially segregated section of Tulsa, north of the Frisco railroad tracks, was variously known as the Greenwood community, "Little Africa," and most often referred to as "Black Wall Street." This thriving community, which by 1921 numbered about 10,000 residents (some estimations place the population as high as 15,000 at its peak), became home to a broad spectrum of businesses that catered to virtually every need of its residents. Building on the commercial benefits of access to the rail line which dissected Tulsa, along with the Oklahoma oil boom of the 1910s, black-owned businesses thrived and the dollars spent by its residents circulated within the black business community for an extraordinarily long period.

Greenwood's business community supplied nearly all of the consumer needs for its citizens. This self-sufficiency was assisted by rigidly-enforced racial apartheid, and thus, behind the curtain of Jim Crow segregation, Blacks created their own bus line and two colleges, including medical schools, 21 churches served the black community, 21 restaurants, 30 grocery stores, 2 movie theaters, a hospital, bank, post office, libraries and numerous schools, as well as jewelry stores, pawnshops, and even brothels. At its apex, the 36-square blocks of Black Wall Street contained as many as 600 successful businesses. Wealthy Greenwood locals even owned 4 airplanes. In the surrounding areas. black agribusiness thrived on the support of the wealth produced within Black Wall Street.

This tremendous success of the Greenwood community was the consequence of two visionary land developers who invested in the area between 1896 and 1906, O.W. Gurley and J.B. Stratford. Both acquired large tracts of land with the specific aim of selling lots only to Blacks. As well, both entrepreneurs built several businesses themselves and grew wealthy, serving the rapidly-developing community. The cumulative wealth of Greenwood residents was celebrated across the country with such notables as Booker T. Washington constantly holding it up as a model of what black self-sufficiency could accomplish. To be a resident of Greenwood at that time was to know a great deal of pride, dignity and self-esteem as its residents dressed in fine garments and had all basic and luxurious needs catered to by people who looked like them and shared the same cultural values. One section of the area contained an expansive row of fine homes occupied by the district's successful physicians, attorneys, land developers and thriving entrepreneurs.

Yet, the most persisting memory of Black Wall Street is the tragic destruction that occurred beginning May 31st and June 1st 1921. Sparked by a rumor that a black shoe shiner, 19-year-old Dick Rowland had made sexual overtures to a 17-year-old elevator operator, a savage militia was formed from within Whites who, living south of the railroad tracks dividing Tulsa into segregated enclaves, had long been jealous of how Little Africa's residents seemingly flaunted their wealth and success. Within days 35 square blocks were torched, over 6000 Blacks were arrested, and according to Maurice Willows, who directed Red Cross relief efforts, the death toll stood at about 300 persons, mostly black yet including white casualties as well. Tulsa law enforcement sided with the attacking racist mobs and was reported to have used airplanes to drop incendiary bombs on the district. It took the calling out of the Tulsa

National Guard by the Governor to bring a conclusion to the pogrom, which destroyed the business district and residences of Greenwood. For many years this terrible massacre was omitted from Oklahoma state and local records. It wasn't until February 2001 that a detailed report was finally released on the incident from the Oklahoma Commission to Study the Tulsa Race Riot of 1921.

Yet, the story of Black Wall Street continued, to teach us all a lesson of resilience. Within five years of the aftermath of the destruction of Black Wall Street, Greenwood was rebuilt into a thriving community again. A few residents fled the area, including J.D. Stratford, one of the founding developers, who had seen his entire fortune destroyed in the riot and had as well been threatened with lynching by the terrorist mob. The renewed success of the area was severely impacted by the Great Depression which began in 1929 and the failure of the railroad line, which serviced the area. Greenwood struggled on but was further undermined by urban blight and population decline in the 1960s. Urban renewal efforts in the early 1970s dissected the area to build a highway loop around the downtown. A few of the 35 original blocks were set aside to create the Greenwood Historic District, which has done its best to keep alive the memory of this once-thriving and wealthy community.

The Civil Rights movement

Many of us from the generation of Baby Boomers and those older retain memories of the great struggles of our parents' generation as well as our own for civil, economic, judicial, and basic human rights. While the antecedence of the Civil Rights Movement can be linked to the long stream of black protests for fair treatment to members of our race as articulated within the Constitution of the United States, it is generally regarded that the 1954 Supreme Court ruling in the case of Brown versus the Board of Education which had been a challenge to "separate-but-equal" racial segregation in Topeka, Kansas, is regarded as the beginning for this period referred to as the Civil Rights Era. The main finding of the decision was the primary challenge to racial segregation in education as well as all other aspects of civil life. Because of the federal government finally agreeing to be on the side of Blacks for the first time since the end of Reconstruction, black social justice organizations sprang to action across the country, especially focusing on the former slaving states of the South. Bitter and protracted struggles took place over the next decade and beyond with notable battles in Mississippi, Alabama, Georgia, Tennessee, South and North Carolina and Arkansas, although virtually no state within the continental U.S. was spared some manner of an activist challenge to the segregated and unjust set of common affairs.

Some of the key strategies by which the Civil Rights struggle made itself historically relevant included (but should not be limited to) massive grassroots organizing and the development of autonomous community empowerment councils, mobilizing religious institutions to engage in civic actions, political education and voter registration drives, campus recruiting activities and development of university leadership structures, unified efforts on the part of black media to bear witness to the spectrum of confrontations which were taking place, support of the movement by entertainers, celebrities, musical artists and other notable persons, outreach to sympathetic voices from outside the black community, sit-ins, marches, protests, and sustained boycotts, and more.

The Civil Rights movement era produced many historical figures of note, some of whose names have become etched upon the very soul of our racial pride. The list of notable Civil Rights leaders is too extensive to cover with due respect here but does include such luminaries as Rev. Dr. Martin L. King Jr., Malcolm X, Ella Baker, Stokely Carmichael (Kwame Toure), H. Rap Brown (Jamill Al-Amin), Fannie Lou Hamer, Medgar Evers, Ralph Abernathy, Daisy Bates, Paul Robeson, James Baldwin, Harry Belafonte, James Farmer, Coretta Scott King, John Lewis, Robert F. Williams, James Meredith, Bob Moses, Rosa Parks, Bayard Rustin, Fred Shuttlesworth, Wyatt T. Walker, A. Phillip Randolph, Hosea Williams, Andrew Young, Walter White and many, many more. Each of these Civil Rights era activist leaders has a notable biography that should be taught to every member of our ethnicity from the earliest stage of education for sustainable power. There were many others, some of whom had questionable roles during the movement era because of selfish intentions, unrighteous or clandestine associations and dubious behaviors. For the sake of the tone of this report, we mustn't focus on such devious individuals herein.

Organizations which served at the forefront of this push for justice, desegregation and equality included such notable organizations as the South Christian Leadership Conference (SCLC), Student Nonviolent Coordinating Committee (SNCC), Nation of Islam (NOI), Congress of Racial Equality (CORE), Ella Baker Center for Human Rights, National Association for the Advancement of Colored People (NAACP), Rainbow Push, Mississippi Freedom Democratic Party (MFDP), Lowndes County Freedom Organization (LCFO, also known as the Black Panther Party), and even extended to black gun clubs which rose to protect the movement's members from racist terrorism.

What is notable about all of this organizing which took place during the Civil Rights era is the coordination which occurred across a broad front of organizations, the sustainability of pro-rights initiatives, the tremendous self-sacrifice that were committed by all community members, the critical role of the black churches in serving the efforts of the struggle, the coordinated support of black journalism and media, as well as the tremendous participation by young people in providing the movement its powerful thrust.

This point of youth participation cannot be overlooked as there is a continuous record of high youth participation in virtually every significant revolution that has taken place in modern history. When we examine photographs and films of the civil rights confrontations, while we may recognize the faces of movement leaders on the front lines, surrounding these leaders and filling up most of the masses within these conflicts were high school and college students as well as youth from across the community. To this date, with the Black Lives Matter movement, we must note that fearlessness and commitment on the part of young people is key to sustainable demands for justice, economic advancement, a voice in governance and the demand for fundamental human rights.

With the passage of the Civil Rights Act, enacted in July 1964 and the Voting Rights Act, signed into law in August 1965, this era of the movement peaked, even though many remnants of the struggle would continue indefinitely. The assassination of noted leaders such as Malcolm X, Rev. Martin King Jr., Medgar Evers, and others, put a painful cap to this era of struggle. From the Watts riots in Los Angeles in August 1965 to a series of urban uprisings during that time which took place in Rochester, Harlem, Philadelphia, Omaha, Newark, Chicago, Washington and Baltimore, it became ever more clear that the struggle for Civil Rights which mainly concentrated itself to a few southern states had not quelled the deep disturbance to the psyche of urban Blacks in the U.S. By the 1970s a new chapter had begun within the Afri-Amer struggle which would display increasing distraction from the type of sustained development and struggle which had been present since the end of enslavement. This new face of black struggle has gone through numerous phases as it still struggles to demonstrate its historical significance.

The rise of China to superpower status

In support of our broad focus on replicable models for *The Repairing*, there are numerous reasons to look closely at the example of China's growth and development from the 1970s. This should serve as an ideal pathway that would move our group forward toward the achievement of our strategic vision. Revitalizing itself from being crushed during the Second World War and its protracted civil war, China's domestic mobilization is itself remarkable for various examples of spectacular transformation.

Topics which could be covered in great depth include the rich Chinese historical and cultural inheritance, long traditions of excellence in arts, craftsmanship and the healing sciences, the role of central planning from a single-party state leadership (which eventually blended with *controlled measures* of free-market capitalism), China's nearly complete eradication of poverty and malnutrition over the span of a few decades, massive industrial infrastructure development, the low level of crime within the nation, the close cooperation with Chinese ethnic enclaves around the world, as well as the great discipline shown by the global Chinese family concerning excellence of education in science, technology, engineering and mathematics (STEM).

For much of the purpose of this research which comprises *The Repairing*, our focus is on China's meteoric rise to global superpower status, today assuming the number one position in the world in GDP/PPP (Gross Domestic Product/Purchasing Power Parity), above the European Union and the United States, who currently occupy the second and third positions. The key to China's rapid wealth expansion is its production of surplus for transnational trade. As well, one of the most important components of this global economic success has been China's deep trade and development relationships across the African continent. If there were any single factor that has assisted China to rise so rapidly in the last 40 years, their reliance upon imported industrial and energy commodities from Africa could be considered to be that key.

In the introduction to Howard W. French's book **CHINA'S SECOND CONTINENT: HOW A MILLION MIGRANTS ARE BUILDING A NEW EMPIRE IN AFRICA**, the author points to numerous keys to the great success that China has enjoyed in its current relationships with African nations. The history of African-Chinese commercial collaboration can be traced back to ancient African trading empires such as Axum which had extensive commerce relationships with China and India, among other nations, during the dominant period of the Horn of Africa empire from 100-940 A.D. Axum "was one of only four major international super powers of its day along with Persia, Rome and China." [12] After their emergence from decades of isolation and internal consolidation of the socialist state, in 1975 Chinese state-run enterprises made their first foray into African mineral extraction with the $150 million purchase of a copper mine in Zambia, the world's 7th largest producer of the valuable industrial mineral.

Fast forward to 40 years later, and China's development partnerships across Africa have risen to nearly $60 billion invested annually, with total Africa-China trade at just under $300 billion, exceeding the United States which had formerly held the top position as a trade and investment partner for emerging African nations. In contrast, China's current African trade is more than nine times that of the United States, which has seen

---

[12] When Black Men Ruled the World: 5 Arab Kingdoms, Cities Dominated By Africans Before Rise of Islam, from the staff of Atlanta Black Star, Oct. 2013 / taken from their website AtlantaBlackStar.com

its share of imports from Africa drop from a high of $113.5 billion in 2008, to $25.4 billion in 2015, a decline of over 77% in 8 years.

I have for years cited statistics on this relationship between Chinese investors, development, trade, and African nations' collaboration. In 2013 China invested some $40.7 billion in African infrastructure development for which it received $210 billion in trade benefits, a ratio of investment-to-trade of 5 dollars in trade for every dollar invested. That same year Afri-Amers spent almost the same amount, about $40 billion on *increased spending* during the holiday shopping months. Similarly, in November and December 2015, Afri-Amers spent $49.7 billion on increased shopping for the holidays – with essentially no expectation or major data to show a wealth-enhancing return on that investment except for the psychological value of consumer satisfaction.

China has profited more than any other nation on Earth from its extensive trade and development relations with the African continent. China's whole globalization effort, which has sustained its rise in GDP by an average of *10.2% annual growth* over two decades, has increased the nation's net worth by 698% over 20 years. A similar expansion in Afri-Amer economic activity, using the somewhat dubious measuring point of $1.3 trillion in *consumer spending*, would have our purchasing power increasing to nearly $10 trillion by the year 2036. Key to such a spectacular transformation would have to include the idea of our taking over the top position of trade with the African continent.

Through the trade and development protocol known as the "Beijing Consensus" Chinese developers, both state-owned and private enterprise, have invested in a huge number of infrastructure projects across Africa, Asia, South America, and even Europe, to include: railroads, highways, airports, harbor facilities, municipal buildings, factories, auto manufacturing capacity, refineries, hydroelectric projects, healthcare facilities, universities, industrial mining, and increasingly security partnerships. While there are certainly reasons to be concerned with the sustainability and quality of some of these projects, for the recipient nations, these trade-for-infrastructure deals yield immense benefit to their citizens as it also brings huge profits to Chinese investors. More recently, China has entered a $50 billion memorandum of understanding with the Central American nation of Nicaragua to plan a future canal route from the Pacific Ocean to the Caribbean Basin which would dwarf the now-dominant Panama Canal. This will signal a major game-changing development affecting trade relationships in the Western Hemisphere.

The takeaway lessons from our detailed inquiry into China's rapid rise to dominance in global trade center upon their focus on massive-scale industrial production from raw materials, seeking off-shore partnerships for domestic wealth generation, and their massive return on investments in developing nations. Nowhere do we witness greater rates of return than that from investments on the African continent and it will be expected to be so for the next century and beyond. This is indeed a powerful lesson for Afri-Amers to achieve self-determination and sustainable development over the next century.

Singapore under Lee Kwan Yew

"I was trying to create, in a third world situation, a first world oasis," Lee Kwan Yew (LKW), longtime Prime Minister of Singapore said in an interview in 2008. When one comes to think of the economic successes of the so-called "Asian Tigers", there can be no better example of a nation moving from the bottom to the top of the world ranking for wealth and industrial productivity than Lee Kwan Yew's Singapore. At independence in 1960, the reported per capita income of residents of this tiny Southeast Asian nation was a mere $428, but after 66 years of somewhat authoritarian rule by LKY's People's Action Party (PAP), the per-capita GDP of the nation had risen by 2015 to $85,300, the sixth highest in the world today, ranking above per-capita wealth of the U.S., EU, Japan, Germany, and the UK.

At independence from the British, Singapore was a backward nation rife with opium dens, urban gangs, slums, and often riotous tensions between its various ethnic groups. Briefly, from 1960 to 1965, it became part of the Malaysian federation of former colonial territories but was expelled from the group because of Singapore's tendency toward autonomy in wishing not to be dominated by the majority Muslim Malay ethnicity. Cast upon its own independence without any natural resources, a territory the size of the city of Chicago, no real infrastructure, and even lacking its own reliable water supply, LKY sparked a renaissance within the Singapore nation whose "only resources are its people and their strong work ethic." Using an authoritarian system of leadership under the dominant People's Action Party, Lee centralized management of national resources, rigidly controlled the media and internal security, while deliberately resisting interference and intrigue from foreigners.

During the era of the Vietnam War, Singapore profited by selling supplies to the American forces while remaining unaligned between East-West hostilities. In 1967 Lee's Singapore was a founding member of the Association of Southeast Asian Nations. Because of his law school education at the London School of Economics, Lee Kwan Yew made great advantage of attracting international investment in the country. Partners such as Texas Instruments, Hewlett Packard and General Electric set up factories in Singapore, attracted by a solid infrastructure, a well-educated and disciplined workforce, low tax rates, and the nation's reputation as clean, safe and easy to set up a business. The standard of education of Singapore students achieved world-class status in STEM sciences, electronic circuitry, financial services, and civic responsibility. English became established as the national language to unify the various ethnic groups which included Malay, Chinese, Indian, European and others, yet each student was also mandated to learn a second language to retain the integrity of native ethnicity.

Over the decades, Singapore built up major infrastructure to rival any modern metropolis of the west. They constructed major harbor facilities, cruise lines, a world-class airport to support the highly-regarded Singapore Airlines, steel mills, oil refineries, extensive roadways, water recycling facilities to help to overcome lacking a natural water supply, extensive high rise housing which was made affordable for all families to own, and all of this succeeded in attracting over 7,000 multinational corporations from the U.S., Europe, and Japan alone to set up facilities in the city-state. In the 2012-2013 Global Competitive Index, Singapore was ranked as the top competitor and its unemployment rated a mere 2%. Singaporean industries include electronics, chemicals, financial services, oil drilling equipment, petroleum refining, rubber processing and rubber products, processed food and beverages, ship repair, offshore platform construction, life sciences and seaport trade.

Lee Kwan Yew, a strongman and visionary, was both loved and feared by his fellow Singaporeans, stating: "Between being loved and being feared, I have always believed Machiavelli was right. If nobody is afraid of me, I'm meaningless." State policies came down hard on political and financial corruption, virtually eliminating such violations from the nation. To maintain the finest leadership class possible, parliamentary ministers, judges, and other top officials were the highest-paid over their counterparts within other wealthy nations. Punishment for many civil violations was public caning, a ruthless but tolerable punitive measure he learned from being educated by British schoolmasters. Drug smuggling in Singapore was punishable by hanging. People were penalized for chewing gum in public, littering, or spitting on the sidewalk. Political dissidence was quashed and Lee's numerous libel suits against the press, including foreign media, were notorious. Although there were attempts to challenge the People's Action Party for power, the phenomenal performance of the government and the prosperity it offered its citizens has kept them in power since independence.

In Lee's later years of rule, Singapore had to acknowledge a crisis of extremely low birthrate, a problem confronting Japan, South Korea, Germany, and other developed nations as well, particularly affecting the European Union. Reversing earlier policies aimed at keeping the tiny nation from too-high population density, by the 1990s, the government was issuing propaganda to increase fertility, especially among highly-educated women. Numerous financial incentives were extended in maternity and parental credits. Total fertility rate (TFR) among Singapore's women today stands at .81 childbirths per woman, making it the *absolute lowest* national birthrate on the planet.

Without a doubt, like Marcus Garvey and the international Negro self-help movement, Lee Kwan Yew was a complex figure. He was repugnant of certain western ideas such as liberal democracy, western decadence, and what he referred to as "wishy-washy idealism." To Lee, "ideology took second place to the pragmatism of how power works." Despite his mediocre passion for electoral processes, nonetheless, it was made mandatory that all Singaporeans participate in voting. His was the appropriate application of tough love for his people to create in Singapore one of the world's great modern economic miracles and to turn this former "Third World" colonial outpost into one of the world's major financial centers. He guided the best and brightest to national leadership through a system of *meritocracy*, wherein civil employees were rewarded for the discipline that they showed in service to society. Lee also raised a national defense system, which included compulsory military service in the armed forces or civil guard that stands as one of the most competent of the Asian Pacific Rim nations. Singapore's military hardware production rivals that of the most powerful armies of the world.

As much as any other aspect of the enduring legacy of Lee Kwan Yew's 30-years as Prime Minister of Singapore, he helped to establish this as "the Asian Century" to displace that of "the Western Century" of the past. There are indeed many lessons for us to appropriate from the accomplishments of this dynamic and visionary Singaporean leader Lee Kwan Yew, especially if we wish to seriously consider the likelihood of "the African Century" ahead.

"I have spent my life, so much of it, building up this country. There's nothing more that I need to do. At the end of the day, what have I got? A successful Singapore. What have I given up? My life." – Lee Kwan Yew

---

Africa Rising - The ascension of Rwanda, Ethiopia & the Congo

Those who have followed my daily webcast on LIBRadio and LIBtv are not at all surprised that I have highlighted the phenomenon known as "Africa Rising" as one of the clearest models of how Afri-Amers can replicate the actions of others to create lasting progress for our particular group. Far outside the awareness of nearly all Americans of every ethnic group, and in bold contradiction to the constant stream of misery regarding the continent that is inflicted upon us by the corporate media, the reality across Sub-Saharan Africa (SSA) actually should lend one to remain quite hopeful. I can assure you that the brief space that I am allotting herein to describe Africa Rising is but a tiny fraction of the needed space to comprehensively cover all of the many aspects of what is taking place on the continent and how this will fundamentally transform the future of not only Africa but the entire world for centuries to come.

Where we last pointed to the examples of China and Singapore as clear models of national ambition which led toward the perception of this as "the Asian Century," I am saying firmly that the 22nd Century (Gregorian Calendar reference, this equates to the 64th Century Kemet calendar reference) will most likely be referred to as "the African Century." In preparation for writing this section of *The Repairing*, I pulled out a legal pad and made a list of the many factors which feed our positive outlook over the topic of Africa Rising. I listed some 28 powerful trends that are pushing the continent forward, some at a very rapid pace. As well, toward the aim of balanced inquiry, I listed another 28 challenges that face African nations which must and will be creatively resolved as the continent achieves its fully-empowered potential. I also frequently highlight how Africa's 55 nations embody this rapidly transforming destiny that we see across the continent. Three of SSA's most dynamically transforming nations are Ethiopia, Rwanda and the Democratic Republic of the Congo, and I consistently point to changes within these nations as best places for us to look for great partnerships in development.

Primary factors which are feeding the Africa Rising trends most certainly include some of the following, each of which could be further explained in chapter-length detail:

- Nations across Sub-Saharan Africa enjoy the world's greatest demographic advantage with higher-than-average fertility (within a geographic space with just a fraction of the population density of Europe or within the Asian Tiger nations), the youngest populations within nations, and the fastest rate of growth of the middle class over any other region of the world.

- Of the world's 31 strategic minerals, Africa contains the largest majority of 16 of them. Speaking specifically of just one, the Dem. Republic of the Congo contains an estimated $23 trillion in untapped natural mineral resources.

- Within the 5 Regional Economic Conferences (REC's) across the continent, the member nations are moving steadily toward integrating their economies and creating multiple pathways which will lead first toward unification within the REC's and, predicted by 2051, the unification of the African Union into a single federated state. Many of us will see in our lifetime a very real entity regarded as the Confederation of African States, which might otherwise be known as the African Union (AU) or the United States of Africa.

- One of the most influential trends of the future which leads to the development of national power is urbanization. Powerful nations have large cities that drive innovation, capital concentration and strategic policy formation. Across Africa, there are about 40 cities with populations exceeding a million inhabitants, of which three of the world's megacities are located in Africa: Cairo, Lagos and Kinshasha/Brazzaville (the latter metropolis bridging two adjacent Congo River nations).

- Africa enjoys the benefits of a youthful workforce, which portends well for the coming decades of sustainable growth through inexpensive labor expansion. This young workforce is becoming more and more educated at home and abroad to facilitate the development of highly-technical industrialization. Numerous tech-based innovations are starting to emerge from SSA nations such as mobile communications banking, organic food production, and alternative energy development. Several "Silicon Savannahs" are giving birth to technology innovation zones across Kenya, Rwanda, Ethiopia, Uganda, Nigeria and beyond. Motor vehicle manufacturing and assembly have recently expanded to six SSA nations, South Africa, Kenya, Nigeria, Ghana, Uganda and Ethiopia, and these auto makers are rising to provide African-manufactured transportation to fulfill the needs of a continental population expected to top 2.25 billion by the middle of the century.

- Within the African Union block of 55 member nations, the greatest area of ocean resources under national control exists above any other region. After confederation, the African Federation will have the largest Economic Exclusion Zone (EEZ, the 200 miles off the coast of any country which is considered to be that nation's exclusive right to economic development), and thus the greatest potential access to marine resources compared to all other nations. Proper management of African marine resources will be key and critical to wealth creation for many centuries to come, for which new generations of marine and biological scientists must train to manage.

- Sustainable non-nuclear energy development across SSA has greater potential for expansion than any other region of the world. Already much of the oil and natural gas production which drives the global economy has shifted away from the volatile areas of Western Asia (the so-called "Middle East") and into African nations such as Algeria, Nigeria, Angola, Equatorial Guinea, Sudan, Ghana, and numerous others. While new oil and gas reserves continue to be discovered across the continent, it is the potential of renewable energies such as solar, hydroelectric, geothermal, biomass, wind, ocean and newly developing energy technologies which will usher the world into a new reality. The rapid expansion of electrification across SSA is expected to generate some $3 trillion of infrastructure creation over the next 35 years.

- African agribusiness is expanding to make the continent the most valuable of the primary "breadbaskets to the world" over the near future. It is forecast that African agribusiness will triple over the next fifteen years to supply $1 trillion annually to the world economy, an expansion of some $640 billion each year over current production. Within that growth of agribusiness are immense opportunities to grow organic foodstuffs, safeguard seed stocks, develop medicinal botany, supply fertilizers for sustainable harvests, expand irrigation systems, build a "Green Belt" to hold back the progress of desertification, create storage systems for large harvests, develop rural processing of farm goods into finished products, and to expand production for African rapidly growing population. Benefiting from the long history of underdevelopment, African agriculture has the chance to move ahead clean and untainted by a century of chemical-based farming. There are more certified organic farmers in Tanzania and Uganda then there are in the U.S. and Canada.

- African cultural and artistic influence is growing rapidly around the world. From the earliest chapters of civilization development, we have witnessed how others outside the continent have adopted much reverence for African arts, pageantry, music, fashion and fabrics, dance, sculpture, coinage, poetic traditions, jewelry, wood crafting and other cultural traditions. Today there is a renewed interest in these creative fields and beyond. Popular music trends beginning in Africa are finding their way into the discotheques and onto airwaves of the world's cosmopolitan societies. African innovation in the arts and humanities will continue to influence world cultural exchanges for many centuries to come. Because of the commonality of culture and civilization across Africa, the expansion of Pan African media communications is anticipated to be quite dynamic over the coming decades.

- Africa still enjoys the greatest diversity of wildlife and nature spectacles of any region of the world. National parks across SSA supply amazing preservation of the spectacle of undisturbed species that can be found. Spanning the African equator, the most diverse and bountiful rainforests hold tourists in breathtaking awe as these regions also harbor species of flora which will provide the basis for healing breakthroughs that can sustain our health. The yearly amount of rainfall across Central Africa, which has created the basis for the greatest hydroelectric generating potential of any region of the world (the Congo and Zambezi rivers alone can provide enough hydro energy for all of Africa and Europe together), also feeds a life-generating zone which, from the dawn of life on Earth, will be humanity's best chance for surviving the disruptive trend toward global warming.

- Investment capital is moving into Africa at ever-increasing rates and the return on investment (ROI) from these numerous capital infusions is encouraging even more capital to be directed into this rapidly developing region. When China can enjoy annual benefits in ROI of 5-to-1 from its rapidly expanding SSA investments, then we can reasonably expect that our equivalent investments should be able to get similar long term traction and success.

I have highlighted just a few of these great advantages which are currently supporting the phenomena called Africa Rising. For the foreseeable future, these trends will continue to expand at sometimes exponential rates of growth, thus further consolidating the likelihood of the African Century ahead. As an accurate and honest assessment of development policies must establish, African nations have a large number of serious challenges that must be overcome for *sustainable* development to continue. While trying to avoid another depressing "litany" of endless problems to occupy our primary attention, I would be remiss to not focus our attention on some of these numerous challenges. These areas of focus would include:

- Lingering conflicts and internecine (brother-fighting-brother) which are nearly always linked to high unemployment, religious and ethnic rivalry, resource competition, the manipulation of foreign powers, and the desperation by which some national leaders ruthlessly seek to retain their grip on wealth and power;

- Healthcare, education facilities, sanitary infrastructure, water, electrification, Internet access, and other modern urban amenities are woefully underdeveloped for the majority of the SSA population. Per capita development and access to these critical functions of society are desperately in need of expansion to include all members of society, across class and ethnic divisions. Primary challenges such as infant and maternal mortality serve as powerful markers of the status of African social infrastructure and must be improved immediately;

- African industrial production must catch up with the immense natural resources which are being extracted. The addition of value to home-produced agricultural products, industrial mining, ocean resources and hydrocarbon fuels is critical toward the expansion of continental economic sustainability. To continue to allow other nations such as France, the U.S., China, UK and others to create inequitable trade deals that ruthlessly exploit SSA resources and retain the wealth for their citizens is insanity. African resources must empower African families and provide a pathway for our children to rise to the top of the world's wealth hierarchy;

- Global warming and the expanding desertification found in several large African regions must be tackled as soon as possible by a massive reforestation effort to build green belts surrounding African deserts. Already, Lake Chad, which has supplied livelihood for as many as 12 million people in Chad, Niger, Nigeria, and Cameroon, has shrunk by as much as 95% over recent decades as a consequence of misuse and mismanagement in addition to global warming. Desertification has thus been a significant contributing factor to destabilization in the region, an example of which is the Boko Haram Jihadist insurgency;

- Environmental awareness and anti-pollution efforts are in dire need of expansion across SSA. Those of us who travel to this region are often dismayed by the callous manner by which areas are disrupted by litter, discarded plastic water cache sacks, huge piles of urban garbage that accumulate around cities, urban slum housing with terrible conditions of hygiene, stagnant waters which breed vector-borne diseases, as well as illegal and unsustainable harvesting of forestry and poaching of large game;

- The current and recurring trend of commodity price depression has particularly hurt African nations as they are so dependent on commodity exports to bolster their economies and sustain national investment. Over past decades this cycle of commodity boom-bust has been one of the primary factors which have SAP'd (Structural Adjustment Programs of the International Monetary Fund and World Bank) African populations and snatched them of their course of development, wealth consolidation and advancing the status of their citizens. While the value of African commodities continues to be set in faraway cities like London, New York, Berlin and Tokyo, African nations will continue to have their economic fates withdrawn, resulting in the ransom of our future development;

- Wealth inequality is a key measurement of the amount of internal conflict within all nations of the world. Across SSA, the GINI Index, which is a measurement standard of the distribution of wealth within a nation, points to nations populated by Blacks as the least equitable distribution of wealth. The ten lowest-ranking countries on the GINI Index are listed as Lesotho, South Africa, Central African Republic, Micronesia, Haiti, Botswana, Namibia, Honduras, Zambia and Hong Kong. The best ranking African nations for wealth distribution currently are Ethiopia, Niger and Sierra Leone;

- While mentioned above regarding the greedy rule of national leaders and internal conflict, the challenge of integrity among African leadership must be raised. Though by no means could anyone ever claim that corruption in African governance is worse than that of western or Asian nations, nonetheless, we must restore faith and credibility for leadership among all Africans everywhere. Western nations spend billions annually to buy favor, access and suppress competition within SSA nations. The corrupting influence of foreign security forces on African soils, to include both foreign military units and private mercenary corporations, is having a long term damaging impact on our need for sovereign development and self-determining security. Most notable, American, French, NATO and British intervention in the security affairs of African nations is bolstered because of their ability to co-opt the loyalties of native military leaders.

- Increasingly, immigration into Africa of large numbers of Chinese, Indian, Arab, and European mercantilists imposes a challenge to the long-term evolution of sustainable African economic development. We have a long and tortured record of being exploited and governed within our own lands by colonial powers and colonist immigrants.

> While the battle to recover lands stolen from African communities a century or more ago continues, it does not serve us well to then be seeing another flood of such immigrants moving into the continent and seizing additional land because of their development financing advantage. We must acknowledge that the population of the planet is constantly shifting and will continue to migrate to where labors are rewarded. Still, the record of such intrusion into Africa should raise a high level of cautionary alarm as we pursue sustainable development.

It is my strong desire to someday publish an entire book on this broad and exciting topic of Africa Rising. Meanwhile, I continue to build an impressive library of books on the subject, read and understand them in detail, and to accumulate a mass of digital research and study it carefully as well. Africa Rising is a dynamic and expansive trend that has shown the potential to redefine the future of global development radically. Within this massively transforming phenomenon, I have become convinced that the fate of all people of African heritage, 1.5 billion strong around the planet, can similarly move upwards across a broad front of progressive advances. For Afri-Amers, the possibilities within Africa Rising are so immense that the overwhelming majority of us will likely just refuse to accept that this is the current reality. It is my most solemn desire that we can properly communicate this empowering information to a critical vanguard of black media, leadership, entrepreneurs and especially toward the education of our youth to manage our sustainable power for centuries to come.

The success of Rastafarianism as a transforming culture

In April 1997 I published the Conscious Rasta Report entitled **MOVING BEYOND RACE-ISM: NEW STRATEGIES FOR A NEW MILLENNIUM**. The theme of the book was that commonly held ideas about race and ethnicity, which had been serving as the basis for Afri-Amer social and political thought, were obsolete. For us to continue along that pathway of racial provocations, reaction and protest without resolution, followed by subsequent provocations, was the classic definition of what Albert Einstein referred to in his timeless quote, "Insanity is doing the same thing over and over again and expecting different results."

As a central premise to the book, I proposed that it was *culture* and not race that should be at the heart of our strategic initiatives to create a more equitable and advantageous reality for our people. Even reference to the word "race-ism" in the title was a new way of defining this phenomenon in a manner that could allow for a fresh approach to the challenges of ethnicity we faced. This research sought to expose that adhering to the *doctrine* of genetic nationalism called "race as a central theme of identity has become limiting and too often a barrier to rational thought." Rather than race, the book sought to consolidate cultural traditions that would shape and transform our common behavioral patterns toward means of sustainable progress.

The key to the new paradigm put forward in the book was what I called "The Six Axioms of Culture." These were a set of integrated themes that are used by anthropologists and social scientists to identify culture and civilization identity. These Six Axioms include religion (or more accurately, spiritual expression), language, traditions (festivities, rituals, ceremonies, etc.), historical perspective, values, and group logic. I also noted the impact of hierarchical ranking among society as another way of showing how notions of race identity were confusing, inconsistent and incapable of ushering us into power for group elevating initiatives.

In direct contrast to the often-quoted phrase by author Neely Fuller (writing in his book, **The United Independent Compensatory Code System Concept: A Textbook/Workbook for Thought, Speech and/or Action for Victims of Racism**): "If you don't understand Racism – what it is and how it works – everything else that you do understand will only confuse you." – my take on this perspective which was served up in my own book stated: "If you don't understand the nature of caste-based-hierarchy, then everything you say about racism/White Supremacy will only sound confusing to others that do understand." While that has stood as a very provocative stance in the face of so much angst over the topic of "White Supremacy," surprisingly, no one ever engaged me in argument to contradict the point that I was making. I suspect that maybe people might have been embarrassed to admit something that might have been so true.

Non-productive arguments aside, within the long history of the evolution of civilizations, these Six Axioms of Culture have loomed large. In the early part of the book, I strived to point out the great contrast between traditions of that called "Western Civilization", which should be more accurately called "Western *Christian* Civilization", were radically different than the set of commonly share traditions which would identify "African Civilization." As the world was moving further toward what former National Security Staff member during the Carter Administration Samuel P. Huntington referred to as the "clash of civilization" and the "remaking of world order", I thought it best that Afri-Amers realized that *culturally* they were either firmly in the camp of the hostile civilization to their own, or were at best sitting on the fence between two seriously hostile forces vying for future viability.

As the book evolved, in the chapter entitled "**The Phenomenal Success of Rastafarianism as a Transforming Cultural Model**" I sought to demonstrate an example of how the creation of a new and disruptive culture can interrupt a group's development and become a massively transforming agent in the evolution of a people. From my own direct and anthropological observations, the appearance of Rastafarian culture on the world scene between the early 1970s and 1990s showed a perfect example of this concept that new cultures do frequently appear within the course of society and that within such cultures behaviors can quickly become established on a vast scale.

Riding on the wings of a wildly popular Jamaican popular music trend, advanced by a vast collection of musical, religious, media and demographic influences, and with its distinct core of radical ways at viewing the world, Rastafarianism spread like cultural wildfire from its Jamaican/African roots throughout the Caribbean Basin, into Europe, North America, Central and South Americas, across the African continent and even made a significant presence in distant Asian lands. By the time indigenous reggae musical groups sprang up in Tokyo calling their musical scene "Jah Pan," we can see that this cultural influence indeed has widespread adherence around the world. Citizens of nations where very little English would be commonly spoken seemed to easily learn to sing along to Bob Marley songs in Jamaican patois dialect.

The reggae-fueled Rastafarian movement had its own distinct set of cultural norms, many of which rapidly transformed common behaviors and traditions, especially among younger adults and teenagers. These included: themes of African roots, a distinct style of dress and the popularity of the "dreadlocks" hairstyle, a newly formed religion centered upon the deification of HIM Emperor Haile Selassie I of Ethiopia (His Imperial Majesty, Ras Tafari), a language richly steeped in Jamaica's patois colloquialism with newly-coined phrases such as "Ital food", "I and I (referring to us together)", "overstanding", "Irie (feeling good)", and Bible-based references to "Babylon" and "Zion" as symbols of wicked and righteous societies respectively. Rasta rituals and traditions centered upon Nyabinghi roots (African traditionalism) which included drumming, chanting and trance-dancing, smoking copious amounts of "the Blessed herb" ganja, avoiding political entanglement with established governments, and most of all celebrating the beloved reggae music tradition that we a primary fueling agent for the rapid diffusion of awareness of the Rastafarian culture around the world.

Within reggae music, one of the dominant themes was the unification of African people on a global scale. The presence of Jamaica's most famous modern son Robert Nesta (Bob) Marley was a perfect complement to the nation's other world-famous personality The Honorable Marcus Garvey as both were primary voices crying out for unification of the race. A vast spectrum of poetic voices championed themes of Pan African unity, peaceful engagement, spiritual elevation and anti-materialism. Among the many voices which sang these themes, David Hinds chief lyricist for the UK-based group Steele Pulse sang these inspiring Rastafarian lyrics in support of the Garvey theme:

Rally round the flag.
Rally round the red, gold, black and green...
Red for the blood that flowed like a river
Green for the land of Africa
Yellow for the gold that they stole
Black for the people that they looted from...

Within countless Rastafarian "reasoning" sessions, fueled by the mesmerizing trance of ganja smoking (cannabis, marijuana), explored all aspects of societal transformation, war, and peace, history lessons, speculation about the future and how a utopian future could be ushered into existence. In contrast to the dominating themes of peaceful coexistence which was consistent within these values and the logic which propelled them, national security agencies within countries who saw the rapid rise of reggae and the Rastafarian culture perceived this as an intrusive threat to their cultural survival; when so many sons and daughters of competing cultures saw that their children were vulnerable to the new ideologies of this radicalized culture, they were confirmed in their xenophobic attitude about this new thing called Rasta. Resistance to Rastafarianism rose to the point of murderous schemes, conspiracies to generate violent political confrontations, the imposition of a pretentious "Drug War" against proponents of the culture, along with other covert and clandestine manners of disrupting these trends.

Nonetheless, to this date, despite decades of anti-Rastafarian machinations, the movement's cultural echoes persist. A large market for Rasta cultural items sprang up around the reggae concerts that eventually matured into a much-expanded, transnational trade in African and Caribbean artifacts as it also stimulated a great increase of production from artisans from across the black community. As well, the new fascination for reggae music stimulated our awareness of musical genres from around the African world and subsequently increased exposure to other inspiring musical artists such as Fela Kuti, Miriam Makeba, Youssou N'dour, Salif Keita, Angelique Kidjo, and many others as it also introduced new audiences to other African-themed styles such as calypso, samba, salsa and much more.

Components of the reggae musical legacy also became part of the foundation of Hip Hop music and culture, which soon followed as another dynamic youth-fueled subculture. Inspired by these calls toward global African cultural unity, countless numbers of Diaspora-born Blacks have successfully migrated to their African homeland with noted spiritual communities with names such as Shashamane, the House of Judah and Black Hebrew Israelites who've become established in Ethiopia, Ghana, South Africa, Senegal, Liberia and other nations. As a transforming cultural model, Rastafarianism is a wonderful example of how African-centered traditions can quickly transform individual and group behaviors toward that which supports unified actions toward Pan African development. As we have done this before, we can certainly do it again.

The global impact of Hip Hop

During my lifetime, we have seen the rise of newly-formed and exciting cultural movements periodically. These historical movements are not sequential; they do overlap one another. As well, they frequently spring forward from common roots yet become distinct because of the convergence of specific trends and influences. Many commonalities accompany these dynamic cultural thrusts which can be found consistently with such movements. For the most part, they emerge from urban youth as this is one of the most dynamic and innovative segments of society. These youths demonstrate deep passion within their lives for things that they have newly discovered. This is due in large part because they are not so deeply bound to the routines of adult life with family, career, debt or social obligations. This youthful thrust forward into new social patterns is a primary outcome of demographic shifts. Throughout history, one can measure the impact of demographics-driven changes which radically alter the larger social pattern, from the French Revolution to the Civil Rights struggles, to the transformation of musical eras and, more recently, the digital communications revolution.

The emergence of Hip Hop culture in the aftermath of the fading of the Civil Rights Movement, the end of the Vietnam War and the crushing of the Black Power Movement comes at a critical juncture in time when a youth population bulge (demographics, again) within the pressure cooker of New York's ethnically-charged boroughs was moved to push its distinct values out into the larger society. While we can analyze this phenomenon from the viewpoints of various social sciences some decades later, at the time, these youths likely had very little indication during the early years that their cultural expression would become the world-changing element of which Hip Hop culture has now proven itself to be. Young people just wanted to have fun, socialize among their peers, celebrate their youthful vitality, meet members of the opposite sex, and talk to all who would listen about their distinct impressions of the world around them. This was all natural and predictable.

I started analyzing this Hip Hop phenomenon early on within the circles of people that I associated with, yet I was still rather late to comprehend just how massively impactful it was to become. My first forays into sociological, anthropological and psychological essays regarding the culture came from my background of investigative journalism into conspiracies. I tried my best not to add my voice to the loud and obnoxious chorus of castigation which was being heaped upon these young pioneers, most often by opportunistic voices seeking political attention or just loud-mouth social critics who seemed to have an opinion on everything. While I didn't necessarily celebrate rap and Hip Hop music myself, I was deeply into the Rastafarian culture during that period, and I could appreciate the phenomenon from the viewpoint of anthropology, a social science which has long captured my passion, thus allowing me a window for deep insights into this dynamic new urban culture.

My research into the emergence of Hip Hop culture, the impact of its traditions on widely replicated behaviors, the political implications of its radical elements, how it was being propagated within mainstream media and a clandestine *conspiracy* to manipulate it all coalesced into my 1997 research report, **RAP, HIP HOP AND THE NEW WORLD ORDER: PLANNED CHAOS IN YOUTH MUSIC CULTURE**. The book broke ground on several fronts and presented several shocking elements about what had been happening within the broader movement out of view of the overwhelming majority of the public as well as adherents of the culture.

To briefly summarize a few of the most surprising revelations with the book were included:

- The so-called Hip Hop generation was composed mostly of the childbearing-age population of black and brown urban residents. I linked this demographic and their fertility potential to the long record of eugenics, population control, and fertility wars. Simply put, toward a scheme to restrict the rising percentage of Blacks and Hispanics in the American population, preventive action was being undertaken to interrupt family patterns and relationships between childbearing-age young adults.

- I revealed that my own 1995 research report, **An Inquiry Into the Death of Eazy E**, demonstrated that the gangsta rapper and label owner was deeply involved in a circle of clandestine relationships that ultimately resulted in his likely assassination, after which his death was fed to the public as resulting from contracting HIV and dying of AIDS; thus this being yet another anti-fertility scheme intended to create massive hysteria among childbearing-age youth of color.

- There existed an organizational structure that tied the influence of media-propagated gangsta rap stars as well as salacious female characters to a much more powerful national security establishment. I showed in the case of several specific individuals how they had become captured within a structure which integrated organized crime, law enforcement agencies, private lawyers, record companies, the courts, and ultimately involving the U.S. Justice Department (FBI), CIA, the White House and psychological warfare operations conducted by the Department of Defense – this was an overarching and broad conspiracy involving the most powerful elements of the U.S. national security establishment.

- The book examined details of the deaths of Eazy E in 1995, Tupac Shakur in 1996, Biggie Smalls (Christopher Wallace) in 1997, and went on to forecast that one of two high profile rappers, whose profiles were examined, was likely on tap to be the next murder victim. I went on to explain how each of these murder victims has numerous covert associations which made them particularly vulnerable to being killed. Among these undercover tendencies were also included elements of Satanic worship and Luciferian cults. Several close associates of these dead rappers were also examined in much greater detail to expose their roles in the broader scheme to pull off the Hip Hop conspiracy.

- I used the book to go further into issues of fertility, reproductive health, eugenics, the promotion of non-child-producing "alternative lifestyles" and the threat posed to the existing power structure by high numbers of childbirths to members of the nation's ethnic minorities if current rates of fertility among non-white women continued throughout several more generations. One of the most important themes of **RAP, HIP HOP & THE NEW WORLD ORDER** was the idea of "*Population Wars, Culture Wars*," that this fertility battle was being carried out using urban youth music culture as a weapon of psychological warfare intended to influence the behaviors of the target population.

- The most important part of the book provided a broad-based set of solutions which would take advantage of the impact of youth music culture and deliberately propagate progressive, developmental ideas into the population which are intended to help the youth rise to their greatest potential, consolidate their artistic creativity into a sustainable economy, and bring a highly competent young leadership vanguard into power and influence. I called this newly-proposed organizational structure the Seventh Millennium Academy of Consciousness (7MAC); elements of which have come to fruition over the two decades since the work was published. Unfortunately, support for these initiatives never extended beyond a small cult following. While the window of opportunity is far from closed, there has been significant setback over the 19 years since publication as one can observe when looking at the statistical data, which indicates the social, political and economic health of America's urban youth population, especially that of Black and Latino youth. All is not lost, but far too many lives have been shattered because of our failure to commit to such an intensive plan for youth empowerment.

There was a very strong element of deliberate conditioning using the power of music, art, and cultural elements that went into the hip hop conspiracy. The cover of the book featured a revealing quote from author and behavioral research investigator Aldous Huxley which stated: "Orpheus has entered into an alliance with Pavlov – the power of sound with the conditioned reflex." These references to the seductive power of music (Orpheus) allied to deliberate behavioral control techniques (Pavlov's dogs) had now come into the hands of social engineers within the pay of the national security establishment. Our youth had become unwitting victim to something so much bigger and more complex than they could have understood and when we sought to alert the larger community and political leadership to the nature of this sinister plot, we were overwhelmingly ignored. Among those who claimed to take this scheme and the evidence I presented seriously, they were, for the most part, paralyzed by the scope of the scheme and couldn't seem to do much more than nod their head and testify, "Man...That's heavy, Bro!"

Over the two decades which followed my investigation, hip hop has impacted global pop culture and economics. It is witnessed in musical styles, fashion, art, social values, traditions, media production and in 2015 even made for Tony Award-winning pageantry on Broadway with the smash hip hop/historical musical *Hamilton*. Daily, one can bear witness to the fact that hip hop long ago rose to a trillion-dollar-a-year spectrum of enterprises. For our ongoing contribution to it all, Blacks are compensated a small but substantial portion of gross revenues generated by the propagation of a culture that emerged from the heart and soul of our talented urban youth. But what significant lessons have been learned about how we should have the capacity to exploit and develop our creative innovation toward our sustainable development?

We do acknowledge that many of the same tools and techniques which have been developed to control, manipulate and restrict the aspirations of a people can also be reversed to serve as methods for empowering the same target group. The power of music, culture and art to preserve, propagate and amplify empowering ideas is something that cannot be further ignored if we are to project ourselves forward into a sustainable future. This deep inquiry into the hip hop conspiracy allowed powerful insights that will remain exceptionally utilitarian for generations to come. We have learned so very much along this course of multiple investigations into history, culture, politics, human rights struggles, rising ethnic and national groups, as well as our mastery of civilization evolution. At a certain point, it is highly anticipated that we will certainly put together the right combination of all of these empowering elements and create an unstoppable master plan for our group elevation.

This moment – our moment has arrived, and yes, we are up to the task of repairing ourselves.

Exponential organizations

While so many of our past efforts toward transforming the race, and proposals for continued actions, have involved grassroots organizing, non-governmental organizations and political aims, the reality is that much of what we can identify as transformative and sustainable development is being done under the agency of private businesses. In certain ways, today's largest multinational corporations are often as wealthy and influential as national governments. According to Forbes, for 2016 the top three of the world's highest capitalized companies are all Chinese financial firms: #1 ICBC (market cap of $3.42 trillion), #2 China Construction Bank (market cap of $2.83 trillion), and #3 Agricultural Bank of China (market cap of $2.74 trillion), with annual sales of $171.1 billion, $146.8 billion and $131.9 billion respectively.

Among top U.S. corporations on the Forbes list, also financial service corporations, include #4 Berkshire Hathaway (market cap of $561.1 billion), #5 JPMorgan Chase (market cap of $2.42 trillion) and #7 Wells Fargo (market cap of $1.85 trillion) with annual sales of $210.8, $99.9 and $91.4 billion respectively. Outside of these financial services companies, the top industrial companies on Forbes' list are #8 Apple (market cap of $293.3 billion), #9 ExxonMobil (market cap of $336.8 billion) and #10 Toyota Motor (market cap of $406.7 billion) with respective annual sales of $233.3, $236.8 and $235.8 billion each.

Pardon my exercise of a bit of data overload here but I want to point out that black-owned enterprises are conspicuously missing from this list. While there is a constant focus on our alleged "Black Consumer Power" of upwards of $1.3 trillion annually, black-owned businesses produce only about 14% of the monies that we spend. Thus our industrial GDP is only around $182 billion annually. Each of the world's top ten corporations produces nearly as much or more than this entire class of 45.7 million Afri-Amers combined. Something is terribly wrong with these metrics. We need to consider doing something at a scale sufficient to fix this failure to measure up to multinational success. While calls for the black community to improve its status through means of economic advancement, it seems quite apparent that practical models for doing so have not been sufficiently developed. If your experience is similar to my own, you have heard dozens of proposals for economic improvement but don't see many examples of them working. Thus it is likely that we are continuously holding up inadequate strategies to make these economic gains that we envision. I propose that some newer entrepreneurial models could be adopted to build a foundation for a powerful advance for our group.

The term "Exponential Organization" is taken from the title of a book by author Salim Ismael. Our analysis of *ExO's* might reasonably begin with a definition of the new business structures. In the introduction to **EXPONENTIAL ORGANIZATIONS: WHY NEW ORGANIZATIONS ARE TEN TIMES BETTER, FASTER, AND CHEAPER THAN YOURS (AND WHAT TO DO ABOUT IT)**, Salim Ismail wrote:

> An Exponential Organization (ExO) is one whose impact (or output) is disproportionally large—at least 10x larger—compared to its peers because of the use of new organizational techniques that leverage accelerating technologies.

The idea of ExO's as such dynamic organizations parallels the exponential growth of computing capacity over the last half-century and is aptly illustrated with an explanation of what technologists call *Moore's Law*, which proposes "that the price/performance of computation will double about every eighteen months," thus the reality of how fast digital technologies have impacted our lives over the last 60 years. One of the central premises of this era of the ExO is that virtually *everything* is being digitized; even to include subtle nuances of our organic lives, our social patterns, interactions between nations as well as the relationship of the individual to the state. It is within this trend toward digitization that new organizations are springing up that can solve commonly shared problems on a massive scale and thus create an ideal environment for rapid business growth and profits.

As an example of the tremendous potential for growth inherent in this ExO class of businesses, Ismael illustrates the launch of PayPal, cofounded by CEO Peter Thiel along with Elon Musk, Reid Hoffman, Luke Nosek, Max Levchin and Chad Hurley. PayPal's radical Internet-based banking service success growth was so rapid that eBay soon purchased them for $1.2 billion:

> ...but the friendships that grew out of it were equally successful. The original team is now known as the "PayPal Mafia, and its members have helped one another on subsequent startups, including Tesla, YouTube, SpaceX, LinkedIn, Yelp, Yalin and Palentir—companies that today have a total market cap of more than $60 billion [as of 2014].

Among the most impacting ideas, trends, new rules, and pathways whereby these ExO's can create such momentum is the establishment within the organization of a commonly shared *Massive Transformative Purpose (MTP)* which can be shared virally within the organization and among its collaborative partners. This MTP serves as a powerfully impacting common vision or reason-for-being for the larger organization which compels each of its employees, partners or participants to collaborate toward this great sense of purpose. The driving theme of this book *The Repairing* is the MTP that for us to be a whole, productive and highly-contributing partner in the evolution of domestic and human society, we Afri-Amers must be united in the accomplishment of Reparations for ourselves, from our resourcefulness, as soon as possible, by every means necessary, and that attainment of such Reparations must extend to all Africans throughout the globe.

Throughout Ishmael's highly-inspiring book, many effective formulas are shared, which have become common to the success of the ExO's examined. S.C.A.L.E. is one such acronym which specifically identifies ways that these new organizations have become leaner and meaner and thus better able to compete against much larger, long-established business competition. S.C.A.L.E. includes 1) staff-on-demand, 2) community & crowd participation, 3) algorithms (smart computer programs to extend productivity), 4) leveraged assets, and 5) engagement. One of the dominant themes throughout the book is the critical manner by which small, *highly functioning teams* can greatly outperform much larger enterprises and this S.C.A.L.E. formula is a good way to comprehend how the "scale" and efficiency of enterprise sometimes favors lean organizational structures over their larger competitors.

Going inside several identified companies which successfully use the ExO model, the author presents another very practical formula identified by the acronym I.D.E.A.S., which stands for the enterprise's technology applications consisting of 1) interface (a digital means of connecting the business with its departments, partners and consumers), 2) dashboard, 3) experimentation, 4) autonomy (flexibility for members to act quickly and creatively toward problem-solving), and 5) social technologies (vehicles by which the community which supports the organization's product or service can interact with the company and the product user's peers, which serves to advance the ExO's MTP).

Another of our favorite books on the phenomenon of these Exponential Organizations is by authors Peter Diamandis and Steven Kotler, **BOLD: How to Go Big, Create Wealth, and Impact the World**. These same authors earlier collaborated on a similar bestseller, **ABUNDANCE: The Future is Better Than You Think**. For those who have followed my daily webcast over the years, the ideas within these books should be quite familiar to you. I do take this curriculum of ExO development very seriously and am firmly convinced that within this set of instructive publications (and I do have several bookshelves of similar and overlapping titles) will project forward within any group that will to commit a creative and competitive dynamic that can allow that group to accomplish its greatest ambitions as it makes its mark on the world of today and tomorrow.

From *BOLD,* we have another very important formula by which ExO's have such great advantage over business-as-usual, and can overcome the stagnation which has too often prevented positive transformation in the world of economic and social development. This formula of which I am so excited is referred to as "The Six Ds", which can be briefly described as the following:

- **Digitization** – All products, services, and business practices are being radically transformed by technology, sensors, communications, algorithms and computing.

- **Deception** – As these rapid developments are implemented, there is a period when the overall impact of these new methods is operating under the notice of competitors, yet the exponential rate of growth eventually greatly outpaces linear growth.

- **Disruption** – This is the introduction of innovations that create new markets while disrupting the dominance of previous ones. The advent of digital cameras is an example of disruption when one considers the fate of film-based photography.

- **Demonetization** – This indicates the arrival on the scene of new business models who can utilize free assets that can compete against old models. Online advertising destroyed the income model for most newspapers, while shared resources such as Airbnb and Uber are creating havoc with hotels and car rental companies.

- **Dematerialization** – This is where the appearance of new technologies or methods make old physical means disappear. The "smartphone" itself has displaced many competing devices such as telephone, camera, video recorder, audio recorder, calculator, data device, GPS locator, dictionaries, and with the growth of shopping apps, even causing brick-and-mortar businesses to disappear.

- **Democratization** – One of the primary ends of all of this 6D activity is that the tools needed to compete become so inexpensive that more serious players can now enter the field of competition. Today's filmmakers are a great example of the disruptive effect of new technologies, which allow the novice to rise to prominence by using available tools most effectively.

Comprehending these and numerous other functions common to successful exponential organizations, I am herein proposing that we should *seriously* consider the formulation of one or more such ExO's for our African-centered strategic planning for global development. Without giving away what I am planning to establish in much greater detail in later chapters of the book, as well as what a few of us are implementing in the background, there are numerous areas which ExO disruptive organizing can be very useful if applied, to include our cultural, economic, political and generational ambitions. As we would seek to implement the right environment where our own ExO mindset is nurtured and cultivated, idea formation can begin to coalesce at such a rapid rate that every member of the community can be excited to a feverish point of active engagement. We must *never* lose sight that "We're a winner and we won't let nobody hold us back. We just keep on pushing!"

Kujichagulia Villages as intentional communities

Earlier, we utilized one of my four published books on Pan African economic development, **THE ROAD TO POWER**. Another of these books which can serve up powerful and practical models quite relevant toward our aim of self-determined Reparations is the Conscious Rasta Report I published in June 2013, **KUJICHAGULIA VILLAGES: A PRACTICAL PLAN FOR SELF-DETERMINATION**. This Kiswahili word of the title is a key principle from our annual Kwanzaa celebrations and is best defined by the Kwanzaa creator as: "Kujichagulia – Self-Determination; to define ourselves, name ourselves, create for ourselves and speak for ourselves." Within this extensive research, we shared experiences from five years of hands-on experience helping to develop three black-owned land projects in Louisiana, Illinois and Virginia, along with assistance with similar developments in Ghana, Benin and Zimbabwe. We have since added one more property in South Carolina as a recipient of our assistance and are in the early stages of expanding to other land projects domestically and internationally. All of these projects are privately held lands whose owners have developed their vision of using the lands for community development, agribusiness, sustainable living training academies, and the preservation of productivity on the land for the benefit of the extended family.

Some of the projects which our Living In Black Family, a group of over 8500 registered members who have linked together over our social media network (www.LivingInBlack.com), have had a lasting impact on these properties. Projects have included: clearing land and building physical structures, building campground facilities and hosting annual retreats, building organic gardens on the properties, planting orchards, building furniture, providing financial assistance for the upkeep and maintenance of these properties, helping to publicize events held on these properties, and participating in community-building efforts which further integration of these properties into the local community. Our international efforts have supplied financial assistance to numerous projects which have aided building infrastructure, supporting schools and training academies, helping to finance irrigation projects, and providing support for travel organizations that bring tourists to these properties.

Yet, within the pages of **KUJICHAGULIA VILLAGES**, our ambitions go much further. The book outlines some 110 means by which these projects can grow into full-blown modern, even futuristic versions of the Black Towns traditions. In the modern technological age, we envision expanding our infrastructure creation on these properties toward the aim of creating diverse and prospering communities of permanent and temporary residents where urban *refugees* can ally themselves with their rural counterparts and share resources for mutual development. Some of our ideas are based upon means of capitalizing already-existent patterns of living and lifestyle common to community functioning. Among the myriad of programs include such categories as:

- De-Urbanized Survival Zones with Construction of Co-Housing
- Healing Resort Facilities and Retreats
- Campgrounds
- Organic Food Production, Food Processing, and Distribution
- Vocational Training Facilities and Innovation Zones
- Convention Center
- Outdoor Amphitheater
- Agri-Tourism and Cultural Tourism
- Sound Stage for Media Production
- Sustainable Energy Development & Training
- A People's University for All Levels and Remote Learning Via the Internet

- And much more (listing as many as 110 distinct, revenue-generating enterprises)

For years, our social media network generated an enthusiastic response among its membership, and we were able to inspire our constituency to support our *Ujima Camping Retreats* in numbers by the dozens. Unfortunately, when more popular social media networks like Facebook came along, active participation from our distinct members dropped dramatically. Much of what we accomplished over the years was quite substantial, and we created a record of collaborative activities of which we were very proud. Ultimately the idea of Kujichagulia Villages development served to be a wonderful model of what could be done with our intentional communities at the most current stage of our development. Far from obsolete, this dynamic model of African-centered rural development can easily be updated and ready to receive a great amount of investment. I have since added a more distinct model of urban development that parallels the Villages but is adapted to nuanced sophistries of urban life. I have been searching for urban organizations and academies willing to take measures to implement such a plan for self-determining and sustainable development. Time will tell whether we can pull off some miracles with such visionary projects.

Summarizing Replicable Models and Historical Precedence

We have offered up this spectrum of 13 practicable models from which key elements for group-serving initiatives and precedence can be extracted. We have shown periods where African people around the world and throughout history have proven themselves to be resourceful, disciplined, and highly-accomplishing. Core values have been identified from within our distinct ethnic journeys as well as parallel achievement from other groups as well. The Repairing continues, these core values and themes must be constantly revisited as they serve as foundation pillars for that which is our envisioned pathway ahead. By all means, complete knowledge and comprehension of this historical precedent are intended to be both empowering and exciting. Knowing with full confidence just how great have been the accomplishments of countless generations of our ancestors, we can gain an inspiring glimpse of the historical record that our posterity should recognize of us.

We are at a major crossroads in world history, and this is even more urgent for our particular journey through this critical corner of the planet. This entire race of 1.5 billion people of African ancestry is eager to see the Afri-Amer segment of the family step up to the full capacity to provide needed guidance and leadership for the rest. We are well educated, skilled and experienced in every field of practical human achievement. With this understanding and the confidence that it allows us, we step boldly forward upon our journey of 24 thousand miles toward this spectacular achievement we call *The Repairing*.

Chapter 6 – Massive Transformative Purpose

"Freedom is never given; it is won." – A. Philip Randolph

"Success is to be measured not so much by the position that one has reached in life as by the obstacles which he has overcome while trying to succeed."
– Booker T. Washington

Vision, Strategies and Tactics

I have come to spend quite a bit of my research efforts on comprehending structural transformation regarding *global development policies*. The world is changing rapidly in numerous ways: peace and security, health challenges, demographic shifts, urbanization, sustainable development, adaptation to climate changes, preservation of wildlife and natural diversity, marine resources management, wealth and income inequalities, a fourth wave of industrialization, changing gender relationships, periodic swings in economic outlooks affecting large regions, the appearance of new competitors in industry and trade, as well as a spectrum of challenges to the fundamental human rights of all who inhabit this lovely planet.

Amid such a broad set of problems and challenges facing this ever-more integrated global community, one can certainly see how some of us might become overwhelmed with personal challenges and thus fail to focus upon macro issues which impact our long-term status.

Throughout our years of study and broadcast through LIBRadio, we have accessed insightful studies, books, and other materials produced by those who have committed to creating means of solving problems, large and small. Developing bold visions of our key role in determining the fate of the entire planet is one of the fundamental lessons that we acquired from analysis of the book **BOLD: How to Go Big, Create Wealth and Impact the World,** published in 2015 from authors Peter H. Diamandis and Steven Kotler. Among the many revealing takeaways from that study are: 1) a critical need for organizations to establish a *Massive Transformative Purpose* (MTP) to unify, excite, energize and compel collaboration within any given group toward achievement of well-defined goals; 2) how the rapid evolution of technology is completely integrated into how communities, cities and entire nations will adapt to a disrupted future; and 3) many executives from today's top-performing corporations, especially in the new-tech fields, have adopted a distinctively different mindset than have those of traditional businesses, and are showing much more concern for issues beyond the "bottom line" of the profit motive. For these reasons and many more, I include *BOLD* in the curriculum of must-read books to understand the future of innovative business growth.

Unquestionably, the future of world development will continue to rely upon agriculture, agribusiness, and rural development as a primary agent of the advance of human civilization. Among the best studies on how global agriculture is in flux, especially focusing on the potential of the African continent to serve as "the breadbasket of the world" over the coming centuries, is the book **THE NEW HARVEST: Innovation in African Agriculture,** by Dr. Calestous Juma. Dr. Juma is a highly credentialed Professor of the Practice of International Development as well as Director of Science, Technology and Globalization at the Belfer Center for Science and International Affairs in Cambridge, Massachusetts. His frequently drawn-upon expertise compliments his absolute expertise in global development affairs at numerous development conferences which take place in, or center upon, Sub-Saharan Africa. His curriculum vitae would encompass much of an entire chapter.

For this analysis, his book *The New Harvest* brings forward many key points where his research is directly applicable toward our stated mission, including 1) there is much rapid change going on in the world of "agricultural innovation systems" and that African nations are well poised to be prime field laboratories for the successful implementation of these new techniques; 2) the combination of large pools of youthful labor and newly emerging education systems are producing a human capacity dynamic that shows immense potential for consolidating sustainable development; 3) that transnational, state and local governance is in great need to adapt to the style of leadership that will properly manage this paradigm shift in global agricultural policies and market expansion, and 4) the role of multi-nation participation in *regional economic communities (REC's)* is among the key factors which will help disadvantaged nations to overcome the crippling legacy of colonial exploitation as quickly as possible. Of all the books that I have collected on Pan African economic development, both historically and of the present, Dr. Juma's book stands as one of the most practical blueprints that we could ever read that helps us to understand the complex nature of modern economic and infrastructure development.

Within this chapter, I've just mentioned two of dozens of books that I recommend for the *serious* student of Pan African economic development. I will include a bibliography at the end of the book for those who wish to similarly pull together a library on the current and future state of the subject. I cannot overemphasize the need to seriously upgrade our literacy in the expansive field of Pan African and global economic development.

During our February 2015 month-long study called "Black History is African History is World History," one of the most powerful and lasting concepts which emerged from that study was "The Six Pillars of Empire." This formula serves as both an accurate predictor of how civilizations have managed to appear on (and disappear from) the world stage, as it also served as a checklist to which we could look at the status of our or any other group and see just how viable would be chances for future survival and prosperity to the group. I will herein remind my readers of these Six Pillars of Empire with a bit more details on why each is such an important indicator of the *evolution and survivability* of identifiable groups. These Six Pillars are as follows, with brief descriptions:

Positive group demographics

It should seem obvious to all but the most logic-challenged individuals that a group's long-term strength is directly bound to its overall numbers, the health status of members, and policies that are dependent on a cohesive population base. Demographics have *always* driven the affairs of nations; *positive* demographics representing the empowering impact of growing numbers with adequate access to sustenance, and *negative* demographics which occur when fertility fails, population aging becomes too prominent, or the group's numbers are too dense to be supported by available sustaining resources.

The greatest nations of the past, along with those of today, are characterized by large populations—modern examples of which are China, India, the European Union, and the United States. Similarly, on the African continent, Nigeria, Ethiopia, Egypt and others are the recipients of what is called "the demographic dividend" by those who study the role of demographics in economic development. On the contrary, once-great nations are on the wane due to a dramatic decline in fertility, excess population density and an imbalance of the elderly-to-youth ratio that best sustains societal welfare. Today, nations in demographic peril include Singapore, Japan, Germany, Spain, Italy, the UK, and others who are all predicted to become even more demographically challenged.

Unfortunately, Afri-Amers have culturally followed the Anglo-American model of *anti*-fertility, and we are ourselves decades into *negative fertility* rates. This steady decline in childbirths causes our group to experience a negative impact from population aging, lack of support networks for aging family members, and a shrinking economic base. High rates of abortion in the U.S., which serve to cripple the nation over the long run, have had an even more devastating impact on Afri-Amers, so much so that our current *potential* population has been reduced by more than a third since we took on this policy of *infanticide*, which is what the procedure was regarded before political propagandists redefined abortion as "family planning." I seriously doubt that, given the real facts on demographics and the rise of national power, black women and men in the US, UK, France and Canada would continue to eliminate as many as 300-400 thousand would-be citizens of our communities every year (the equivalent to the entire population of a mid-sized city such as Miami, Oakland, New Orleans or St. Luis). This devastation has been ongoing for 40 years now in the U.S. and has eliminated an estimated 17-18 million Afri-Amer babies along with the descendants who might have been born to each aborted female.

Fortunately, we have the choice to identify as members of a *global* African family, and as such, we can reap the benefits afforded from the greatest demographic advantage on the planet today. More than merely a shift in identification, by functioning practically within a singular global African ethnicity, we can assure our viability all over the planet for many centuries to come. Per my demographic projections for Afri-Amers over the coming decades, we have approximately 50 to 55 years to get this right or by 2070, we will have been nearly completely *ethnically cleansed* from the American population.

At present, the cumulative effect of rapid reproductive degeneration amounts to a discreet form of "race suicide." We can certainly do better than this, but it requires that we plan and act as if we are at least well-informed of the critical role of demographics in the evolution of civilizations. In the simplest terms, toward the aim of basic survival, Afri-Amers only have one choice and that is to recover our group's demographics as well as to integrate our population of 45.7 million completely into the global family of African people, currently at 1.5 billion and increasing at the fastest rate of any ethnicity on Earth.

Comprehending demographics in the greatest sense for its impact on the evolution of civilizations, it is profoundly true that **there is great strength in numbers**.

Development of natural resources to industrial production

A hallmark to the presence within the world society of any identifiable group is that the people comprising the group have some measurable set of talents, skills, crafts, tangible production, service or other distinct contribution to industrial progress. Strong groups produce a wide range of products and services which are needed within the society. If locally available natural resources are available in abundance, then with the proper contribution of indigenous labor, the group will produce sufficiently to empower itself with *internal commerce*. One can examine the whole record of human history and find some distinct measure of group-serving production taking place.

The special history of enslavement lent a peculiar twist to this formula of group members producing for their own empowering consumption. What the enslaving parties did produce was the slaving system itself and their chief contribution to it was the violence and physical means of capturing and enslaving others to perform their labor for them. This model has, for the most part, become obsolete (although forms of enslavement persist to this date; some might argue that "wage slavery" is the modern form of the same model) and replaced by a volunteer national labor force. The bottom line is, within a healthy economy, members of the nation or group will create a spectrum of products and services for which they will be primary consumers. When a group produces less than what it needs, and that includes less than sufficient to trade for those needs which it doesn't produce, that group is in an impoverishing cycle. At that point, the group or its members become dependent on public welfare from others to attempt to fill the deficit.

Throughout this book, I frequently return to the *consumption versus production* equation and this is especially pertinent to the current state of Afri-Amers whose production of an estimated $182 billion annually in goods and services is but a fraction of the widely believed $1.3 trillion in consumption, which ultimately produces an impoverishing cycle. The ration here is $1 produced for every $7 spent. The imbalance is filled in by trading the labor of members of the group for wages which can sustain this level of consumption. Because the labor is traded at an inequitable rate of exchange compared to workers in the larger society (black workers are still compensated at a rate of about 70 cents for every dollar that a white worker makes), and this is not only ultimately impoverishing to the group but a form of indentured labor just a few steps away from enslavement.

Because we do not produce enough with our labor to satisfy our consumption needs, then we end up bargaining away from 30% to as much as 70% of the value of our labor to purchase that which is not being produced by the group. This impoverishing equation is the reason that so-called "Buy Black" campaigns are doomed to failure because there are not enough of the right Black products to purchase; we cannot live on hair care, sports, and religion alone. So, it should seem apparent that the second of the Six Pillars of Empire has also failed to supply Afri-Amers with a current pathway toward imperial development. We MUST drastically scale up the creation of products and services.

Creation of an internal trade system

As previously stated, this deficit of producing less than the rate at which we consume is ultimately an impoverishing trend. The intention behind "Buy Black" campaigns is worthy, yet our strategies for supporting such campaigns with increased production need be revisited. Opportunities abound all around us to capture existent markets and make great headway in relatively short periods. By accurately examining our consumer/producer trends, we can leverage these patterns and redirect consumption toward the support of increased production. One clear example of this is the area of food consumption, specifically *full-service supermarkets*. Looking across the spectrum of such enterprises in the U.S., we frequently encounter such names of favorites such as Publix, Trader Joe's, Fareway, Kroger's, A&P, Costco, Walmart, Target, Whole Foods, Sprouts, Albertsons, Aldi and many more. Yet, when scanning through this list of more than 200 national and regional chains, only one Black-owned chain can be located: **Calhoun Foods Grocer** in Montgomery, Alabama, founded in 1984 with five supermarkets and 300 employees. There are a small handful of Black-owned stores, but none with the economic clout of a chain. [Update: From a total of 15 stores at its apex, Calhoun Foods Grocer closed its third-to-last store in the Spring of 2017, thus no longer qualifying as a supermarket chain. The founder, Greg Calhoun, died in December 2018 at the age of 66 years.]

Yet, annually Afri-Amers spend a projected $80 billion at such full-service supermarket chains. Just 10% of this annual consumer spending could provide sufficient capital for purchasing already-existing stores that are frequently being sold off by larger chains. The A&P chain filed for bankruptcy in 2015 and set up a plan to put as many as 151 underperforming stores on the market for an average selling price of around $1.9 million each. Thus an entire chain's worth of 25 stores, five times the size of the only Afri-Amer controlled chain, could have been acquired for less than $50 million, one-sixth of one percent of what our group spends annually in this sector. With the acquisition of a distribution network such as that of full-service supermarkets, an entire supply chain can be activated. In food services, this can include real estate, agriculture, agribusiness, food processing, transportation, marketing and equipment supply. As well such a distribution network can be used to distribute a spectrum of products that compliment grocery stores. Looking at the top 10 employers in the U.S., 5 of these are firmly established in the food services industry with a cumulative total of 4 million employees among them. These top retailers, which include mega-giants Wal-Mart, Costco and Target, also carry many diverse products in addition to their groceries.

One can find other sectors wherein already-existing patterns of our consumer spending can be captured as we organize to increase industrial production and gross domestic product. At a certain point, it should be expected that we achieve the capacity not only to produce that which our group members require as consumers but to then expand manufacturing capacity toward producing surplus which would then be traded outside of our customer base. Logically it follows that an expansion of trade would extend across national borders to maximize our profit from excess capacity. Yet, current models of Afri-Amer business development insufficiently weave together diverse geographic regions.

What, might we imagine, would be the benefit of the previously-mentioned Calhoun Foods grocery chain of a once-high of 15 stores in Alabama expanding its operations to other cities with large black populations? Montgomery has a population of 206,000 Blacks, ranking 9th within the U.S. for the largest *percentage* of the black population, yet doesn't rank even in the top 30 largest U.S. cities when we consider the numbers of Blacks at a lower proportion of these cities' entire ethnic mix. If a chain of 5 stores can service an average of 41,500 Blacks-per-store in

Montgomery, then consider what might be the impact of the chain expanded to include New York, Atlanta, Chicago, Washington DC and Philadelphia with a combined black population of 9,660,000 Blacks? – Proportionately, that would require 233 additional stores to serve this larger market with the same number of customers potentially serviced per store.

What is it that prevents investors in these larger cities from seeing the value of taking a retail chain model and expanding upon it? Things could be so much better if we deployed this type of strategic planning. Unfortunately, in general, the black economy is going the way of decay and degeneration and this trend impacts black supermarkets as well. While it does maintain businesses in other Alabama cities, Montgomery-based Calhoun Foods closed its last store in its founding city in June 2015. This is, unfortunately, an all too common plight among courageous and visionary black entrepreneurs in America. The model of full-service supermarkets has proven itself to work very well across this nation. Yet it seems that Blacks are currently not prepared to compete in this huge segment of our national economy. (At last word, Calhoun's is now down to its last two stores in Selma and Tuskegee, taking it below the "chain" threshold of three stores.)

Beyond groceries and food supply chains, we can identify a broad spectrum of enterprises encompassing every aspect of what is needed to satisfy consumption within advanced economic societies. Isolating these opportunities and planning strategically to capture market share, we could soon be developing Black-owned enterprises toward the aim of creating a robust, competitive and sustainable *internal market system* to serve the consumer needs of 45.7 million Afri-Amers along with another 2 million African immigrants living among us. This should not be too complicated for us to comprehend and upon which to act.

Production of surplus for external trade

As was stated before, the richest man in world history is listed as the great Mansa Musa, Sultan of the Mali Empire. Our study needs to clarify the basis for the incredible wealth of the Mali Empire (whose indigenous name was the *Nyeni* Empire, named after its capital), which at its apex spanned the modern-day nations of Senegal, southern Mauritania, Mali, northern Burkina Faso, western Niger, the Gambia, Guinea-Bissau, Guinea, northern Ghana and Cote d'Ivoire. Included in the empire were over 400 cities.

The key reason for the rise to eminence of the Mali Empire was its immense trade. It contained three huge gold mines, and it is said that the empire taxed its precious metals with precision, to include gold, copper and salt mining. It is reported that at its height, one of the Mali Empire centers of development Timbuktu, supported a population of 200,000 people and contained an abundance "of doctors, judges, priests, and other learned men who are bountifully maintained at the King's cost. This regional center of culture and learning Timbuktu "was larger and wealthier than London, Paris and Rome." [13] Caravan trade traversed the entire northern African region, the most famous was the pilgrimage by Sultan Mansa Musa to Mecca in 1334 for the Muslim Hajj.

Our key lesson from this outstanding incident in world history is to acknowledge the critical importance of not just producing goods and services sufficient to supply the consumption needs of our indigenous population but also to produce sufficient surplus for transnational trade. This is a rule that remains consistent throughout every narrative of the rise of great empirical states. All the world's great empires were engaged in extensive trade including the Ancient Egyptians (Kemetians), Axum, Romans, British, Mongols, Ottomans, China's Qing Dynasty, Spain, France, the Mayans, and today the European Union, United States and China.

As we Afri-Amers would also aspire to write our names into world history for glorious achievement, it should be for activating a powerful system for industrialization and production of a spectrum of goods and services, including arts and humanities, for which global commerce will have high demand. We can already witness the ways that black music, fashion styles, dance, and art are highly recognized for their world-class appeal. Black scientists have made a great reputation advancing scientific achievement in fields of biology, botany, social sciences, space

---

[13] Mansa Musa & the Kingdom of Mali, from GoHistoryGo.com

technology and computer technologies. An impressive line of black inventors has made their mark within a spectacular listing of important inventions, to include such practical inventions as potato chips, the traffic signal, the light bulb filament, gas masks and hundreds of others. Yet, glaringly missing from this impressive listing of black inventions is the corresponding industrial dominance which Blacks should have galvanized around each of these landmark inventions. As is the case of modern Hip Hop culture, we invent it and others take our inventions to the bank on a massive scale.

This failure to capitalize on our creative labors and to create industry sufficient to compete within the global marketplace is not written in stone. We can put together the right type of investor capital infrastructure to seek out and develop this deep wellspring of black creative inventiveness. Our present economic state compels us to alter our course and become much more disciplined towards our sovereign development. A vast set of new challenges faces the world today wherein our record of accomplishment and unique cultural values would favor us as likely problem solvers. As an example of such qualification, within the field of natural health Afri-Amers have produced some of the most outstanding scholar-practitioners of our generation. Yet, too often, our indigenous and inherited healing skills are overlooked and ignored, for which our group pays a terrible price in the number of people injured and killed each year by toxic practices of westernized medicine.

Our vanguard leadership will organize to identify and develop this spectrum of creative and inventive talents with which members of our group have been so extraordinarily blessed. We will solve the challenge of building the right type of education and investment infrastructure so that we don't continue to "piss away" our resources with endless rounds of pointless consumerism. We strive to find the right combination of data-based evidence linked to a compelling narrative that will convince increasingly larger numbers of our thought leaders to collaborate towards this aim of *The Repairing*; we are left with no other choice – we've run out of time for indecision. Just the money spent by Afri-Amers during November and December 2015 on increased holiday shopping, according to my projections totaling some $49.7 billion, would have been sufficient to support a massive investment pool for global development for our group-serving infrastructure which would approach state-of-the-art within 2-3 years. Yet we thoughtlessly squandered this opportunity in 2015, just as we did in preceding years.

As I write today and share these strategies on my daily webcast, we are just two months away from the November-December 2016 shopping frenzy. During this upcoming holiday season, will we once again squander away another opportunity to secure a powerful global trading empire for the temporary satisfaction of seasonal consumerism? I don't think that the continuation of this pattern is inevitable. This decision is yet ours to make but it will require more than superficial calls to boycott Christmas and to buy black. Turning this holiday shopping season with its increased household spending into a nation-building program for community sustainability will require a precise and accurate plan with plenty of collaboration across the spectrum of potential partners.

Security and expansion of territory

One of the hallmarks of each of history's great empires is the might of its military. Toward the goal of wielding a strong army, a nation must already have in place the other five of the Six Pillars of Empire: enough young men to be in military service, production of military hardware (or enough trade commerce to purchase weaponry); and so on. Beyond the concept of a strong military as merely the ability to impose death and destruction at will upon another group, herein, we are looking at the mere existence of such a force as evidence that the nation has advanced to such a stage of state capacity.

As our analysis of the history of struggles within America against terrorist militias such as the Ku Klux Klan, there have been periods when black men were called to military service, outside of government sanctioning, to defend their basic human rights. For historical examples of such black militias we can examine the record of the Deacons for Defense, The Monroe, North Carolina chapter of the NAACP under the leadership of Robert F. Williams who formed a National Rifle Association (NRA) chapter and stood down Klan attacks, the Black Panther Party for Self Defense, the Fruit of Islam as the paramilitary wing of the Nation of Islam, the Black Liberation Army, the Black Guerrilla Family, the most organized of the street organizations (so-called "gangs") Chicago's Almighty Black P. Stone Nation, the New Black Liberation Militia, and the current New Black Panther Party which was created by a brilliant scholar and modern son of the Garvey vision, Khalid Abdul Muhammad.

Today the threat of racist violence and terrorism has far changed from what was commonly experienced after the end of Reconstruction, during Jim Crow apartheid, or within southern states during the most hostile period of our battles for civil, judicial, economic, and human rights. Yet, black lives and neighborhoods remain in such dangers that we cannot let up our struggle toward securing these communities along with all members of our group.

Within the boundaries of what goes for black urban communities, social and economic conditions have combined with lax government policies to create zones of high crime. Economic inequality, long a major factor of America's history is an engine of desperation which drives mental disorders, degrades education, constricts pathways toward upward social mobility, increases the likelihood that a drug-and-crime-based illicit economy will take hold, and isolates large numbers of young males and females outside of the mainstream of national society, thereby greatly increasing the chances that they will mature into lifestyles that increase the chance of criminal prosecution and incarceration – upon which the vicious cycle of intergenerational social mal-adaptation continues into another generation. We must always keep in mind that these young people represent our prime childbearing-age population. Beyond a doubt, the existence of insecure black urban ghettos has a strongly negative impact on fertility and demographic strength.

I determine that most of our recent and ongoing efforts to curb the high rate of crime, violence and insecurity which plagues black urban populations will continue to fall short because of the *Theory of Cumulative Causation* as was espoused by Gunnar Myrdal writing in AN AMERICAN DILEMMA: The Negro Problem and Modern Democracy. Within this theory, as we have mentioned before, no single facet of the challenges facing our people is disconnected from many others; I have identified some 14 critical areas of societal engagement that span this range of challenges. To the extent which we currently understand this interrelatedness of social problems, our efforts toward socially engineering a new *Culture of Success* for these communities must be based upon a complex mix of programs and actions which reinforce this entire spectrum of human interactivity.

Security is a precious right of all citizens of a nation just as is freedom of expression, healthy living, education, liberty, and the uninhibited pursuit of one's life goals. Keeping its citizens safe is generally the highest priority of a nation. Some of the world's safest nations have prioritized creating the highest quality of life for their citizens – this follows or supersedes anti-crime priorities – most likely because such a society has evolved largely beyond the widespread demonstration of criminal tendencies. Unfortunately, the United States is not such a socially progressive society and, as it has increasingly shown in the decades that followed the struggle for civil rights, America is more apt to increase state force to *contain* its citizens' protests than to work to resolve points of grievance permanently. As such, if it is community security that we need to move further along our course of sustainable development, we as Afri-Amers are thus challenged to secure ourselves to the best of our abilities.

The causes of failure of us to secure ourselves are numerous. These include both obvious and more nuanced factors. Chief among the problems is the persistence of wealth and income inequality, even within the black community itself. Beyond the firewall of racial segregation, the lives of well-off and less well-off Blacks were closely intertwined; we worked together, worshipped together, educated our children together and shared in benevolence which looked out for the integrity of family and community. Thus, a program to propagate increased security within the black urban experience must include means of once again bringing together seemingly disparate black income classes that became separated after the Civil Rights era.

Failure to develop a robust and expansive industrial economy has pushed too many of our youth to the margins of subsistence, requiring a new vision of productivity to provide our youth with economic stability. Idea formation toward illicit social behaviors is constantly propagated within media and entertainment, thus requiring us to distance ourselves from America's obsession with violent movies, television, and video gaming. As well, one of the primary values which have persisted within this nation is xenophobic fear of others unlike us and ethnic hostilities; unfortunately, these anti-black ethnic hostilities have been internalized to too great extent – Our redemption must include the acceptance of our physical characteristics, cultural traditions as well as our identity in the world as people of African *ascent*.

I always do my best to put such opinions in the context of credible research whose findings are consistent with the best available data-based evidence. One of the key research findings which I have taken from social research of the Pew Charitable Trust Foundation is this link between wealth and income disparity within a nation and the level of violent crime that takes place within that nation. In the aftermath of "The Great Recession of 2007" and the subsequent "economic recovery," the evidence shows that the widely-proclaimed recovery was inconsistent across wealth classes, with the middle class and the poor lagging behind and the wealthiest 7 % of households largely enjoyed the limited benefits of a recovery.[14] The impact of the real estate finance debacle was reported to have cost the nation's "minorities" an estimated $260 to $360 billion in lost home equity. Across all ethnic groups, this loss is believed to have totaled $7 trillion in home equity value.[15] This massive and rapid loss of wealth inflicted on our already-marginalized community cannot but produce a tremendous amount of social stress on black neighborhoods when so many families suddenly find that the major investment of their lives is stripped of its long-term benefit of equity accumulation.

America's cities have become some of the most violence-plagued localities on Earth, certainly within the boundaries of the most developed OECD nations (the Organization for Economic Co-operation and Development, a coalition of 35 of the world's most wealthy and developed nations). Amid the third wealthiest nation on the planet, the

---

[14] A Tale of Two Recoveries: Wealth Inequality After the Great Recession, by Benjamin Landy, August 2013, The Century Foundation

[15] Race and the Housing Cycle: Differences in Home Equity Trends Among Long-Term Homeowners, by Jacob Faber and Ingid Gould Ellen, Housing Policy Debate, 2016, from Routledge, Taylor & Francis Group

cities with the highest percentage of Blacks hold the reputation as being the most dangerous. It will be almost impossible to turn around our degenerating urban social/economic status if this poverty-linked violence and insecurity continue to plague our districts. Any solution for decreasing urban insecurity which does not include advancing the social, economic and political status of urban youth, appears to be doomed from the start. The very same youth who would be serving the defense corps of traditional societies have today become tagged as the leading threat to municipal security. Tragically, this high level of urban insecurity has recently spawned the growth of an ever-more-threatening (and extremely expensive) militarized police response; and the vicious cycle escalates.

Within *The Repairing*, our vision is to propagate a set of broad-based paradigm shifts that will allow for the advance of *real security.* As real security spreads, it will naturally follow that the business climate within these districts will begin to expand sustainably. Coupled with stabilized and expansive demographics, communities will grow, in turn feeding the need to invest more of our surplus into more supportive infrastructure and geography. This is how great empires expanded their national boundaries. This new territory will need additional labor to fulfill the expansion of industry and this upward cycle should be expected to continue indefinitely until the core civilization itself runs out of momentum.

Under ideal conditions, the core of human nature is empathetic, creative, resourceful and generous. Each of these noble characteristics is best nurtured in a secure and stable environment. We owe it to our children to make their world a better place for them to raise another generation to follow their own. We cannot allow ourselves to fail this most honored tradition of protecting our communities and enterprises from internal and external dangers.

Education of youth to sustain power

It should be naturally expected to follow that, upon securing these first 5 of the Six Pillars, a stable and wealthy nation would seek to perpetuate its successes for the benefit of future generations. This naturally follows for successful families and communities to similarly elevate their children to a new pinnacle of empowerment using ever-increasing resources gained during each generation. I frequently remind our community members, especially the youth, that "As we reach for the stars, we must remember that we stand upon the shoulders of giants." Over the long course of struggle which followed our emancipation from enslavement through the Civil Rights era, it was always a given that our children would grow up healthier, wealthier and better educated than their parents' and grandparents' generations. This evolutionary trend is reversing itself in recent generations and that we are witnessing the actual *devolution* (de-evolution) of significant portions of modern American society. This divide is occurring just as we see the trends of industrialization, globalization, scientific advance and upward social mobility for many developing countries all moving humanity forward.

I have become convinced that our mission to properly orient our youth for this global paradigm shift, that the fundamentals of what I've termed *Scientific Futurism* must serve as a core curriculum for these young people's sustainable advancement through education. Scientific Futurism can best be defined as "a method of using scientific investigation to predict future social events and trends."[16] In a later chapter, I will further delineate the 16 interrelated disciplines which form the basis of future studies. I will also share a list that I have compiled of 15 critical careers of the future for which our young people must be educated. Currently, a large bulk of urban education has placed our youth in danger of being left behind socially, economically, technically and politically. Highly informed professional critics of education have consistently decried the manners by which public education in this nation has become so inadequate, especially within stressed communities. This trend of failure to educate our youth to adapt successfully to rapidly transforming industrialized societies has got to reverse itself if we are to succeed for generations to come.

There are several disruptive trends and *megatrends* which are occurring across society, and this is especially true with regard to the future of

---

[16] IDEAS ABOUT THE FUTURE: A History of Futurism, by Burnham Putnam Beckwith, 1984

production and commerce. Interruption in the way that education has traditionally been proffered within society offers new opportunities to expand our group-serving capacity, or conversely, threatens to leave black urban and rural youth even further behind their peers in other parts of the globe. The world's most rapidly-advancing societies, currently favoring the so-called *Asian Tigers*, have highly prioritized education in science, technology, engineering and mathematics (STEM). This is consistent with Marcus Garvey's admonition that we *must* educate our youth to achieve scientific mastery.

Building upon our Honorable Ancestor's vision, we *must* educate our youth to manage, maintain and expand our vision of an African Global Empire from the middle of this 21st Century to its apex and dominance over the 22nd Century of modern history; which corresponds to the 64th Century if we choose to use the oldest accurate solar calendar of the ancient Nile Valley Kemetic Empire as our most fitting reference point to serve our perspective of the history of civilization.

It is often said that "A journey of a thousand miles begins with one step." There can be no more important steps toward our global redemption than these Six Pillars of Empire, which I have covered within this extended chapter. Ours must be a *massively transforming mission* that engages powerful visions, strategies and very precise tactical steps toward a well-defined set of future goals. This is not any manner of simplistic endeavor that is being proposed, yet the very nature of any civilized person should make these transformative motives natural and easy to rationalize. We have already shown our innate ability to craft powerful empires throughout history. This chapter has illuminated must-needed and critical steps along our pathway to the restoration of our imperial glory.

We must now set upon this glorious journey of thousands of miles and decades of disciplined focus. We step forward, focused on a point on the distant horizon, one step after another, after another until we have once again rediscovered our rhythm of life. Ours is quite a magnificent journey made even more inspiring by the great masses that are at our sides and at our back on this journey forward.

Chapter 7 – Structural Organization

"The thing to do is to get organized; keep separated and you will be exploited, you will be robbed, you will be killed. Get organized and you will compel the world to respect you." – Marcus Garvey

---

I trust that by this point, you are starting to feel the same excitement which has overtaken me as the book author. I've had a deep burning desire to get this material out of the folds of my psyche for the past year and more. Beyond personal drives and ambitions, this work is a lifetime tour-de-force, which, if done correctly, can inspire an historic transformation in the lives of many millions of persons, even billions on a global scale. What I want my readers to understand is that my entire life of scientific inquiry, community organizing, disciplined studies and futurist orientation has prepared me for this task at hand. I know that I am imminently qualified, sober and rational in this endeavor.

What excites me further is that I am confident that I have attracted a circle of associates in various parts of the world who are just as qualified as me to serve within this transformative leadership vanguard. Over 14 years of serving as a radio talk show host have allowed me the tremendous privilege of deep engagement with the finest intellects of this generation; I can claim that without hesitation or apology. I have also interviewed way too many who thought they had profound insights for landmark change but were deceiving themselves and as many as would take them seriously. There is a difference between a well-studied, insightful and accurate visionary and a self-inflated loudmouth who bum rushes his or her audience with unfounded theories, hyperbole and superstition. It has not always been the easiest task but I have managed to separate myself from the constant stream of useless, unfounded, or reactive noise that poses as "progressive conversations." Quite simply, our great mass of 45.7 million Afri-Amers did not get into this current mess of affairs because we have accurate and productive leadership. Much of the reason for our spectacular dilemma is because we have a lot of bad leaders and engage in a lot of meaningless dialog and banter.

The good news is that we can do better. We can *do* better because we *know* better. Many of us know yet have kept quiet so as not to stir up hostility and resentment with our self-criticism; this is again part of our problem. Because it has been an unwritten rule: "Thou shalt not criticize popular black leaders in public" (least others will be listening and use our criticism as points of attack). This "11th Commandment," as it has been called by one of my scholar friends, is a big handicap to our movement because it allows for intellectual stagnation to go on for decades. I will return to this point later when I further map out strategies to increase the educational level of our leadership.

The good news is also that the masses aren't quite as unprepared for change as many of our public pessimists have claimed. Contrary to popular belief, Afri-Amers are *not* stupid, naïve, vain, or dishonest people with questionable morality. To our detriment, we are *too American* and not enough African, but that can be fixed with the right amount of exposure to an optimized set of African cultural engagements. Yes, for generations, we have been duped (hoodwinked, bamboozled, had, misled, tricked and connived) into believing that we are merely darker-hued Americans (what I *used* to call "chocolate-covered crackers" until I mellowed out over the years). Certainly, too many of us eat like Americans and pay a high price for such behavior.

In other ways, our lifestyle has been corrupted by adopting a spectrum of Americanisms, but these can be corrected over time; they must be corrected for us to survive. The empowering factor, even within this maladaptive behavior, is that we can be enticed to function within widely-adopted group behavior. If hostile external forces are directing the group, then the outcome will be detrimental to long term viability. But, if skilled individuals are engineering the culture which shapes behavior within the group, and on such scale that it now presents as the group's traditional behavior, then a massively-transformed outcome can be brought to bear. This challenge of *inner-directed* verses *externally-directed* will is very important toward the future status of the group.

Social engineering (SE) is the process by which large scale behaviors become established by deliberate and willful planning. SE can have various aspects of engagement and involves collaborative engagement across a base of highly-affecting social agencies. Decades ago I discovered the following brief formula for social engineering in the highly-acclaimed book **THE HIDDEN PERSUADERS**, by Vance Packard:

> "Sufficient financial backing for regular utilization of mass media, constantly to communicate the desired objectives to the 'common man.' New values can be deliberately created, disseminated, and adopted as personal and collective goals highly desirable of achievement. But the concerted effort of the major social institutions—particularly the educational, recreational, and religious—must be enlisted with the ready cooperation of those in control of the mass media... By utilizing the various tested devices, our modern genius in advertising may alight upon simple phrases well organized in sequence and timing, and coordinated with other efforts geared to realize the 'grand design.' But there are required a host of laborers with plenty of financial backing." [The quote is from sociologist Philip J. Allen, Univ. of Virginia][17]

Among the social agents mentioned by Prof. Allen in this 26-part formula are 1) financing sources, 2) mass media, 3) the grassroots ("common man"), 4) educational, 5) recreational (leisure-time activity), 6) religious institutions, and 7) marketing professionals. I have become convinced that this formula is still highly practicable and have adjusted it somewhat to fit our contemporary application. One of several formulas which I have introduced within my books on self-development, which is somewhat an extension of Prof. Allen's instruction, is The Six-Part Partnership, by which I am claiming virtually *anything* that we wish to

---

[17] Excerpted from The Hidden Persuaders, by Vance Packard, pgs 236-237

accomplish that will affect the larger target group, can be essentially guaranteed to succeed as we can assemble this Partnership.

I will briefly describe each component of The Six-Part Partnership, each of which could be further explored in one or more complete books of detailed, nuanced research. I am convinced that this should be one of the most critical courses of teaching for any leadership vanguard. These six collaborations of which I speak are 1) grassroots, 2) NGO's, 3) public sector agencies, 4) the private sector, 5) institutions of higher education, and 6) mass media. We can further explore each as follows:

Grassroots Stakeholders

It has become easy to see mass movements in the form of iconic figures who served leadership roles particularly well during an era of struggle. Thus, the Civil Rights era might be perceived as individual actions of the Rev. Dr. Martin L. King Jr. or any one of several prominent clergies who've served on point for the struggle, along with strong leadership of Fannie Lou Hamer, Stokely Carmichael (Kwame Toure) or other such noted personalities. Yet this is not an accurate assessment of the history of this era and its numerous campaigns of struggle, resistance, boycott and protest. More so, it was a vast and relatively faceless mass of grassroots activists moving together in coordinated activity. The "Grassroots" represents The People in the most elemental fashion. It is not just those who are mobilized in the streets but also their peers, family members, neighbors and such. This mass forms the broad and most stable base of the pyramid structure that elevates the leadership to prominence and provides a solid foundation upon which all subsequent structures can be erected.

The Grassroots represent the target of, and how, empowering ideas and motivating propaganda is best diffused into the larger society. Social media thrives from many of these Grassroots voices who are particularly adept at attracting a response from a large number of people; this being the highly-desirable "viral" spread rapidly among the "common people." In an ideal formulation, Grassroots people aren't divided by ethnicity, class, religion, geography, political affiliation, or other hierarchical division. Yet, getting together such disparate collectives of people to be able to assemble and guide such an idealized notion of a "grassroots community" can be quite an elusive task. Upon accomplishing a sizeable assembly of Grassroots membership, visionary leadership shapes them into pretty much any form necessary to cause widespread societal change. Hence, political parties, marketing agencies, civil organizers, and religious communities spend the bulk of their efforts to galvanize a powerful Grassroots community and to direct them to sustained specific actions that benefit the greatest numbers of those being organized in league with the visions of the organizers.

Another critical function of the Grassroots community, just as the roots of lawn grass are critical to holding the soil together in the face of steep slopes or heavy rain, the health of the entire community is measured by the health of the masses of members. Too often, we have been led by deceptive forces to see the health of the nation as the status of the wealthy, powerful, celebrity or "beautiful people." They will promote the idea that the national economy is healthy when Wall Street executives receive exorbitant bonuses and shareholders get significant dividends. We should know better than to fall for this ruse. We declare that it is the health, prosperity and security of our families, grandparents, children in public education and young people making their way into adult life that are true measures of the prosperity and vitality of the world around us. As such, the Grassroots have great significance within our strategies to build unstoppable coalitions.

Non-Government Organizations (NGOs)

As Grassroots get better organized, they inevitably give birth to mission-serving development agencies – *Non-Governmental Organizations*. NGOs can range from small community committees with no formal structure to multinational structures such as Greenpeace, the International Committee of the Red Cross or Doctors Without Borders (Médecins Sans Frontières). As community organizers and activists follow the admonition to "Get Organized," forming an NGO is the logical next step as it doesn't require a lot of capital to bring an entity into being. At some point, to facilitate the acquisition and organization of greater resources, as well as to create special tax status toward the aim of raising larger amounts of money, NGOs formalize themselves with *non-profit status*.

NGOs are indeed powerful organizations that, like government agencies and corporations, can have tremendous influence in the development of national and international affairs. They tend to operate in areas of human development such as development, health, environmental protection, niche group policies, politics, as well as various sectors of social and economic development. Included among the top 20 largest and most influential NGOs in the world today are included such familiar names as The Wikimedia Foundation, Partners in Health, Care International, Médecins Sans Frontières, Cure Violence, Mercy Corps, and the Clinton Health Access Initiative. [18]

Among the most powerful and influential NGOs serving the Afri-Amer community are extensive systems of religious institutions. As Charles S. Johnson wrote in **GROWING UP IN THE BLACK BELT**:

> "The church has been, and continues to be, the outstanding social institution in the Negro community. It has a far wider function than to bring spiritual inspiration to its communicants. Among rural Negroes the church is still the only institution which provides an effective organization for the group, an approved and tolerated place for social activities, a forum for expression on many issues, an outlet for emotional repressions, and a plan for social living. It is a complex institution meeting a wide variety of needs." [19]

In the extensive research series, I conducted in the mid-1990s, which I called "**MINISTER, THOU ART BOUND – THE COLONIZATION OF THE BLACK CHURCH IN AMERICA**," I listed some 14 critical functions that the black churches have served throughout our long and challenging history as a subgroup within the U.S. This should serve as a powerful standard for correctly analyzing the historical, present and future roles that are bound to our religious non-governmental organizations.

---

[18] Top 100 NGOs 2016 / From NGO Advisor

[19] GROWING UP IN THE BLACK BELT: Negro Youth in the Rural South, Charles S. Johnson 1941

1. Spiritual & Psychological Support Center
2. Educational Facility
3. Tax Collection Agency (Tithes)
4. Communications Center
5. Business Networking Hub
6. Town Hall Center
7. Leadership Training
8. Health Advocacy
9. Social Support Network
10. Political Action Center
11. Political Refuge
12. Cultural Repository
13. Historical Repository
14. Conference Center

Within the Afri-Amer community, NGO's represent the highest level of political influence that we have amassed in the last century. Organizations such as the NAACP, Urban League, Rainbow Push Coalition, 100 Black Men of America, National Action Network, and Jack and Jill of America have been on the frontlines of organized struggle for the advance of our status within the U.S. There are hundreds of non-profits serving Afri-Amers, most established in urban centers, working in a wide variety of critical affairs to include "healthcare, daycare, entrepreneurship, minority business grants, minority business loans, scholarships, internships, equal opportunity, civil rights, and more." [20]

There should be no doubt that strategic efforts to advance initiatives for sustainable development *must* reach out across this spectrum of NGOs to benefit their already-existing infrastructure, tax benefits, staffing and experiential insights into the areas which we intend to develop. While there may be some negative history or political baggage that we may have associated with any of this vast collection of non-governmental organizations, there is a wide variety of such agencies that can be incorporated into our strategies for group advance, sovereignty and sustainable growth.

[20] Top Black Organizations and Non-Profits, BlackNews.com

Public Sector / Government Agencies

For so many reasons, it would be foolish to overlook the value of public sector government agencies as part of our essential partners for group-serving advancement strategies. The resources that can be accessed through the proper utilization of government assets, political insiders, and local governance, are immense. While we have witnessed a gross amount of government agency misbehavior at all levels of governance, as well as rabid criticism of the political processes, within this report, we have an obligation to accuracy. Listed below are samplings of the vast resources which can be tapped and integrated into our strategies for *The Repairing*.

Grants, loans and employment – Raising funds for our initiatives will remain a constant challenge for decades to come. Until the consolidation of group-serving endowments, capital investment funds, and other permanent funding sources, we can expand our currently functional capacity to access government-sponsored grants, loans, tax exemptions and targeted development programs. It is a requirement that we can deploy a cadre of grant application writers who are committed to the specific goals of nation-building within the group. As well, most elected officials are aware of available funding from government programs that can be targeted for our needs. These politicians will also serve as a key interface between various of the other critical partners, as they do readily access the media, universities, foreign diplomats and a spectrum of NGOs.

Small Business Administration – One particularly important government agency that assists community economic development is the U.S. Small Business Administration. Primary focuses of the SBA are centered on 1) negotiating the complex maze of business startup, 2) managing your business, 3) how to get funding assistance with loans and grants, 4) obtaining government contracts, 5) accessing business development education, and 5) tapping into local resources which assist business development including NGOs.

Within municipalities, a system of National Small Business Associations (NSBA) serve as local partners to the federal agency. Within these organizations, young entrepreneurs and existing businesses can get access to training, counseling, mentoring from experienced executives, advice on how to access resources, peer-to-peer networking, and direct access to many grants and loan sources. Under the NSBA one can access business services, resources, property and medical insurance, as well as disaster relief.

SMEs (Small and Medium-sized Enterprises) are the very backbone of the nation's enterprise. While large corporations get so much focus and attention within the press and governmental influence, it is the much greater network of SMEs that serve as the base for the greatest economic engagement of a healthy nation. As we have seen the disproportionate ascendance of large corporations and cookie-cutter retail industries across municipalities, the health of SMEs has suffered and therefore, the economic health of the larger community is put in jeopardy. The utilization of SBA resources is vital toward our goal of revitalizing urban and rural enterprise development.

U.S. Census Bureau – Our development programs will require us to produce substantial amounts of data-driven research. The federal Census Bureau is one of the best sources for us to get the right type of data which can serve the basis of market research, allocation of our sometimes-scarce resources, demographic trends, locating concentrations of our population and perspectives on the collects up-to-date data include: population statistics and projections, fertility rates, ethnic makeup of the citizenry, economy, business, education, emergency preparedness, employment, family and living arrangements, health status, housing, income and poverty, international trade, and numerous public sector data.

One example of the type of data which one can access from the Census Bureau, which would be quite useful for *The Repairing*, is the recently released study entitled: **New American Community Survey Statistics For Income, Poverty and Health Insurance Available For States and Local Areas**; September 15, 2016; Release Number: CB16-159. This document features "Statistics for More Than 40 Demographic and Economic Topics Provide Detailed Profiles of Communities Nationwide." Details, statistics and trends are shared on poverty, income, income equality, health insurance, along with other topics within the latest American Community Survey. The Census Bureau describes this annual survey as:

> The American Community Survey provides a wide range of important statistics about all communities in the United States. The American Community Survey gives communities the current information they need to plan investments and services. Retailers, homebuilders, fire departments, and town and city planners are among the many private- and public-sector decision makers who count on these annual results.

Not all of the Census Bureau data can be precisely accurate and, as such, must be correlated to other databases for more precision. I cannot overstate this point of vetting information for accuracy as well as being up to date. Nonetheless, when one is looking for a quick glimpse at data sets that reveal the makeup of the American population, this stands as a great go-to source.

USDA funding for rural and urban development – The relationship between the United States Department of Agriculture (USDA) and Blacks is not one for which the federal government should be proud. In 1997 a class-action lawsuit brought by Timothy Pigford, joined by 400 other black farmers, was brought against Sec. of Agriculture Dan Glickman and the USDA for racial discrimination against black farmers in the allocation of farm assistance and loans between the years of 1981 and 1996. The case, Pigford v. Glickman, was settled in April 1999 in the U.S. District Court in the District of Columbia. Yet the settlement which provided for monetary compensation of $50,000 along with loan forgiveness and tax offsets, did very little to make up for the long and deep injury to Afri-Amer agriculture for the decades of exclusionary policies which were entrenched within USDA policies.

Further pressure by an expanded class of farmers has forced the Obama administration to expand compensatory payments greatly, yet there can be no denying that it is much too little to compensate for the damage which was caused by USDA discrimination. As of the latest reports, payouts from the settlement of lawsuits against the USDA have topped $4.4 billion with legal fees topping $130 million. At best, we can state that the federal agency has become more transparent and less likely to be caught in such blatantly exclusionary racial policies against Blacks, Native Americans, Hispanics and women, all of whom have been the victims of USDA discrimination. During the Obama administration, the USDA is still occasionally involved in scandals over its failure to support Blacks and one incident involving USDA administrator Shirley Sherrod and Sec. of Agriculture Tom Vilsack shows that even under an Afri-Amer president, the agency cannot overcome its legacy of racial discrimination.

Some current USDA policy moves should be incorporated into our strategies for increasing food sovereignty, urban gardening, and expansion of rural agriculture and agribusiness production. The USDA.gov website shared an April 2016 news release of a program **USDA Unveils New 'Urban Agriculture Toolkit' for Urban Farmers and Agri-business Entrepreneurs** that provides funding and other assistance "to help entrepreneurs and community leaders successfully create jobs and increase access to healthy food through urban agriculture." The release read in part:

> Industry estimates show U.S. local food sales totaled at least $12 billion in 2014, up from $5 billion in 2008, and experts anticipate that value to hit $20 billion by 2019. The numbers also show that these opportunities are helping to drive job growth in agriculture, increase entrepreneurship and expand food access and choice.
>
> USDA's Toolkit is an electronic document that helps urban and small farms navigate more than 70 helpful resources, including technical assistance and financing opportunities. It focuses on some of the most pressing challenges confronting urban producers such as land access, soil quality, water resources, capital and financing, infrastructure, market development, production strategies, and applying for federal, state or private foundation grants. University extension service partners in Chicago and Indianapolis helped develop cost estimates for starting urban farms and the toolkit includes information on best practices and check lists for start-ups and early-stage producers planning outdoor or indoor operations.

It went on to list many of the resources included in the Urban Agriculture Toolkit, which could be of great utility to our partnerships whose mission includes food sustenance and job creation.

- The Natural Resources Conservation Service provides technical and financial assistance for drip irrigation and seasonal high tunnels to extend the growing season.
- The Farm Services Agency extends microloans that provide up to $50,000 in financing for equipment, working capital or other expenses.
- The Food and Nutrition Service provides assistance to help urban farmers become authorized to accept SNAP, WIC, and Senior Farmers Market Nutrition Program benefit cards.
- The Agricultural Marketing Service Farmers Market Promotion Program serves grants that support direct-to-consumer marketing activities in cities, and Local Food Promotion Program grants that support food hubs, farm-to-retail, and related projects.
- The National Institute of Food and Agriculture's Sustainable Agriculture Research and Education (SARE) is a program of support for field trials in urban settings and urban farm planning and marketing guides.

Libraries and Museum facilities – There is always a great need to find space for conferencing, holding small group meetings, information and data access along with other empowering activities that can utilize government-owned resources. Because the citizens own public libraries and museum facilities, then it is only fit and reasonable that we should have a strong say over how these resources can best be utilized. As we can observe that the proliferation of Internet-based culture has been somewhat displacing the vital importance of libraries and museums from public attention, it seems only fitting that our strategies for uplifting community and family development would step into to fill this void and reestablish these facilities for their critical importance toward our sustainable development. Because of budgetary constraints, many of these facilities will charge a fee yet these fees tend to be quite nominal and easily accessible to small organizations.

Libraries are also one of those areas of public sector employment where Afri-Amers have enjoyed a respectable presence. Finding allies within these facilities should be convenient. Librarians are a class of career with special skills for research and organizing of information. Within my own life's accomplishments, these facilities have always shown to be of great value. Much of our grand scheme for elevating our group involves raising literacy to its greatest potential and therefore support from, as well as the support of libraries, should prove to be a great investment of our resourcefulness.

As with libraries, museums serve a broad set of functions for the community, especially their task of preserving the nuanced heritage of the group that they serve. Museums are true national heritage and there can be no greater example of such preservation for Afri-Amers than the Harlem-based Schomburg Center for Research in Black Culture. The Schomburg is a unit of the New York Public Library system, with a specialized commitment to research into Afri-Amer, African Diaspora and African culture, history and living experiences. The museum is the living legacy of its visionary founder Arturo Alfonso Schomburg. In addition to its extensive and exclusive archives of research into the global black experience, it provides facilities for community development with the Langston Hughes Auditorium and Atrium, along with the American Negro Theater and other facilities.

In most major metropolitan areas there are similar museums centered upon the whole Afri-Amer experience, to include Philadelphia, Chicago, Los Angeles, Dallas, Oakland, Cleveland, Baltimore, Atlanta, and many other cities; according to Wikipedia "Between 1868 and 1991, there were about 150 African-American museums established in 37 states." As I write, tomorrow September 24th, 2016, the Smithsonian National Museum of African American History & Culture will have its grand opening on the Washington Monument Grounds. It is quite an ambitious project and should serve to be a major center of activity for events, ceremonies and traditions serving the promotion of our unique experience as well as the preservation of our wonderful global historical legacy.

Our task of managing the engagement of public agencies, libraries, and museums will have an important and cherished place within our strategies for self-development.

Overcoming resistance from hostile government administration – As I write, the U.S. is just 1 ½ months from the 2016 election and the very real possibility that either Donald Trump or Hillary Clinton will be inaugurated in January 2017 as president. For a good reason, political analysts who can remain unaligned to either of the two major political parties have sounded numerous alarms over the ideologies, records and loyalties of both candidates. I have similarly looked behind the candidates' policy speeches to their actual record of actions which can help us to determine their commitment to justice, fair distribution of wealth, policies toward disaffected groups, foreign policies and a basic commitment to human rights. Regarding both Clinton and Trump, we quite likely might expect our freedom, access to opportunity and basic human rights are due to be further constricted.

For those among us who pay close attention to these matters, this increasing hostility from government administrations has been worsening for decades. Without going into excruciating detail, my analysis shows that in the last 60 years, since the assignations of Pres. John Kennedy, Malcolm X, Rev. Martin L. King Jr. and Sen. Bobby Kennedy, we have witnessed a federal government which, along with its state agency partners, has become increasingly hostile to our genuine achievement of "life, liberty and the pursuit of happiness." In the aftermath of the "new Pearl Harbor" of the 9/11 events of September 11th, 2001, we have seen the steady creeping and rise of a pseudo-fascist state that is increasingly restricting legitimate human rights. As well, we cannot overlook the role of state and municipal administrative activity posing various threats to our sovereign development – not all of the dirt done against us is limited to the federal government.

We cannot continue to be compliant partners with suppressive governance. We have grown accustomed to permanent warfare against nations who have done nothing directly to attack the U.S. or its citizens. The national security establishment has increased pressure on U.S. citizens who are merely acting upon their duty as citizens to create a more fair and equitable society. The national security establishment is peering into every corner of our lives even though most of us are not at all engaged in activities that threaten this nation. We must be ever vigilant of oppressive governance.

Urban revitalization and empowerment zoning – One of the many places that public agencies have shown great potential to serve our vision of *The Repairing* is supporting the growth of innovation zones, regional technology clusters, revitalization investment and other efforts to generate sustainable economic growth. As was mentioned earlier, some of these policies have been detrimental to the integrity of black communities, such as the "urban renewal" policies that cut up our communities with municipal highway construction. Ongoing "gentrification" of formerly strong black neighborhoods is problematic and is being fed because of local government policies. Our task is to see these policies and trends as distinct advantages. Here again is where our motto of "Get in, get in early, get in deep" comes to our advantage. We must take the initiative to assure that these urban economic investments include us in all phases of development: viability studies, environmental impact analysis, architectural designing, investment, construction, as well as developing commercial and entrepreneurial spaces within these newly revitalized zones.

While recently in Baltimore, upon arrival, I tuned into local media to get a feel for what was taking place currently in the city. News stories of the day detailed the Port Covington redevelopment project, an industrial area in South Baltimore intended to provide renovated facilities for mixed-use urban commercial use. The position of Baltimore's black leadership was to protest that the Port Covington redevelopment didn't carve out enough local jobs for residents. Issues of homelessness, unemployment, income inequality and racial exclusion are no doubt a significant and ongoing problem in Baltimore and most other large cities in America. It is my definite position throughout this book that we need to graduate from reactive protesting and to push ourselves as an organized group into the forefront of design of these urban revitalization projects, invest along with others, and expect to reap all the benefits of such visionary and productive developments – Let's trade our trend toward *protesting* for the more productive trend toward *investing*!

By deftly maneuvering in and amongst various public agencies, we get access to up-to-date information where these commercial and community development projects are to appear as well as to participating in the economics of such projects. This consistency of access is perhaps the greatest reason to *not* abandon the local voting process because we are disgruntled over the quality of candidates for national office – we need merely to shift our focus toward local politics and the means of accessing the flow of development capital that makes real change happen on the local level.

Infrastructure construction and contracting for government services – I have a twin brother who is highly accomplishing in business, economics, money management, and such. He spent the bulk of his career working in the field of diversity contracting for a major aerospace corporation. During his career, he arranged to have over a billion dollars allocated to "minority-owned" businesses doing contracting for the company's NASA related technology development. Of course, this "minority" also includes women, but I want to emphasize the point that there are tens and even millions of dollars in government contracts in virtually every field of commerce.

Federal, state, and municipal governments arrange for private contracting in a broad spectrum of industries including sustainable energy, green businesses, veteran's affairs, healthcare, highway construction and infrastructure development, import-export services, education, community development, biomedical research, housing and human development, and financial services. Many career professionals will eventually form their own corporation from which to enter this lucrative field of contracting for government services as a means of boosting their career up to the next level.

As well, contracting for infrastructure development and government services does not have to be limited to domestic agencies. Developing nations around the world are eager to access the expertise experience of contractors from the most developed industrial/technological economy in the world. Putting ourselves into a position to be able to compete for these contracts successfully will require our disciplined organization and we are fortunate to have a spectrum of qualified coaches to engage the process.

I can recall a conversation with an Afri-Amer man who was just about to retire from 30 years of working in the field of municipal sanitation services; his experience was in management for a sewage treatment plant. I asked him about his plans for retirement (he seemed to be reasonably healthy at retirement) were and his response was not specific about anything more than enjoying not working. I tried my best to plant a different vision within his mind. With his experience, knowledge of sewage treatment methods and technology, connections to other experts in the field and such could qualify him to start a contracting firm. With his own corporation, he could market his expertise in developing countries.

Across the African continent, rural-to-urban migration is driving the rapid growth of huge metropolitan areas, most of which are struggling to provide modern sanitation systems of water treatment and sewage management. Many of these countries, such as Angola, Nigeria, South Africa, and Botswana, have large *Sovereign Wealth Funds (SWF)* of billions of dollars which they can invest in development which consolidates the wealth of their nations. As such, this individual could get massive funding to launch his corporate enterprise, contract with these and other governments to create these municipal facilities and create an entire spectrum of permanent jobs by providing a service that was increasingly needed for continued urban development. Unfortunately, I received no follow-up from this man that would indicate his interest in becoming such an *Ultra-High-Net-Worth Individual (UHNWI)*. Too bad – It was a great idea for which his career experience would have qualified him.

We have the intention of taking a second look at all of us who have career experience within this complex, technology-driven industrial economy. I am convinced that every one of us possesses such a skill, craft, experience or career talent that can be utilized to transform our reality. Translating our experiences into contracting services for public agencies is something that must be taken seriously toward the aim of *The Repairing*.

Private Sector / Business Community

So far, our Six-Part Partnership has engaged the grassroots masses, non-governmental organizations and government agencies. To no small extent, our trust and faith in the ability of public sector agencies to adequately respond to our specific group needs have been over-extended and overly-dependent. Governments can help but it is much more likely that we will get even more progressive traction by our interactivity with the private sector/business community. The good news is that there are many more businesses with which we can collaborate than there are public agencies.

Within the modern capitalist economy, private sector activity is the *real* driving force behind many societal advances. Private and public corporations supply the bulk of research and development into new and disruptive trends and technologies. Profit motivated companies have risen to dominate those areas of our lives which we share as citizens from the food supply system, to recreation, healthcare, higher education, media, real estate, infrastructure creation, entertainment, innovation and industrial creativity. One thing which Afri-Amers must demonstrate is increased capacity to *compete* within the private sector, where the history of capitalism has often presented the most ruthless and cutthroat policies for exploiting markets. Because it so much conflicted with traditional African values and traditions, the 500+ year history of mercantilism has not been kind to the global population of Africans.

Mercantilism, also called "commercialism," is a system whereby a country builds wealth through protected trade, striving to amass precious metals, such as gold and silver, as a measure of the nation's power. Unfortunately, we Africans suffered the greatest under the European mercantilist system as they not only stole our gold, precious metals, gems and other commodities but also harvested our African population to further extend their exploitation through agricultural production in the colonized lands. Today, the face of mercantilism and capitalism has transformed and it serves our best self-interest to acknowledge, comprehend and move in the direction of this newly emerging global economic order. Too many of us are still stuck believing that the economic world of today is run like it was hundreds of years ago, and this is a fatal error of comprehension.

For one of my recent studies, I accessed data on the status of some 2.584 million black-owned businesses in the U.S. Collectively, their performance is not particularly impressive. On average, these businesses produce about $58,000 to $80,000 of gross income annually, per varying sources, and most of these have no employees (sole proprietorships whose owner is likely employed outside of their own business). As pointed out earlier in this book, while Afri-Amer "consumer power" is reported as high as $1.3 trillion annually, because our businesses only produce about 14% of that amount in goods and services, we are at a serious deficit. The 6 of every 7 dollars that we are forced to spend outside of our group could theoretically provide leverage for us to construct collaborative deals with sympathetic businesses which will benefit them with loyalty from such a large demographic and can benefit us by gaining us more sustainable development for our investment.

I cannot overemphasize the critical importance of negotiating new deals with this nation's business sector. Our needs for sustainable development are great, and we can begin to appropriately fill this need by seizing opportunities to collaborate with existing businesses. Blacks spend large sums of money on such staples as housing, food, transportation, healthcare, insurance and pensions, personal care, apparel and education. These expenses serve the great bulk of our annual expenditures, but other expenses include donations to charities, entertainment, alcoholic beverages, tobacco and a comparatively tiny amount on reading. In most of these areas, our spending patterns are not supporting the growth of powerful corporate entities under the control of our group members. Obviously, in the short run, we must develop partnerships.

Social Business Enterprises (B-Corps) are a new class of corporations that are either specifically designed to address a social problem or otherwise committed to doing the greatest good within the broader business environment. SBE's can be either for-profit or non-profit but are most assuredly committed to doing what is in the best interest of both the public and the corporate entity. The growth of social businesses is one of the exciting frontiers of the new global business environment. Philip Kotler's excellent book **MARKETING 3.0: FROM PRODUCTS TO CUSTOMERS TO THE HUMAN SPIRIT** provides numerous examples of such social businesses and their corporate mission to engage in practices that have the greatest public benefit. Social enterprises help communities to stretch disposable income, increase household income and increase the distribution of products and services not previously available to those whose needs will best be served by increased access.

Towards the aims stated in *The Repairing*, it will serve our best group self-interest to seek out and partner with this spectrum of socially responsible businesses and use our collective consumer clout to assist these benevolent capitalists in gaining greater clout and dominance within the national economy. *Forbes Magazine* publishes The **Forbes Impact 30 List**, which names some of the top social enterprises in the world, spanning such businesses as information technologies, venture capital, education, healthcare, human resources and leadership development, along with a spectrum of goods, products and services.

As well as collaborating with social business enterprises, Afri-Amers can do a much better job of acknowledging the growth of exponential organizations. While we are often quick to consume the products from these new and fast-growing enterprises, the idea of partnering with Ex-O's toward the aim of long term and sustainable economic growth has largely bypassed Afri-Amer leadership. Many of these nouveau riche companies started as risky ventures and would have loved to have support from such a large and potentially impactful demographic with as much disposable income as the 45.7 million Afri-Amers. Yet, sadly we are too often too late to embrace the trends which usher in these disruptive businesses and thus come onboard solely as consumers and not producers. This is even more ironic when we consider that significant black inventions form the basis of some of these new enterprises which produce exponential growth.

What is critically needed is a well-funded set of think tanks linked together, whose research serves the economic needs of our group and our larger global family. Across the vast spectrum of private sector enterprises, there are solutions to persistent challenges, opportunities to transform our economic fate, and pathways upon which we can create intergenerational wealth, prosperity and sustainable sovereign development. Finding the capital to endow this vision of a vast intelligence-producing structure is most certainly *not* beyond the capacity of a group that spends $1.3 trillion annually servicing its own consumer needs. With the right strategic planning and tactical engineering, our already-existing experiences in business enterprise development can fill that great void between the $7 that we currently consume versus the $1 that we produce.

Colleges and Universities

One of the valuable societal resources which is often overlooked, as we seek to transform our circumstances regarding political, social, economic, and judicial status, is the vast network of colleges and universities serving the nation. As I listen to the exhortation of numerous community leaders, lecturers and empowerment advocates, I find that few of them even attempt to include these facilities in their schemes. For so many reasons, we need to correct this exclusion of institutions of higher learning from our strategic initiatives as soon as possible. Here are just a few of the critical resources which this nation's excellent class of colleges and universities can supply for our development strategies.

- **Facilities** – Most of this nation's colleges and universities have a spectrum of valuable real estate assets to include libraries, laboratories, auditoriums, theaters, amphitheaters, sports stadiums, transportation, classrooms, dining rooms, convention halls, and ICT technology. For these facilities to be replicated within our communities or business districts would likely entail hundreds of millions of dollars within every metropolitan center. We would be best to develop already-existing relationships with administrators and faculty to access these priceless resources.

- **A large student body** – We began our Six-Part Partnership with the Grass Roots as the foundation of our empowerment as well as the critical role that young people have played in every successful struggle we've undergone. Here on these campuses, we can find thousands, even tens of thousands of partners that are willing to aid our strategic initiatives for group development. These youths have already risen above numerous limitations and social stresses to achieve the status of college admission; therefore, we know that they have great potential to be highly productive, focused and committed citizens. These youths also have a great need to interface with the larger society for which they are developing the skills to lead in the decades ahead. We cannot lose if we can successfully engage and galvanize the creative efforts of college youth.

- **Research institutes** – People are striving to immigrate to America because it still has the finest class of colleges and universities of any nation. On many of these campuses is the absolute cutting edge of research into technology, agriculture, future trends, biotechnology and healthcare research, political, cultural and economic think tanks, along with advanced research into critical geophysical sciences toward sustainable management of the ocean, water, mineral and environmental resources for the future. Some of this nation's most powerful campus institutes have endowments more than 100 million dollars; there are a few, such as the Massachusetts Institute of Technology (MIT), whose annual output in affiliated enterprises is over $1 trillion in annual economic activity.

- **Healthcare facilities** – While we have issued a great deal of caution about the way that Afri-Amers have been abused by hospitals, the medical industries as well as human experimentation, there will be an advantage to our group through developing closer working partnerships with university-based healthcare facilities. Part of their utility is to keep our people out of the unsafe practices of the larger medical-pharmaceutical cartel. Many universities have outreach programs to increase nutritional awareness, maternal and child health status, the risks associated with certain lifestyle patterns, as well as the most cutting edge and up-to-date peer review research on causes and solutions for a spectrum of chronic diseases. Much of the research which I have cited in my numerous books on health emerges from university research laboratories and I can assure you that this information is empowering when used in the right manner by people who genuinely comprehend what such research findings mean.

- **Agriculture extension services** – Because one of the most fundamental policies of any nation is how to feed its population properly, an impressive array of agriculture and agribusiness practices have been and continue to be developed using campus facilities. From seed collection and preservation to biotechnology research, pest prevention, organic farming techniques, increasing yield production, soil management, water management, and more, there is always cutting edge food production research taking place across the nation's spectrum of colleges and universities. As well, many of these universities will send graduate students, interns and academics into the field to assist local farmers with their challenges to maintain the integrity of their sustainable harvests. The single case of the development from Alabama's Tuskegee Institute under the tutelage of Booker T. Washington and George Washington Carver can provide Afri-Amers with a prime example of the dynamic leadership potential that these campuses harbor. This is another of the critical functions of higher education that can help to provide our flailing HBCU's (historically black colleges and universities) with a newly-charged massive transformative purpose to keep them in place and competitive for the century ahead and beyond.

- **Cutting-edge academics** – We as African people have come a long way all along the course of human civilization. Some of our greatest achievements have been associated with the development of great academies of learning in the Nile Delta, Timbuktu, Tuskegee, Howard University, the Atlanta Campus Center, and many other places. The key to our successes in each of these institutions has been the persistence of our academics and intellectual class. While there continue to be questions as to the quality of commitment that many academic professionals have been displaying in recent decades, there should be no question as to their immense value for the sovereign development of our group. Yet, these academics need much greater support from the larger group. They need support in the form of honorariums, book publishing, campus institutes, conferences, radio and TV production facilities, documentary and cinematic film production, other communications technology as well as marketing services for the brilliant ideas which are anticipated to spring forward from this group during our highly-energized vision of *The Repairing*.

- **Libraries** – In talking about the value of public agencies for our Six-Part Partnership, we earlier pointed out the primary value of libraries for community and economic development. Over my life, especially during the critical phase of early adult socialization, it was within campus libraries that I acquired the zest for information, which has become one of the driving forces of my life. While I was never formally enrolled in a college or university – merely taking a community college class in Japanese language and two online certifications in Early Childhood Nutrition (from the University of Southern California) and Global Health Policies (from the University of Copenhagen) – it was settling into libraries for many hours a week which became a great source of my intellectual development. On the campuses of California State University Long Beach, UCLA, USC, Emory University and Johns Hopkins University, that I was grounded in advanced academic research. Not only was I spared the challenging expenses of university enrollment, but the pace at which I could learn on my own in these libraries was far faster than the burden of being in a classroom with students of every level of accomplishment. Campus libraries are treasure chests full of the wisdom of the ages, cutting-edge peer-review scientific publications, rare collections of books and concentrated research from some of the finest minds of each generation. We can and must revive the spirit of literary excellence within our young members as well as all other age groups among our people.

- **Transnational partnerships** – One of the greatest advantages of access to university campuses is access to foreign exchange students along with Pan African student organizations. The youth who can successfully migrate to the U.S. on student visas represent a special class of the best and brightest, most politically connected, and most ambitious youth of their nation. Many of them are challenged by the high expense of attending college in the U.S. and thus are amenable to friendships with locals and others who take an interest in their education. Some of the most notable leaders across African history as well as from other Diaspora countries attended their university studies in the U.S. Colleges also participate in overseas study courses that can be invaluable toward acclimating young leaders to the challenges of an extended stay in developing nations. I have interacted with immigrant students numerous times and they present themselves as outstanding young academics and productive citizens. Further, one can access foreign language studies, along with other cultural resources and traditions on most urban campuses. By engaging and supporting international students while they are young, we can assure ourselves of influential long term partners and associates when these youth graduate and return to their home countries to begin their careers and ascend into the leadership class within their homelands. An investment in African immigrant students is an investment in leadership on the continent for decades to come.

- **Technology innovation** – Repeating the fact that America has the finest system for the higher education of any nation on Earth, we can increasingly look to universities for cutting edge innovation within a spectrum of critical areas. Noted innovation campuses within the nation include such universities as Arizona State, Stanford, Massachusetts Institute of Technology, Georgia State, Duke, Univ. of Michigan, Harvard, Florida Institute of Technology, and numerous others. Among Historically Black Colleges and Universities are listed such outstanding innovative institutions as Spelman and Morehouse Colleges, Howard, Hampton, Tuskegee, Xavier and Fisk Universities, as well as agriculture, mechanical and technical universities in North Carolina, Florida and other locations. We can match the needs of our development strategies to campus resources on these and many other colleges and universities, and we will tap into deep and competent capacities that can assure that our visionary engagements will have the absolute best chance of ongoing success. There can be no denying that technological innovation is an important component of modern economic and societal development. Thus, the better we can tap higher education and college resources for assistance in these areas the better will proceed our group-elevating initiatives.

- **Large scale endowments and benefactors** – Accessing investment capital has consistently been a challenge to the sovereign and sustainable development of our community. While the whole of the HBCU community of colleges is quite challenged regarding operating budgets, we can still look to these institutions to be in direct contact and interaction with the wealth of the nation. What is needed is to create mutually supportive relationships between community-serving NGOs and campus administration. Because so much of the investment capital within the body populace is being squandered on frivolous consumerism, there is the potential to redirect a percentage of this spending toward investing in long term institution building. Those wealthy who do support colleges and universities, especially non-HBCUs, are well connected in financial services and other wealth building enterprises. They have much to teach the public about creating wealth-producing institutions and can also be a great beneficiary of efforts on the part of our grassroots to do better at channeling their spending patterns into real estate, industry and financial services. The campus environment should seem particularly well suited to serve as a common ground upon which to bring these people together. Among the many loyal campus benefactors are athletes and other highly-compensated professionals who owe much of their foundation for life successes to their university experience.

- **An extensive network of alumni across society** – Many of our most notable professionals across the spectrum of productive leadership honed their skills within the college experience. These include artists, scientists, engineers, politicians, journalists, authors and medical professionals. Most of them remain connected to their alma mater through various connections, ranging from initiate societies to supportive alumni, adjunct professorships, professional athletes and numerous other connections. Accessing the broader community leadership from the common basis of campus relationships should, therefore, be a natural strategy for rallying the best and brightest toward community development. I am convinced that one or more of the numerous Black Greek societies could marshal enough resources to leverage the securing of critical infrastructure such as markets, industrial production facilities, real estate, urban innovation zones, or agribusiness enterprises. Galvanizing these organizations for our long term development, increasing such investment will no doubt be a daunting challenge; this we know for sure. Some of these Black Greek associations have as many as 900 chapters and members estimated to reach as high as 150,000. There is an organization made up of the nine historically Black Greek letter organizations called The National Pan-Hellenic Council (NPHC). Should this organization become energized with a massive transformational purpose such as *The Repairing*, there is a great chance that their membership could take a powerful leading role in accomplishing many of these distinct goals which we have laid out. Beyond these societies, numerous other alumni associations can be identified and called upon for their specialized set of organizing skills.

Mass Media

So much of the behavior that is widespread within society can be attributed to cues taken from mass media programming. The power of mass media to shape human behaviors in large part has increased steadily since the creation of the printing press in the 15th Century. A century ago, the Garvey Movement made its greatest successes in no small part due to Marcus Garvey's skills acquired as an apprentice in the printing industry and the widespread distribution of the UNIA publication The Negro World, which was published between 1918 and 1933. In the years that have followed that historic milestone, numerous print, broadcast, and cinematic media have conveyed powerful narratives about the Afri-Amer and African world experience, which have helped to shape our image of ourselves on our pathway to national and global empowerment.

Unfortunately, much of the media images that reflect this society's view of our people has been distinctively negative propaganda. One of the most tragic consequences of centuries of *white supremacist* propaganda against everything black has been the seeding of inferiority, angst, non-competitiveness, and anti-African sentiments within the minds of far too many of our people. Those who have deliberately instigated this constant stream of anti-black propaganda are not only intentional in their slander but have developed a vast set of marketing tools that are reinforced by a depth and mastery of the use of propaganda as an offensive weapon. They have become so accomplished at molding a negative set of images of our Being, that too many of us have bought into the myth of white supremacy and black inferiority.

Many researchers have pointed to the proliferation of anti-social behaviors that are constantly being modeled within television, movies, videos, and music. "If it bleeds, it leads" is an often-quoted summation of the way that local and national news coverage consistently paints the image of Blacks, especially the youth, as dangerous predators, unfit to be accepted as citizen-partners within the larger society. The wonderfully empowering genre of hip hop and rap music became victim to a slanderous media cabal which twisted the creative ideas of the genre's creators toward the proliferation of the image of predatory young black and brown criminals, prowling America's urban streets with nothing but crime and mayhem in their hearts. "Violence is as American as apple pie" is a quote that has its roots in the era of militant black struggle. And this pie is being consumed constantly throughout the media resulting in this nation being tagged as the most violent prone of all the wealthy developed nations. People whom one would hardly ever encounter in the real world invade our homes daily, creating deeply seated anxieties and fears for personal security within the psyches of people who are far removed from such dangers.

I can recall the excitement which accompanied the appearance of Black Entertainment Television (BET) in the early 1980s. The novelty of seeing this level of black-owned cable television engagement certainly energized the community across the nation. According to the online biography of BET co-founder Robert L. Johnson (along with his wife Sheila), the company "became the first African American-owned company to be listed on the New York Stock Exchange." The success of the network continued to develop for the next two decades under black ownership until Viacom acquired it in 2000; the sale netting more than $1 billion. The Johnsons became the wealthiest black household in the United States.

Unfortunately, stewardship of the ideological communications emerging from BET's programming was not sufficient to keep the network from contaminating the Afri-Amer cultural environment. The network rose in large part due to the impact of the new genre of music videos and the explosion of rap and hip hop music into entertainment economics. The cable network which had caused much excitement upon appearance steadily deteriorated into the single greatest degenerate influence upon the young people of the community. This coincided with a time when our youth were being increasingly isolated socially, politically, economically, and largely due to the rise of the illicit urban economy, pushed in huge numbers into the burgeoning incarceration industries. While BET cannot be blamed for this larger set of detrimental policies affecting our youth, we can firmly state that our failure to use the network to *socially engineer* national development for Afri-Amers to offset America's social problems serves as one of the biggest blown opportunities in our history since emancipation.

The ability to amplify one's voice through mass media is an exceptionally empowering capacity, and this applies to voices of empowerment as well as degenerate ones. Toward the aim of empowering our Six-Part Partnership, we must master the use of mass media to generate the type of mass response that can guarantee our campaigns. These days there is a vast spectrum of digital communications pathways that are proving useful for rapid and in-depth penetration of our ideas to those who we've targeted for collaborative organizing. A new collection of *over-the-top technologies (OTT)* has come on the scene in this era of information communications technologies (ICT), the Internet and mobile communications. We can add great value and momentum to our Pan African organizing efforts by mastering as many of these digital communications pathways as our resources can support.

Our plans toward socially engineering an abundant, sovereign and sustainable society will unquestionably require the capacity to transmit empowering ideas across the void which separates our people from their rightful destiny. Digital communications allow us to communicate within our locale and across continents within seconds instantly. The newly available filmmaking tools have empowered The Lion to now taking primary responsibility to correct the narrative of The Hunt. It is especially encouraging to witness the uninhibited use and mastery of these new communications tools by our younger members, some of whom are building lucrative careers by taking these new tools to heart and producing transformative programming.

Behavioral Modeling within mass media programming is an ideal way of diffusing desirable values, characteristics, and cultural patterns across broad geographical spaces to a susceptible audience. We have long complained that the hostile external group uses these methods against us, yet within *The Repairing,* we take primary responsibility for making sure that our initiatives result in sustainable empowerment. There is a vast library of research to confirm that social engineering through mass media is not only possible but has been in play and has been influential for more than a century.

My book **MISSING ASSETS: THE CULTURAL, BIOLOGICAL AND PSYCHOLOGICAL ORIGINS OF INFERTILITY** cited the writings of population researcher Elizabeth Liagin-Sobo who had this to say about the use of cultural communications to proliferate anti-fertility lifestyles among target communities:

> "...for population control to succeed, a great deal more must be done than to merely establish family planning centers and to provide surreptitious funding for local advocacy campaigns. An entire spectrum of variables affecting the desire to have children must be influenced – from basic economics and government programs to family relations, personal expectations, lifestyle, cultural tradition, concepts of land sharing and private ownership, wealth production systems, ethical standards, and even religious beliefs. Taboos must be breached, the bonds that unite family and community must be undermined, and sufficient disruption must occur to literally disorient the targeted communities and make them vulnerable to the imposition of external cultural forces.
>
> ...Nothing can be left to chance. To be effective, an intervention in the media must be thorough, careful, persistent, and extravagant. It must be capable of penetrating the minds of the audience at the subconscious, as well as the conscious level. It must systematically create an illusion on a massive scale, while at

> the same time remaining discreet enough to give the impression that the false doctrine represents a spontaneous change in the target society itself. [21]

Comprehending what was just shared, we can acknowledge that this media-propagated culture of scarcity and defeatism can be deliberately reversed using the same propaganda tools which have been deployed against us. It requires careful strategic organization by a team of intellectual scientists who are adept at scripting cultural communications and must be marketed to our masses with the same skilled capacity, which sells soft drinks, fast food restaurants, automobiles and popular television programs. There is a vast library of published research that can be accessed which instructs how to master cultural communications for political and marketing purposes, as well as their use as weapons of warfare and conquest. I and many others have trained for decades to wield these "weapons of mass instruction" with precision and skill toward the aim of our noble, group-serving empowerment initiatives.

To summarize this extensive chapter on the nature of structural organization, I trust that you find this Six-Part Partnership to be an indispensable formula for building unstoppable coalitions and accessing many layers of already available resources. While it might be easy to perceive the theoretical value of getting collaboration between the grassroots, NGOs, public and private agencies, universities and mass media, putting this formula into direct practices will be the only true test of its validity. This requires the guidance of masters of social engineering and cooperation across this broad base of collaborative partners.

We have run out of time for pontificating, hypothesizing, and endless debate over which formulas are meritorious or not. The future is at stake for our masses within this country as well as throughout the world. As such, we don't have time to waste. We must act immediately to galvanize the right mix and depth of resources and apply them with skilled deliberation to this task of *The Repairing*.

---

[21] Working Paper #3 PROPAGANDA, CULTURAL IMPERIALISM & POPULATION CONTROL: Ideological Communications in the Southern Hemisphere, Information Project for Africa.

Chapter 8 – Capital Investment

"Now is the accepted time, not tomorrow, not some more convenient season. It is today that our best work can be done and not some future day or future year. It is today that we fit ourselves for the greater usefulness of tomorrow. Today is the seed time, now are the hours of work, and tomorrow comes the harvest and the playtime."

– W.E.B. Du Bois

For the purposes of *The Repairing*, our group ultimately consists of 45.7 million Afri-Amers, in partnership with some 2 million continental-born African immigrants along with another 1.45 billion people of African Ancestry around the world. In so far as demographic capital, this is enormous compared to other ethnicities on this planet, only exceeded by the global population of Chinese ancestry. With such a broad global population, we have the human capital to accomplish virtually anything that humanity historically or currently is capable of doing. I cannot overemphasize the critical importance of such demographic and human capital potential toward the aim of dynamic transformation within our group and for the whole of humanity. In so many ways throughout this book, I have endeavored to implant the concept within the consciousness of my readers that *we are a GREAT PEOPLE*, and as such we should be naturally expected to accomplish what great people do.

One of the core functions of any great organization is to assemble the investment capital necessary to do strategic development which will benefit the whole of the group. Recently a report was highly-publicized among Afri-Amer intellectuals and journalists, published by the Washington, DC-*based Institute for Policy Studies and the Corporation for Enterprise Development*, entitled **The Ever-Growing Gap: Failing to Address the Status Quo Will Drive the Racial Wealth Divide for**

Centuries to Come. The most cited statistic within the report pointed out that current economic trends in income and wealth disparities between ethnic groups, the nation's richest class and the general population, have placed the black household in dire straits. Among many publications and across social media, the most cited portion of this report read:

> If average black family wealth continues to grow at the same pace it has over the past three decades, it would take black families 228 years to amass the same amount of wealth white families have today.

Without belaboring the point and falling into the seemingly endless trap of lamentation over this forecast, my immediate point of contention arose over the question of "why do Blacks always compare themselves to Whites, even when such comparisons take our sense of esteem down to misery and lamentation?"

Should we, as African people living within this wealthy nation, stop comparing ourselves to others whom we are not and begin to compare ourselves to African people around the planet, we would quickly determine that we are the *wealthiest* Africans within a quite sizeable global population. By accepting the identity of being African on this planet, our sense of self shifts nearly completely from being a permanent underclass to that of an upper class with an immense potential to affect changes that will benefit the whole group. With that understanding in place, we can begin to engage in proactive efforts to confirm our fundamental understanding of who we are and what our responsibilities should be.

I can assure the reader, our status as citizens of the United States, especially our seemingly poor economic performance, will be best enhanced as we become much better players on the global stage. Only then will this nation's members respect us for the great potential which we display.

From this position that we truly are a Great People, wealthy, experienced, skilled, diverse and now committed to transforming our group and the world with this *massive transformative purpose* of The Repairing, let us look at a spectrum of development investment vehicles which can handle the financial capital which, combined with our demographic and human capital, will cause rapid, sustainable growth for our global family.

Within the cutting edge of Europe and America's rapidly changing corporate environment, a class of businesses referred to as *Socially Responsible Corporations (SRCs)* are now springing up and making a big difference in the enterprise environment. SRCs are profit and non-profit businesses whose model is based upon "mission-driven enterprises." These corporations conduct their business while advancing social change and human development in sustainable ways. SRCs can range from traditional for-profit entities who expect to return profits to their shareholders, to nonprofit, tax-exempt entities, hybrids of both nonprofits and for-profits in collaboration, or two new classes of corporations: Benefit Corporations (B Corps) and Low-profit Limited Liability Companies (L3Cs) [22]

One of our favorite books on the new face of corporate responsibility by Phillip Kotler is **MARKETING 3.0: FROM PRODUCTS TO CUSTOMERS TO THE HUMAN SPIRIT**. The book gives dozens of examples of these new businesses and how they have set upon developing their business model to create a new relationship with their customers and value chain partners. *Forbes Magazine* publishes **The Forbes Impact 30**, which is a listing of the top socially responsible corporations in the world whose successful business experiences are based upon the mission to do good in the world while pursuing profitability and sustainability. Across the spectrum of areas that impact the lives of our group members, we see a great need to create vehicles such as corporations which can impact our group on a massive scale. As such, I encourage the development of Small and Medium-Sized Enterprises (SMEs) which have studied and modeled themselves upon this wonderful new class of SRCs. There is undeniably a great dearth of such enterprises operating within and upon the behalf of the Afri-Amer community and our transnational partners.

---

[22] Social Enterprise Q&A: What is a Social Enterprise? By Mollie Cullinane, March 2014, from Cullinane Law

Another range of *social corporatism* is the development of co-ops as vehicles for community development. As non-profits, these are ideal ways for community-based NGOs to organize shareholders toward solving challenges facing regional groups. Co-ops are being developed in fields of housing, food production and distribution, micro-financing, education, local markets, and commercial real estate. As our overall transformative mission continues to expand, it should be expected that co-ops will become a vital area for progressive development. Like other social businesses, co-ops are not in business to generate profits for shareholders but are here for the definite purpose of addressing social challenges.

I frequently ask of my audience or in conversation a question which has been nearly impossible for people to correctly answer: **Who is the richest black man in America?** His name is Robert F. Smith, founder and CEO of Vista Equity Partners and, according to *Business Insider*, has a current net worth of $2.5 billion he is the 268th wealthiest man in America. As founder of this equity investment fund, which was the highest performing among its class in the U.S. in 2015, Robert Smith has primary decision-making power over this powerful corporation. His central focus for developing the company is to take an equity stake in the development of enterprise software, the software which powers the backbone of most corporate ICT functioning. The nation's top-performing equity fund in 2015 "regularly returned 30% to investors," according to *Business Insider*. From the Vista Equity Partners' website, a brief description of their investment practices follows:

> Vista currently manages equity capital commitments of over $14 billion and oversees a portfolio of over 30 software companies that employ a combined approximately 30,000 employees worldwide. Since Vista's founding in 2000, Mr. Smith has overseen over 200 completed transactions by the firm. During that time, Vista has managed capital for hundreds of limited partners, including many prominent public, private and corporate pension plans, endowments, family offices, and high net worth individuals.

> Under Robert Smith's leadership, Vista has exclusively focused on the enterprise software, data and technology enabled solutions sectors. Mr. Smith is a member of the investment committees of the Firm's funds and currently serves on, or participates on, the boards of many of the Vista Flagship and Foundation Funds' portfolio companies.

Equity funds are a type of mutual funds or private investment funds that buy ownership in businesses, most often in publicly-traded common stock, which show potential for rapid growth and development. As one source describes them:

> The common denominator with an equity fund is the desire for fund management to find good opportunities to invest in businesses that will grow, throwing off ever-increasing gushers of profit for the owners, as opposed to a bond fund or fixed income fund, which uses shareholder money to make loans to companies or governments, collecting interest income. [23]

Equity funds can be focused on regional investments or what are called *geographic mandates*, such as international, global, worldwide, or domestic equity funds. They can as well be focused on *market capitalization* and are classified by the size of their fund base as Mega Cap, Large Cap, Mid Cap, Small Cap and Micro Cap Equity Funds. For our purposes, the attractiveness of equity funding is strongest because they can be arranged as private funds, they can issue bonds, they do pay dividends to investors, they have a record of growth in dividends per share much faster than the stock market as a whole, and they can be targeted at specific markets, industries or sectors such as ICT, healthcare, commodities, real estate or industrial production. All of these priorities fit our vision of how business enterprise growth within *The Repairing* will unfold over the coming seasons, years and decades.

According to *Private Equity International,* the top five performing private equity funds in the U.S. for 2016 are #1 Blackstone, #2 Kohlberg Kravis

---

[23] What Is an Equity Fund?: An Introduction to Equity Funds for Mutual Fund Investors by Joshua Kennon / September, 2016, TheBalance.com

Roberts, #3 Warburg Pincus, #4 Advent International, and #5 The Carlyle Group. The top-ranked **Blackstone Group** is currently reported to have $336.4 billion in Total Assets Under Management as of December 2015, comparatively equivalent to the GDP of nations like Norway and Ukraine. While Blackstone's investment of public funds ranges across "private equity, real estate, hedge fund solutions, non-investment grade credit, secondary funds and other multi-asset class strategies," the business also provides a wide range of financial advisory services. I hope it is obvious to the reader why a private group of our own could learn a great deal as we develop the right type of economic research and development capabilities to comprehend how the powerful world of private financial capital has advanced leading-edge investment capacity.

One area of equity investment fund activity is the creation of *investment-grade bonds*. Per *Investopedia*, "A bond is a debt investment in which an investor loans money to an entity (typically corporate or governmental) which borrows the funds for a defined period of time at a variable or fixed interest rate." Many of us remember the popularity of U.S. Savings Bonds as a simple preferred investment that many families purchased in the past. I can remember our father buying us savings bonds as Christmas presents. Typically, a bond will mature over 4-10 years and bring a modest interest rate expected to exceed the rate of inflation. Investment-grade bonds will have a rating issued by one of the popular rating companies of BBB or higher and have been judged by the rating agency as safe and likely to meet payment obligations to where banks can invest in them.

For the purposes of *The Repairing*, I am suggesting that we create **a Reparations Bond** that would be very specifically arranged to provide capital for a large private equity fund which will provide investment capital to underwrite the nine foundations of Reparations which we outlined in detail earlier in Chapter 2.

The idea of a "Reparations Bond" is a very radical departure from literally all of the various schemes for Reparations that I have examined over the years. It does have its historical precedence within Pan African economic development as the Universal Negro Improvement Association (UNIA) under the leadership of the Honorable Marcus Garvey had a parallel investment of stock in the Black Star Line for members of the UNIA. It was a private investment instrument whose intended purpose was for the sustainable economic development of the global community of African people.

As the historical record clearly shows, problems did arise because of betrayal on the part of some of those who invested in the UNIA stock shares, failure to adequately manage the investments, opposition from a hostile federal government along with other governments to the ambitions of the UNIA, as well as inability to quickly solve the challenges to the UNIA stock funding when they did arise. These setbacks cannot be overlooked individually or as a group. We cannot afford to abandon such needed investment strategies simply because we had one or more catastrophic failures in the past. There have been other investment schemes since then which have been implemented, which have similarly had a remarkable failure. Nonetheless, as the current state of transnational investment and development demonstrates, there is a tremendous success awaiting us as we finally get it right on a global scale.

When nations get their act together and can build sustainable wealth through the development of natural resources beyond mere service of their domestic needs, but move firmly into the realm of transnational trade and wealth accumulation, they can then create *Sovereign Wealth Funds* for further development, financial security and for creating powerful transnational partnerships. Turning again to *Investopedia* for definition, "A sovereign wealth fund (SWF) consists of pools of money derived from a country's reserves, set aside for investment purposes to benefit the country's economy and citizens. The funding for a sovereign wealth fund (SWF) comes from central bank reserves that accumulate because of budget and trade surpluses, and from revenue generated from the exports of natural resources."

A critical key to the capacity for deploying a Sovereign Wealth Fund (SWF) is first achieving financial reserves. This first entails creating above and beyond mere subsistence. Because of financial booms that emerged largely from commodities extraction (such as oil and minerals) certain African-peopled nations have amassed large SWFs in the past decade to include, in order of size: Botswana, Trinidad and Tobago, Angola, Nigeria and South Africa. The five largest SWFs in the world are held by Norway, the United Arab Emirates, China, Saudi Arabia and Kuwait, and these are not all state-controlled funds. Norway's Government Pension Fund-Global has a reported $871 billion of reserves available for investments. Like the private equity funding models we analyzed earlier, SWF's have made their impact "investing in real and financial assets such as stocks, bonds, real estate, precious metals, or in alternative investments such as private equity funds or hedge funds," according to a Wikipedia entry on the topic.

These are just a few of the numerous means by which the capital necessary for such a massive undertaking as *The Repairing* can be assembled and managed. I am asking my readers to think outside the traditional box of conventional thought, which has restricted our creativity. There is so much that we can do. We don't have a lot of time for indecision as the pace of this transformation of the global economy, along with our status of economic health, demands our immediate, deliberate and precise action.

Chapter 9 – Training Leadership for a Sustainable Future

As we reach for the stars, we must always remember that we stand upon the shoulders of Giants.
The future belongs to those who are best prepared to create it today. – Keidi Awadu

---

For optimized long-term continuity of this or any other strategic plan, a collaboration of leadership must become established across generational divides. Every successful group owes much of its accomplishment to the supreme efforts exerted toward progress from the generations which preceded it. At this time, toward accomplishing the initiatives laid out in *The Repairing*, many great transformative efforts must be implemented, yet we must keep in mind that we are not acting only for the benefit of our self, but also for our children and generations to follow. One cannot overemphasize the importance of this critical need for the transfer of power from older to younger generations.

The value of forward-projecting research as an essential part of a leadership education curriculum is imperative. For a good reason, a broad spectrum of education advocates has stressed the importance of educating our youth to excel in fields of science, technology, engineering and mathematics (STEM), cultural awareness and identity, world history, economics, financial management, psychology, languages, and sustainability. I agree that such studies are essential toward creating *whole citizens*, capable of positioning themselves as healthy contributors to progressive democratic societies. For those youth who can master such a spectrum of studies, there is another even greater level of leadership development studies which can be mobilized toward the creation of a highly accomplished leadership vanguard.

Over decades of focused research, I have come to greatly appreciate the value of the study of *scientific futurism*, which utilizes methods of scientific analysis versus "crystal ball" forecasting when determining what the future will likely produce. Scientific futurism is the stuff that guides the most influential think tanks and research institutions which serve great national powers. A broad set of interrelated disciplines which constitute this forecasting method include the disciplines of demographics, science and technology trends, economic patterns, geology, and planetary resources, sociology and culture, politics, environment and climate change, psychology and the humanities, alternative futures analysis, health and biology, history, anthropology, as well as trends analysis and the ever-changing state of education.

Scientific futurism thrives on data-driven criteria, which means that its methods produce significant amounts of patterns, evidence, data trends, subjective and objective observation, as well as an intense debate as to which outcomes are more likely to occur based upon the presentation of differing scenarios. Society has popularized forms of futurism based upon esoteric mysticism: astrology, numerology, "casting bones," reading auras, palm reading, talking with disembodied spirits, etc. My intention is not to insult those that utilize these practices; they should be recognized as an extension of culture, religion, and spiritual expression. Yet, when it comes to scientific futurism, our methodologies are quite distinct and I desire to instill within our future leaders the ability to utilize these various tools and disciplines toward the aim of *traversing the future*.

What follows is the briefest possible description of these various disciplines which constitute the state of the art of scientific futurism. While these descriptions are necessarily brief, I encourage the reader to take time to explore these cues much further.

Demographics

Demographics is defined as the analysis of statistical data relating to the population of any nation or subgroup within it. Examining short- and long-term demographics allows groups to determine which trends empower or disempower the group. Key aspects of demographic analysis include fertility factors, the percentage of various age groupings, migration, sheer population numbers, military-age population numbers, ratio of elders to working population, family status, population density, and the ever-changing ways by which people within any identifiable group change the ways that they replicate themselves for the sake of future generations. Tracing the expansion of population numbers throughout world history follows the rise and fall of empires closely. The most powerful nations in the world today are also leaders in population numbers even though this status can be directly challenged when women within any given society stop giving birth in the same numbers that preceding generations did so.

Today the greatest demographic advantage among nations has been assumed by the peoples of Sub-Saharan Africa. Fast-rising superpowers like China, India, and Brazil have been beneficiary of great population rise in the previous half-century. Earlier, the British, American, German and Japanese empires rode their strong demographic numbers to powerful influence over colonial outposts. At present trend, Japan, the European Union, Russia and a few of the Asian Tiger nations are in a demographic free fall. On the contrary, the highest fertility on the planet is shared by rising powers in Africa, western Asia (the so-called "Middle East"), along with parts of Central and South America. When rising demographics coincide with sustainable development, peace and equitable distribution of wealth, these elements signal that a nation is to be expected to move swiftly up the hierarchy of rapidly-developing nation status.

As my associate, Ahmad Ali stated during a call into my daily webcast, "Demographics is destiny." I completely agree that such a pronouncement is a fundamental truth.

Science and technology trends

The modern history of the world records major epic shifts due to significant breakthroughs in science and technology; no period of history doesn't correspond to such transformation. We have now entered what is being referred to as "**The Fourth Industrial Revolution**," accurately described by the World Economic Forum as such:

> We stand on the brink of a technological revolution that will fundamentally alter the way we live, work, and relate to one another. In its scale, scope, and complexity, the transformation will be unlike anything humankind has experienced before. We do not yet know just how it will unfold, but one thing is clear: the response to it must be integrated and comprehensive, involving all stakeholders of the global polity, from the public and private sectors to academia and civil society.
>
> The First Industrial Revolution used water and steam power to mechanize production. The Second used electric power to create mass production. The Third used electronics and information technology to automate production. Now a Fourth Industrial Revolution is building on the Third, the digital revolution that has been occurring since the middle of the last century. It is characterized by a fusion of technologies that is blurring the lines between the physical, digital, and biological spheres. [24]

We are witnessing this era where virtually *everything* is being digitized; turned into some form of a computer-managed and data-driven matrix. Even the complex parts which make up mechanical instruments, or the management of agriculture, are controlled and directed by flows of digital data. As such, the ability of the leadership of any group to see these trends and the long-term impact that they wield over society is imperative. To continue our collective failure to see these technology trends in advance or real-time occurrence is one of the self-limiting trends which has caused the obsolescence of Afri-Amer leadership of

---

[24] The Fourth Industrial Revolution: what it means, how to respond, by Klaus Schwab, January 2016 / WEForum.org

recent decades. One hopeful trend among many of our youth is their fearlessness in accessing new technology tools and trends. While this can work greatly to our advantage, we do have to make sure that those tools are used in an optimally productive manner rather than just another generation of *electronic variances* that distract our people from productivity toward sovereign development.

There is a major difference between acquiring the latest technologies for consumerism versus innovative productivity. To advance within this current matrix of rapidly-shifting industrialization, we must train a loyal collective toward acquisition and mastery of current technologies along with advances in biotechnology, nanotechnology, robotics, artificial intelligence, the "Internet of Things", self-driving autonomous vehicles, energy storage, 3-D printing, quantum computing, and more.

Similarly, science is another area where we have a great need to reinforce our competence, again of critical importance for developing leadership competence. Science can span a broad range from economics to health, industrial production, forecasting social trends, environmental protection, engineering, linguistics, natural resources, and communications. Our people, and especially the youth, must develop supreme confidence in their ability to master the entire spectrum of earth sciences from the very earliest age of comprehension. The very evolution of civilization was predicated upon the application and mastery of a spectrum of sciences beginning within the earliest Africa-based societies.

For us, promoting the proliferation of science academies, STEM studies, science fairs, and competitions, as well as media which highlights the competence of our global African members within these fields, will go a long way to motivate younger generations toward elevating a highly-competitive vanguard prepared to lead the entire world toward a revitalized state of sustainability and non-destructive advance of material culture.

Economics

Throughout this book, we have taken many forays into the spectrum of means by which our economics can be transformed from stagnation into dynamic productivity. We must instill in younger generations the capacity to consistently realize the advantages of short-term sacrifice for long-term gain in all matters of future economic growth. For scientific futurism to be applicable in the field of economics, our studies must go so much further than mere money management or household budgeting. They need comprehensive studies and hands-on experiences in micro and macro financing. The vast field of global development economics is critically important, especially when we consider the growth potential of 1.616 billion people of African heritage whose nations shelter the greatest base of natural resources on the planet.

Sectors such as foreign direct investment (FDI), equity funding, market capitalization, production for local consumption and foreign trade, income and wealth equality, traversing the maze of small and medium-sized business entrepreneurship, agribusiness, real estate financing, and cashless banking must all be integrated into a natural curriculum that emphasizes how these factors might be expected to transform over the coming decades. These studies can be implemented early in life in the form of gaming that mimics what is being actualized in the real world.

When it comes to many of our current leaders, it seems all too apparent that they are severely lacking in genuine comprehension of the depth of variables which have impacted our economic fate in the past and present, and can be expected to become even more *effective* in the future. We are obligated to correct this deficit within our future strategies to educate our youth toward the mastery of leadership for sustainable economic growth.

Geology and planetary resources

There can be no ignoring of the impact that resource development has had over the past 500 years of world history. The role of geology and planetary resources over the coming centuries should be expected to become increasingly critical as population growth and density reaches critical mass over the century ahead; the world is approaching a population peak expected to top out between 9 and 11 billion in the century ahead. Beyond the mere management of natural resources within any one nation or region, the whole of humankind will be challenged to come up with viable solutions to creating sustainability and preventing the collapse of human civilization into the worst forms of misery and exploitation based upon notions of scarcity.

The future will increasingly be influenced by technologies allowing for the exploration of deep-sea environments, exploiting extraterrestrial resources, and even the likelihood of subterranean living and working facilities. Energy needs will increasingly challenge us to come up with unique and sustainable solutions. Training our youth to manage the future of geological and planetary resources must begin with an essential sensitivity and empathy for all things living. In this current era of mass exploitation of our fellow humans, reducing other species down to the level of their utility for human exploitation, an irreverence for the sanctity of Nature, and an ever-pressing drive to extract profits at the expense of sustainability, our future leaders must be deeply embedded with values and morals which put an end to these uncivilized practices. We need to raise generations of leaders with true compassion for all manifestations of life and the discipline to forego short term and selfish benefits in favor of those activities which elevate the collective human spirit.

Sociology - culture and society

Again, our focus here is on training our youth along with older leaders in means of using the disciplines of scientific futurism to advance the status of the group. I cannot overemphasize the critical importance of truly comprehending the role of culture as a foundation for guiding the behaviors of group members within the current social construct of our communities. Toward understanding the overall role of culture in guiding our lives, it is necessary that we not only comprehend the *six axioms of culture* but as well how these are undergoing certain fundamental *paradigm shifts* as society evolves.

To comprehend and master future trends in culture and society, our leaders will have expertise in a wide spectrum of spiritual experientialism, how ethnic groups observe traditions, how perspectives of history can differentiate, as well as comprehend the various ways that morality, values, and logic run distinct based upon perspective within society. Even the very nature of language and communication are rapidly shifting, for which our viability will demand flexibility and comprehensive understanding.

Sociology is the science of how people fit together to make up a functional community or nation. What is the importance of the presence of young professionals at the beginning of their working career to the stability of a neighborhood? What is the healthiest ratio of seniors to workers within a municipal setting, and how is that affected by technology shifts? What can be done to reverse the destructive trends of marriage failure, single parenthood, below-replacement fertility rates, and the increasing presence of "gender alternative" households within our ethnicity? Toward building healthy and sustainable communities, concrete tactics must be found for these challenges and many more which will appear over the decades to come. Comprehension and mastery of the social sciences will be an absolute prerequisite for our group to advance a highly competent leadership vanguard to guide us toward a permanently sustainable future.

Politics

I will admit that an increasing political cynicism has accompanied my own intellectual and academic maturity; to a great extent, it is prompted by the poor quality of political leadership which has ascended to dominance within the United States. Yet, the academic residing within me accepts that it has not always been so bad as it seems and that it is quite likely to get better within some future period. Despite my current conviction that the private sector is a more influential factor over societal evolution at this point, it should be accepted that selected political leaders will continue to be elevated for the foreseeable future. As such, we need to create fresh means and mechanisms by which such policy-leaders are well-prepared to manage public assets and to provide the leadership required for key strategic and tactical engagements.

It might be easy to imagine that it will be a new process of leadership selection, which will come along soon to replace the electoral structure which our people are currently experiencing. New technology breakthroughs could combine elections with social media and campaign finance reform to usher a more authentic leadership to the forefront. As such, it will remain necessary for our group to have a defined process for bringing an optimized leadership cadre to maturity to manage our common affairs. I also envision that future trends will see the convergence of politics with the massive increase in alternative news and information streams. This could prove critical toward allowing a new, more authentic leadership to gain access to the vast base of stakeholders whose democratic self-interests need to be addressed.

We must also imagine that what might be considered old might become renewed once again. At various junctures in world history, the most effective African-centered leadership was essentially *socialist*, not to confuse indigenous Pan African socialism with other forms of communism, socialist-fascism, democratic socialism, and centralized-planning socialism under an authoritarian state. This Pan African socialism of which I speak has deep organic roots in the traditions of village life wherein the Elders and Chiefs of these regions guided the shared development of those under their trust with empathy and benevolent authority. I stand quite optimistic that our future development as a global African population exceeding today's 1.6 billion will give rebirth to the spirit of indigenous African socialism as a primary foundation for shepherding the group forward into and beyond the century ahead.

Environment and climate change

Among the chief determinants of life on planet Earth over the immediate centuries ahead is humanity's relationship to the environment. Dramatic news of major changes in weather patterns, global warming, desertification, record-breaking storms, and drought all press the need for our responses to be more complimentary to the idea of sustainability. The impact of a world population now expanded to a current 7.7 billion and growing ever more rapidly towards 9.25 billion by 2050, raises our awareness of the many ways that national habits impact environmental integrity. Agricultural practices have a strong impact on the quality of water, soil, and chemical toxicity of the larger environment. Rising ocean levels due to melting polar ice caps will cause increased stress to coastal regions where much of the world's population is residing. For these and so many other reasons, leadership for a sustainable future must bring forward real and timely environmental solutions.

In a world where everything is somehow connected to and impacting upon everything else, this climate change *wild card* threatens to seriously upset civilization-development. Energy production systems that rely upon the burning of hydrocarbons, such as oil refining, diesel and gas-fueled transportation, natural gas, coal-fueled generators, and wood-burning, all put immense stress on the environment as they add increasing greenhouse-causing carbon dioxide to the atmosphere. The threat posed by aging nuclear power generators and the hundreds of thousands of years of residual radiation that accompanies these facilities stands as another great challenge to the integrity of the land, with the Japanese nuclear disaster at the Fukushima generating plant dumping some 400 tons of radioactive water into the Pacific Ocean daily for five years now.

The solutions to these and other environmental challenges to arise over the century ahead demand the ascendance of new leadership with long-term futurist vision. Africa must manage its tremendous land and sea resources in a much cleaner manner than is presently taking place on the continent. The Sahara Desert continues to expand as do other desert areas on the continent. Lake Chad, traditionally the 2nd largest African inland body of water, which has served a local population of 12 million, has shrunk some 95% in the last half century, a possible harbinger of global warming-related threats to appear within future decades. Seasonal floods in certain areas are still quite problematic despite the possibility that aqueduct infrastructure development could help to balance the impacts of flooding and desertification.

Everything is not doom and gloom regarding the environment, especially across the equatorial belt of the African continent. Immense rainforests, unlimited hydroelectric generating potential, a great diversity of plant and animal species on the continent are still great advantages to African people. We must guide multiple generations of leadership, which can comprehend all the subtle nuances of Nature's complexity. These new leaders need to work to inspire mass participation across the entire population to defend the environment and cease dirty and unsustainable industrial practices which have been created by those in other parts of the planet but compromise Africa's pristine environments; these outsider nations are acting toward the aim of trying to protect their environmental integrity at the expense of developing nations.

Psychology - Humanity and the individual

Traversing the future sustainably and developmentally requires the management of people at every scale. One of the significant trends that has a major impact in determining the quality of future life is *urbanization*, the migration of young people from rural to urban areas as they pursue their professional adult life. From the smallest social units of the family to communities, municipalities, mega-cities, nations, regional coalitions, and continental-sized populations, interactivity among citizens is integral to the health and sustainability of the larger society. What factors will impact our future desires for consumption, productivity, peaceful coexistence, ability to form families, how we serve as model citizens, spend our leisure time, or the factors which affect one's ability to make personal changes that best serve the larger group's best practices?

The "shaping of men's attitudes" is a primary occupation within politics, merchandising, business marketing, news reportage, and enforcing security within a nation. We can most certainly see how the influence of newly appearing communication technologies has transformed the psychological state of societies who've come into widespread adoption of television, radio, cinema, literacy (or conversely failing literacy), and now the Internet.

To manage complex societies and diverse industry requires deft management of the population regarding social engagement, worker productivity, consumer behaviors as well as individual mental health. Constant shifts highly influence scientific futurism in public attitudes and behaviors. As the pace of transformation of media and communications continues at an ever-more accelerating rate of change, we will need to train our future leaders to be firm but empathetic guides to help everyone to progress to their greatest potential within the most critical needs of the larger group. New research of the mind sciences and workings of the human brain promise both new opportunities and new dangers, depending on the fundamental values of those who are sponsoring and conducting such research. The negative impact of ever-more-stressful environmental influences is pushing too many toward the edge of social and political inclusivity. To contribute to a more just and equitable society, the management of people has got to improve over the dangerous state that it has become today.

STEM education

It appears all too obvious that to traverse the future successfully, leadership must have a powerful working knowledge of how we must organize education in science, technology, engineering and mathematics, the so-called STEM studies. Again, our focus on scientific futurism is not just mastery of education but to recognize and analyze trends over time. Regarding this specific population of Blacks within the U.S., Caribbean, throughout the Americas as well as across the African continent, we have generally been on the short end of competent mastery of STEM education and related entrepreneurial engagement.

One of our primary handicaps is our extremely poor outcome regarding public school education. Across the U.S. for the years 2011-2012, the "four-year adjusted cohort state graduation rates for public high schools" placed graduation at the rate of 80 percent for all nationalities. Blacks graduated at a rate of 69 percent compared to 86 percent for Whites and 73 percent for Hispanics. For black graduation rates, Texas came out on top, with 84 percent graduating compared to the low of 51 percent for Minnesota. [25]

For so many reasons, a person's ability to successfully matriculate through public education is connected to virtually every aspect of their social, economic, and political viability within the larger society. The

[25] State High School Graduation Rates By Race, Ethnicity, by Mike Maciag, Governing: The Future of States and Localities, December 2012

world is becoming ever more competitive within the global economic sphere and our specific group is being severely handicapped by our poor performance in the field of education. The careers of the future will not be as dependent upon unskilled labor as was the reality a century ago.

To compete in the workforce of tomorrow, those entering their adult-life careers today must demonstrate a high level of competence in one or more of the STEM sciences along with several other life skills such as functional multilingual abilities and a high level of communication skills. Should one analyze recent decades of trends within these STEM science studies, it should be obvious that these fields are rapidly shifting constantly. As well, the pace of transformation within these scientific fields can be expected to increase over time. STEM-based industrial societies are at the top of the hierarchy of the world's most advanced economies. For us to be competitive within this nation or any other nation within which we find ourselves, as well as in the global arena, we are simply going to have to highly prioritize research, training and accomplishment in the rapidly changing fields of STEM education and application.

Health and biology

There can perhaps be no more important area where rapidly-transforming trends can impact one's quality of life than the fields of health and biology. As a practicing futurist for so many years, the data that I am continuously examining regarding health and biology keeps me excited. I have developed an interest in disease prevention, the evolution of complementary medicine, analyzing risk factors for developing chronic disease, the changing metrics of health statistics for national and global populations, and especially the compelling research into the future of longevity and high-quality life extension.

Looking at the evolution of cancer from a very rare disease in ancient times (incidence rate of one-quarter of 1 percent in Kemet/Ancient Egypt) to today expected to exceed 1 of every 3 Americans during their lifetime, gives a great example where the scientific futurist approach can be beneficial toward prevention. The field of life extension is even more exciting with the very real possibility that people alive today (me *definitely* included) will live to be far more than 100 years before death, as well as being able to live well, work and function superbly into their 90's and beyond.

Future trends in healthcare favor those of us who are developing careers in personal healthcare management in direct contrast to the recent rise of dominance by corporate health providers, Health Maintenance Organizations (HMOs), and insurance industries. The era of omnipotence from large pharmaceutical and medical cartels has reached its apex and is handicapping itself by the persistence of extremely high cost and low performance. Too many people are on prescription drugs despite their desire to maintain natural health. OTT based technologies and information delivery systems are making many of the basic functions of medical practitioners more and more obsolete. Things are changing rapidly and there are increasing numbers of the population who want to take back control over their health destiny.

Similarly, with biological research and development, fields of genetics, stem cell research, fertility treatments, the creation of synthetic organs, new medical diagnostic tools, nanotechnology, and the increasing knowledge of how natural botanicals can assist our biological integrity – these and more exciting new frontiers are appearing at ever-more-rapid pace. To prepare our group leadership for these newly-empowering trends in health and biology is imperative if we are to remain a healthy, competitive, vital, and non-dependent segment of society. To retain the reputation of being the sickest subgroup within the sickest of the developed nations, is an unacceptable status for Afri-Amers, especially when we have so many brilliant and insightful natural health scholars within our midst. We must continue to transfer this mastery to younger generations for sustainable future development.

Education

As the world is moving firmly into the Fourth Industrial Wave, structures that educate the populace to adapt to this major paradigm shift properly must also need to adapt radically. Futurists are producing waves of studies and forecasts which envision how education will transform over the coming decades. What we do know is that the cutting edge of innovation will not be constricted to how public education currently serves the masses. Key questions constantly appear, for which answers are sought that have massive potential impact for this world of tomorrow that is being forecast.

In what manner will private education assist students in competing at higher levels? Will brick and mortar colleges and universities can compete against the new wave of online education? What spectrum of interrelated academic disciplines will best prepare our youth for rewarding and long-lasting careers? How much can a family expect to spend to educate their children to succeed in an increasingly competitive global labor market?

Answers to these and other education-related questions will push the boundaries of futurist research for many generations to come. The existence of a somewhat rigid educational hierarchical elite within wealthy societies poses challenges which the ever-advancing nature of technology will allow each of us to project ourselves forward upon our ambition. As well, because education is so closely tied to other futurist methods, such as demographics and STEM sciences advance, this leadership, which we are bringing forward, must be impeccably disciplined, forward-thinking, precise and dynamic.

Education is a primary vehicle for national competitiveness and for allowing any individual to advance their status within society; this has been the fact for centuries and will continue to be so for centuries more to come. There can be no doubt that the future of education will make radical and disruptive departures every decade for a long time to come. We need to assure that African leadership remains as close to the very forefront of these transformations as our collective resourcefulness can allow.

I must stress the point that education to lead our group must be life-long reinforcement of the critical facts, trends, and relevant histories, and must produce an integrated comprehension of what challenges are before us. As I write, last evening I had the experience of watching an hour or so (as much as I could tolerate) of a CSPAN presentation of a forum called **Minorities and Economic Opportunities**, presented by the

U.S. Department of the Treasury. This panel featured the mayor of Atlanta Kasim Reed, the founder of Operation Hope John Hope Bryant, and Kim Saunders, CEO of Eads Group, a financial consulting services corporation. While I am sure that these three panel members are sincerely concerned about elevating the lot for Afri-Amers, I was horrified at their lack of competence toward answering questions put to them by the host of the panel. Their responses were rambling, long-winded, nearly completely avoidant of specific responses to pointed questions, and in general, seemed to indicate to me that we have the wrong type of leaders in place when it comes to our economic advancement.

In contrast, the following discussion featured former Atlanta Mayor and U.N. Ambassador Andrew Young. His presentation was all about details of the history of economic affairs during the years of his mayoral tenure along with that of his processor Mayor Maynard Jackson. Ambassador Young's responses and details to attention were very pointed and revealing, even though his advanced age had left a few deficits in his memory.

From my armchair listening to the questions and non-answers from the discussion on economic development, I was extremely agitated as the performance of these economic leaders confirmed the worst of what I've suspected about Afri-Amer leadership – quite simply, they generally don't know what to do. Too many of these leaders emerge from a selection process that relies on personal charisma, oath-taking (Greek society connections, etc.), corporate nepotism, affirmative action (a kind of non-challenging selection of leadership) and other insider-connected processes. Our future demands a much better-educated, precise and responsive leadership, especially regarding self-determining economics and all other aspects of our group's sustainable advancement.

History

Let there be no confusion that scientific futurism demands that the futurist be adept at historical analysis. History is a continuum, and it is not cliché that *the past is the present is the future*. Malcolm X emphasized this in his monumental speech **Message to the Grassroots** when he informed us that "history is best qualified to reward our research." Many historical patterns and trends tend to be cyclical and repetitive. Historical research allows one to develop the critical talent of comprehending nuance, details of complex situations, and how to bring notice to subtle influences which could have great consequence. Historical perspective allows for more credibility for our future projections; some claim to forecast future developments yet have no valid historical references to bolster their predictions.

For the futurist, history is alive. It speaks to us as we are observing real-time events of the current moment. History is also relative and non-fixed. Some events have happened in the past, which continue to resonate and influence the present and can be predicted to continue to impact the future. Look at the sordid history of political assassination in the U.S. during the early and mid-1960s, these killings still impact the integrity of, and trust in the American national leadership. History is like the waves that resonate outward as a stone is thrown in a body of water – even though the waves may become subtler, they continue to move molecules far away from the epicenter of the impact.

A great place for any group to look for a body of students from which to cultivate a new generation of scientific futurists would be to pick from the top students of history in university studies or within study circles. Futurism does require that the adept *not* be bound to any particular historical episode, especially not bound by what has become referred to as "post-enslavement trauma disorder" or other disordered relationship to the past. Those who cannot let go of past traumas, especially those episodes that injured others and not oneself directly, will not be able to free their psyche to explore the present and future in all of their nuanced details. Such people tend to project these past sufferings into every aspect of what else is going on in the world or might be expected to occur in the future. There is a difference between enslavement to perpetual victimhood and the stream of liberated creativity that must serve as a foundation for accurate future projection.

Anthropology

The Merriam-Webster dictionary defines *anthropology* as the following:

1. The science of human beings; especially: the study of human beings and their ancestors through time and space and in relation to physical character, environmental and social relations, and culture;

2. Theology dealing with the origin, nature, and destiny of human beings.

There is a multiplicity of important themes within these definitions, to include science, sustained direct observation, heritage, history, geography, behavior, environment, spiritualty, natural order, archeology, and the evolution of civilizations. As such the discipline of anthropology becomes an incredibly powerful tool available to those pursuing scientific futurism. To the anthropologist, the world is one big, dynamic cinematic spectacle. To consider ancient artifacts that depict the often-mundane aspects of daily activities of long-departed populations is like stepping out of time and imagining this direct experience all over again. To be effective, a futurist must be able to unbind themselves from time, space and personality and to *become one* with the subject of their precise interest. The disciplines of anthropology develop just such capacity. The most *practical* anthropologists, even those not formally affiliated with a research or academic institution, have best equipped themselves with this talent for slipping through boundaries of "normal existence."

And as the definition of anthropology also suggests theological, religious, and spiritual foundation, I feel this link to spirituality as a proper infusion into our futurist projections, an even greater imperative for Pan African futurists to generate *holistic research.* Restoration of a glorious civilization, which we know to have once been our widespread reality, will require us to also see our world in real-time terms as scientists, priests, healers, from the perspective of dutiful Wise and Esteemed Elders, and as a functional national security council. This holistic approach to solving existential challenges to the group will be greatly enhanced as more of our leaders consolidate these scientific disciplines. I can think of no discipline more essential to being able to adequately manage the affairs of our group as that of the science of anthropology.

We have got to get serious with our academics in this critically-important contribution to the sustainability of *The Repairing*.

Trend analysis

Of the many things that occupy the attention of futurists is observing influential phenomena in real-time. This is referred to as *trend analysis*. Essentially, this is the result of a developed skill to see history occurring in real-time. To repeat: **The past IS the present IS the future.** Therefore, trend analysis is something that we need to take seriously for our current mission.

Wikipedia has the following informative definitions of trend analysis when applied in the field of future studies:

> Trend analysis is the practice of collecting information and attempting to spot a pattern or trend within the information. In some fields of study, the term "trend analysis" has more formally defined meanings.
>
> Although trend analysis is often used to predict future events, it could be used to estimate uncertain events in the past, such as how many ancient kings probably ruled between two dates, based on data such as the average years which other known kings reigned. ...In statistics, trend analysis often refers to techniques for extracting an underlying pattern of behavior in a time series that would otherwise be partly or nearly completely hidden by noise. A simple description of these techniques is trend estimation, which can be undertaken within a formal regression analysis.
>
> Today, trend analysis often refers to the science of studying changes in social patterns, including fashion, technology, and consumer behavior.

The National Intelligence Council publishes a report every five years, the latest one entitled **GLOBAL TRENDS 2030: ALTERNATIVE WORLDS**. Within this extensive futurist projection report, one can see the various pathways which are causing the greatest changes in the world, as well as the manners by which these trends will affect the U.S. Among the trend categories under examination within the highly regarded NIC reports, are the following:

- **Megatrends** – Including such powerful forces of change as Individual Empowerment, Diffusion of Power, Demographic Patterns, and Food, Water, Energy Nexus. These megatrends are predicted to be the biggest drivers of change in the world of the coming two decades.

- **Game Changers** – To include Crisis-Prone Global Economy, Governance Gap, Potential for Increased Conflict, Wider Scope of Regional Instability, Impact of New Technologies, and the Role of the United States. Significant and surprising changes in these categories can have a major disruptive impact in wide regions of the world.

- **Potential Worlds** – Stalled Engines, Fusion, Gini-Out-of-the-Bottle, and Nonstate World. Indicative of either positive or negative outcomes, these potential worlds require intensive study of future trends and the drawing up of numerous maps by which to ideally respond to what changes may manifest.

This periodic report from the National Intelligence Council is but one of many such futurist publications that we can access and examine the way that powerful institutions and agencies have set upon the task of trends analysis. As well, it should be obvious that Africans can take greater responsibility for producing such reports themselves. I am aware of such future trends analyses being produced by continental African organizations such as the African Development Bank Group and the African Union. Other such reports are prepared to reflect future African trends by the United Nations, World Bank, International Monetary Fund and other agencies.

Geography

A definition of geography (from Dictionary.com) includes a diversity of topics such as the study of the geo-surface area, examining climate, elevation, soil, vegetation, and land use, the scientific inquiry into these areas as well as "the arrangement of features of any complex entity." It should seem obvious to any scholar committed to scientific futurism how these various categories of geographical relationships should be examined in sufficient detail to be able to map out some manner of traversing the complex interaction between these sectors.

Little did we know in high school geography classes how critically important this study would be for our long-term sovereign development. As I write, just today, I was responding to posts within the social media that purport to expose sovereign threats to the Sub-Saharan nation of the Democratic Republic of the Congo. Yet, the report being cited was several years old and based upon a very narrow set of points of examination. I wrote in the thread in protest that this tired, old narrative about DR Congo was misleading and was likely to leave the readers in a deficit of comprehension about the latest and future trends that were being manifest in DR Congo which indicate that it was rapidly moving toward status as one of the worlds *Rapidly Growing Economies*.

It serves us well to have within our midst this research that emerges from trends analyses of geography-centric changes. It can be usefully valuable to not only correct outdated and distracting propaganda, but better yet, will serve as a foundation for energizing and exciting our motives toward capital investment, training our younger generation of leadership, and moving us away from prejudice against our global family members. The facts of the matter regarding the geography of the African continent, along with other nations with predominantly African-heritage populations such as the CARICOM nations, Africans have a distinct geographical advantage in virtually every category. We can best serve our own best self-interests by understanding these advantages and creating deliberate pathways to exploit our advantages for sustainable economic, social and political development.

As well, there are strong indications that the unification and confederation of the 55 states on the African continent will take place during the middle of this century. As a Confederation of African States / African Union, the ocean waters extending up to 200 miles off the coast of this CAS/AU will rule over an internationally recognized *Exclusive Economic Zone (EEZ)* within which all commercial exploitation of ocean resources will be under primary control of CAS/AU governance. This EEZ will be the largest such exclusive zone of any nation on the planet, providing more square miles of oceanic real estate than the landmass of the vast African continent. This massive geography of Africa's continental real estate conjoined to its marine EEZ designation serves as the indisputable largest base for the world's greatest natural resources under control of any nation.

Quantum Physics

During July 2015 / 6255 on LIBRadio, I committed to a month-long series of broadcasts on the broad topic of *Quantum Advancement*. It has been my intention since producing these 50 hours of broadcast research to ultimately write a book on the topic, an effort that could likely take several years to write because of the complexity of this actual topic. Regarding this investigation and inquiry into *scientific futurism* to use this all as a basis for accomplishing *The Repairing*, I wish to point out a few areas of our research into Quantum Advancement and why it is imperative to our stated mission and our massive transformative purpose.

- Reasoning and creating from *First Principles* instead of analogy – "First principles" is a physics way of examining the world and the universe beyond our world. It breaks phenomena down into the most basic components and then imagines from that point. This stands in contrast to analogical innovation, which takes an existing product or service and merely improves upon it. According to First Principles thought, the most innovative and disruptive new industries, designs, and patterns are appearing which have the potential to generate the most radical paradigm shifts in the way that things are done.

- We are realizing the potential for quartz crystals and other natural geological phenomena to usher in radical new means of affecting electromagnetic design, construction, and management. We can make the reasonable assumption that Nature has perfected certain designs for managing the subtlest aspects of Life. Our ancient African ancestors seemed to comprehend this at great scale and incorporated this natural scientific wisdom into structures such as the pyramids, obelisks (tekhenu), tomb burial items, and other "Tekken-ology."

- Western governments, in their endless pursuit of profits, have suppressed some of the most advanced research into alternative energy development. In particular, the genius of one European-born scientist Nikola Tesla had the potential to so completely revolutionize energy supply, that there is strong evidence that he had unlocked the key to free energy before his death. Immediately after his death, U.S. federal officials entered his apartment and confiscated thousands of pages of his research, much of which had never been published, and virtually all of which has never been shared since. Tesla had pushed far into the realm of quantum physics and was mapping out strategies for using the Earth's magnetic field as a source of unlimited energy.

- Other aspects of ancient Egyptian (Kemet) civilization are available for our development at this point in our journey into the future. Techniques of Kemetic yoga, martial arts, health maintenance, astrology, and cosmology could all be adopted, adapted and developed as means of extending our focus, capacity, and mastery of a spectrum of sciences of the mind, body and spirit. In no uncertain terms, humanity was more advanced in certain important categories 5000 years ago in the Nile Valley than it is today.

- The frontiers of science have pushed us to a bold new assessment of the very forces of the Universe. The most cutting-edge research into gravity, dark matter and dark energy, time-space warping, black holes, and the possibilities of interstellar travel all will accompany a major transformation of our understanding of ultimate reality over the coming decades. What new powers lie in this future of exploration for the fate of humanity to solve so many fundamental challenges? Is it possible that breakthroughs in our comprehending these essential cosmic forces will take us back to many of the earliest conceptualizations of the forces of Nature, Life, and the Universe that were known to scientists during the earliest phases of African continental civilization? Our self-determining African scientists must be on this front line as well.

- While there is so much attention committed to the current and future impact of global warming, and there should be such great concern, there is another area of Earth sciences that should also merit our attention. The Earth has a powerful magnetic field that protects us from being annihilated by solar radiation as well as wielding immense effect over the world's weather patterns. Any major shift in the planet's magnetic field could cause a catastrophic impact on the ozone layer, power grids, increase cancer rates, cause a shift in the magnetic pole, and other severe atmospheric effects. What we don't know today will be known in much greater understanding shortly. Which of our youth will be trained to master these quantum sciences which help us to understand humanity's ultimate relationship to such powerful forces of our planet's Nature?

- Quantum science is also taking us deeper into the functions of the brain, neurological system, and the subtle energy forces within the human body. What we do know is that what we observe on the macro level within the world and solar system we inhabit, also has its parallel correspondence on the micro-level within our cellular biology. Many of our habits, indulgences and unwitting exposures do impact us on the level of neurobiology, and it serves us best to bring our comprehension of such influences up as high as possible before we suffer irreparable harm. The knowledge we now have about the impact of malnutrition, alcohol, marijuana, pharmaceutical drugs, endocrine-disrupting chemicals, and other unnatural corrupters is so much greater than these understandings during previous generations. The quantum science of the brain, energy forces within the body, and the electrical functioning on the cellular levels will continue to expand at exponential rates. What will be humanity's relationship to mind, body and soul as another century passes? Will we evolve to become an ever more subtle, capable and adaptable species? Or, conversely, are we already witnessing devolution among modern humankind due to the impact of a spectrum of environmental stresses, pollution and self-indulged toxicity?

15 Critical careers of the future

Across the U.S., there are numerous innovation centers, some of which are quite renowned, like California's Silicon Valley, the Massachusetts Institute of Technology, and the Silicon Hills area of the Austin-based University of Texas. Within these and dozens of other innovation hubs around the world, experienced industrialists are collaborating with a dynamic young generation of tech pioneers toward a broad set of future-defining research. Their works span a vast set of tomorrow's most effective innovation, to include: IT, bioscience, biotechnology, electric vehicles, wearable electronic devices, automation, robotics, new materials, polymers, computers, clean energy, LED technology, semi-conductors, electronic engineering, nanotech, medical devices, battery technology, digital media, telecom, avionics, aerospace, sensors, artificial intelligence, ag-bio, ag-tech, life sciences, retail innovation, defense technologies, optics, entertainment, autonomous driving vehicles, wireless communications, home automation, the future of housing, 3D printing, and even more. [26]

I have previously researched and published what I consider to be a valuable and instructive list of *15 Critical Careers of the Future* for which we need to be guiding and educating our youth now to prepare them to manage the global affairs of the African collective population for the decades and even centuries ahead. The future belongs to those who are best prepared to create it today. These critical careers include:

1. Space-based systems
2. Wildlife management and nature tourism
3. Child birthing, prenatal care and post-birth support for child and mother
4. Research and development for science, industry and systems management
5. Biological health sciences, neuroscience, and molecular biology / bio-tech
6. Robotics and human-machine interfaces (not transhumanism)
7. Macro development policy experts

---

[26] Extracted from THE SMARTEST PLACES ON EARTH: Why Rustbelts Are the Emerging Hotsponts of Global Innovation, by Antoine van Agtmael and Fred Bakker, 2016

8. Ocean resources development and management
9. Renewable energy specialists and systems engineers
10. Infrastructure development, engineers and construction management
11. Information and communications technology (ICT) & cybersecurity
12. Agribusiness, from farm to processing to markets
13. Cloud-based banking development and management – the digitization of money
14. Mass media, entertainment and communications production – ideas distribution
15. Development investment management

Undoubtedly this list could be expanded to include a vast number of viable careers that would serve our young workers well. I have strived to create a list that is somewhat outside the box of our current conventional thought. Some of these careers, such as entertainment and media production, are deeply ingrained within every generation and can be expected to remain and transform for the immediate future ahead.

There will undoubtedly appear new career trends as the larger society moves further into the *Fourth Industrial Wave* and for which new styles of education need be developed. Another important point is that each young person needs to be individually analyzed for their distinct and unique personality, talents, interests, and natural abilities. Here is where our strong insights through scientific futurism must be combined with empathetic listening and imagining what each person can best bring to societal progress. As I listen closely to young people's voices across society, I feel ever more confident and impressed the way that so many of our youth are developing intellectually and experientially.

Summary

I hope that you, the reader agree that this has been a very important part of this whole strategic vision of *The Repairing*. There should be not one dissenter among us to the idea that we need to do a much better job of carefully cultivating those who would aspire to serve our Noble Race as leadership. As well, the leaders which we do put in place must be capable of guiding each generation along a sustainable course of development spanning all sectors of our group activity and across the entire spectrum of our immense talent and resource base.

Within these 15 various categories for scientific futurist studies, along with the **15 Critical Careers of the Future** that I have just highlighted, there is a demand for highly-focused, sober and competent engagement. We cannot take these studies lightly; we cannot fake our way through to the future which mastery of these subjects would bring about. We are a Great People as we are *serious* people as well. To bring up a vanguard of scientific futurists who are highly competent, multi-disciplined and competitive for the benefit of the group will require a significant investment of time, money, and focused scholarship. This is the stuff by which great nations place themselves on the grand stage of human civilization. We have a powerful and highly-motivating vision to create something at this time, with available resources that will certainly astound the world and empower our posterity toward a never-ending future.

We are an immensely talented people. We should thus expect spectacular success from our generation.

Chapter 10 - Gaining Consensus with Stakeholders

"Glorious shall be the battle when the time comes to fight for our people and our race." – Marcus Garvey

To move forward deliberately in the self-interest of the mass of people who form the base of our civilization period, we need to formulate strategies that directly address their fundamental needs for identity, self-esteem, prosperity and security. At this point, I feel it appropriate that we propose an updated "message to the grassroots," but to do so properly, let's begin by sharing the opening paragraph from the more well-known Message from our honorable ancestor, Malcolm X, El Hajj Malik al-Shabazz:

> We want to have just an off-the-cuff chat between you and me — us. We want to talk right down to earth in a language that everybody here can easily understand. We all agree tonight, all of the speakers have agreed, that America has a very serious problem. Not only does America have a very serious problem, but our people have a very serious problem. America's problem is us. We're her problem. The only reason she has a problem is she doesn't want us here. And every time you look at yourself, be you black, brown, red, or yellow — a so-called Negro — you represent a person who poses such a serious problem for America because you're not wanted. Once you face this as a fact, then you can start plotting a course that will make you appear intelligent, instead of unintelligent. [27]

[27] Excerpted from Message to the Grassroots, by Malcolm X, Nov. 10, 1963, from TeachingAmericanHistory.org

We are once again in great need of such an "off-the-cuff" conversation in a deliberate and easily-accessible language directed toward all of us of a common African heritage. And this major problem for America which Malcolm X pointed out in 1963, not only remains but has grown in intensity in many ways since that historical period. The increasingly tense period leading up to the November 2016 national election (which stands exactly four weeks from the time I write this paragraph) reminds us once again of the immense xenophobia (fear of *The Other*), suppressed racism, anti-black propaganda, and desire for exclusion of our members from centers of power, which has always been the backbone of America's unnerving relations with people of African heritage.

As difficult as it sometimes seems for this author, there is a need to "reach the people where they are" and share a conceptual framework for transformation in an easily comprehensible language. Contrary to the traditional tale of the Lion and the Hunter, this "digitized Lion" is tasked with creating the right media through which to reset the narrative of who we truly *are* and what to make of our long-term relationships with those among whom we live that are so often hostile to our presence. We truly have something very important to share and cannot risk the masses slipping through our grasp because we have not helped them to comprehend our New Message to the New Grassroots completely.

It is only fitting and natural that the masses would project the demand for black leadership to "Give us something we *really* need," and stop manipulating our people for short-term political or monetary gain and narcissistic self-aggrandizement. Our people need mental and spiritual food, *real food*, something that will excite, educate and empower them toward sustainable accomplishments. The black community has become fed up with being lied to, manipulated, their spirits pumped up and then dismissed by a long chain of slick-talking imposter leaders who work our emotions and past traumas within their deftly-crafted spin of fact, fiction, mythology, hopes, dreams and deceptions – all toward the aim of wasting our time as they play us like a cheap musical instrument.

Freedom and dignity are at the very core of fundamental societal values that run common to all stakeholders within our extended group. We seek and demand freedom from poverty, exclusion, injustice, sickness, hunger and malnutrition, from economic pressure, being cast upon our own resources within devitalized sections of cities, and feeling robbed of the surplus generated from our labors due to the crushing pressure from the greedy class which dominates the larger society. This fundamental need for dignity seeks to reassure every woman, child and man that they are valued, relevant to the benefit of group advancement, considered a part of the national treasury and worthy of being appropriately compensated for the quantity and quality of our work on behalf of the society within which we live. We have pride, self-worth, moral esteem, a strong sense of purpose in life and need to feel appreciated as whole human beings.

As well, it serves as essential advice that we, within the larger society, do not continue to repeat the mistakes of the past. Don't ignore or overlook the youth, for they are the essence of the change and transformation which are so critical for sustainable progress for our group and the nation. Contrary to the excess of negative propaganda that has isolated and offended so many of the younger generations, these youths bring great value to the world. Each has been born for a reason and should naturally be powerfully-motivated to want to make their mark on history through the introduction of new ways to live while enjoying all the wonderful benefits of youthful vitality, enthusiasm and creative energies. These younger members of society must be invited to work in close collaboration with the mature working generations as well as with the Wise and Esteemed Elders of society. We have got to do a better job of loving our youth to full empowerment.

"**Harambee** – Let's all pull together." This Kiswahili word should loom large over the common-unity (community) that serves our global African family. As has been pointed out throughout the book, within the body of individual talents found within our Noble Race, we have everything we need to demonstrate as great or *greater* successes in life as any other ethnic group. We should reasonably appreciate the accomplishments of other ethnic groups because each of them has brought some measurable value to the progress of human civilization. Yet all is not on a course of planetary sustainability; therefore, we must plan for an elevation of leadership that can bring viable solutions to some of the more pernicious problems of the past and present, along with new challenges to be faced in the immediate and long-term future.

One of the strategies which have been proposed for the benefit of African leadership consolidation is to conduct a *plebiscite (a narrow-focus election)* for the people. For the most part, most of us who were born outside of the continent are direct descendants of those who were kidnapped, enslaved, brutalized and forced to accept the identity of the enslavers. Many of us carry the names of the plantation owners who violated our fundamental human rights. The religion that they upheld ended up displacing our indigenous spiritual systems. We were stripped of our native languages (even our natural ability to function in more than one language, dialect or idiom as was the case in our West African societies). In every critical aspect of cultural identity, we were forced to change from who we were to what we have now become – and it doesn't necessarily work well for the majority of our people.

Who are we and what is our true reason for Being? Many of us have been reduced to *survivors*, merely moving from day to day, month to month, with a severe limitation upon our greatest visions of Being something vitally important to our family, community, metropolis, nation or family of humanity. Some manner of unifying action which re-establishes our core identity should be brought to bear which can set us again on the pathway of practical "nationhood" and put us back on our course of civilization history.

Conducting a plebiscite for our people could go a long way toward resolving this deep-set identity crisis which haunts our presence within this or any other nation within which we are identified as an ethnic minority. I know of no authoritative individual within my family lineage who had ever decided to relinquish our family's African ethnic identity and turn our posterity over to America; no one individual could or should even have the *authority* to take the family line and attach it to a colonizing nation. With a plebiscite, we can plan for correcting this crisis of national identity. As I have stated throughout this book, as *Africans*, bound to an entire continent of 55 nations and with contribution from multiple national groups coursing through our bloodlines, we represent the embodiment of the African Union. It should, therefore, seem quite fitting that we should have the opportunity to have a sovereign determination as to whether we are an integral part of the African Union future as embodied in the AU's master blueprint for the future **Agenda 2063**.

Because of the advance of our computer-based, mobile communications-assisted present, and future state of development, the idea of creating a means of conducting a widespread narrow-focus election should be more practical than ever. In the era of paper ballots and voting machines, pulling off something as ambitious as a plebiscite would have been much more difficult than today when we can pull an app from the Internet which can be installed on mobile devices, tablets and computers. We see computer apps that are very popular in use for music, streaming media, fantasy sports, recipes, daily horoscopes, celebrity gossip and personal communication. The idea of creating an app that will help to consolidate the identity of as many as 45.7 million of African heritage within the U.S., along with large populations in numerous other Diaspora nations, is an idea whose time has arrived.

With the **Afro-Plebiscite App** (for want of any other designation), we can settle the fundamental question as to whether we wish to relinquish our ancestral identity and throw our future and fate into that of these former colonizing powers within whose nations we are currently domiciled. The App could also become a forum for debating the merits of other important decisions that would be made on behalf of the group. It could serve as a communications pipeline to offer alternative solutions or points of analysis for hot-button issues that arise that impact the broader group. In so many ways, such an Afro-Plebiscite App could develop into a powerful, effective, unifying and motivating platform. The first questions to be decided are WHO we are and WHAT is our determined fate?

Beyond resolution to such existential questions, we then need to organize our group into a body politic that can negotiate within the parliament/congress of the nations within which we live. After years of sitting on what I knew to be a great idea, just this past week, I began to share the idea of our need to create our political party and have as such just pronounced the necessary formation of a ***Reparations Party* (www.ReparationsParty.org)**. At present, this vision is quite undeveloped but we do have great reason to assume that a political union with its foundation based upon the **9 Foundations of Reparations** could become quite an attractive core focus for our political, economic, judicial and social organizing. The U.S. Census Bureau reported that 17.8 million Blacks voted in the 2012 presidential election (which fell by 765,000 to 16.4 million in 2016[28]), thus giving us an idea of the *potential* voting power of our own, self-determining political clout.

Throughout history, and especially the post-colonial history of African independence movements, the role of a strong centralized political party has been critical towards our freedom and sovereign development. Unifying political parties have had such success across the African continent and elsewhere (such as China) that we must now accept the probability that the formation of a strong, centralized political power entity would also serve our immediate and future drive to consolidate our leadership authority. Ultimately, this centralized leadership must come to govern specific communities of our people, especially those concentrated in both urban and rural geographic locations.

For some eight years, I have involved myself and many others of our Living In Black social media family in collaborative partnerships which we call our **Kujichagulia Villages Projects** as new working homesteads. The properties we have been working on are privately held rural locations in Louisiana, Illinois, Virginia and South Carolina. As well, we have collaborated with several properties in Ghana and Benin as well as contributed financially to other similar developments in Rwanda and Zimbabwe. In my book **KUJICHAGULIA VILLAGES: A PRACTICAL PLAN FOR SELF-DETERMINATION**, I discuss our history of involvement with these landholders, specific contributions we have already accomplished, as well as a much larger vision of how the Villages can evolve into a powerful future model of revitalization, community development, training academies and problem-solving institutions which can commit

---

[28] Black voter turnout fell in 2016, even as a record number of Americans cast ballots, by Jens Krogstad and Mark LopezMay 2017, Pew Research Center

to a wide range of challenges facing the group. For too many reasons to explain within this new book, those of us who have participated in the Kujichagulia Villages are very proud of the legacy which is the consequence of our building tangible projects which last for many years, adding value to these landholdings. Ultimately, we have defined as many as 110 specific profit-generating functions that can be created, produced and enacted within these Kujichagulia Villages.

Similarly, we have envisioned a series of urban-based land development projects as well. In contrast to the "gentrification," which has disrupted longstanding black neighborhoods and displaced many residents, we see *revitalization* as our preferred pathway to creating sustainability within these same urban geographies. The idea of producing for our group empowerment, consumption, self-governance and sustainable development is one that is particularly suited for the urban environment and should thus serve as a powerfully unifying achievement.

Despite the persistent trends which have made too many of our neighborhoods desolate areas, bereft of employment, security, quality consumer retailing, and lacking in group esteem, futurist-minded researchers strongly consider the trend toward urbanization that has risen around the world as an empowering factor toward national development. We must get this right and get it in order; we have run out of time for critical strategic mistakes. There are numerous models of these urban innovation zones which have come into our possession, which we know could be replicated using resources already accessible to Afri-Amers who have become motivated to act in a coordinated fashion.

When the time arrives when we have created an authentic consensus with and for our people, it will become apparent that we will then arrive at a position that we can use our new capacity for continued collaboration and collective decision making. There should be no shame in wanting to preserve our identity as a distinct people with a long and spectacular history. The idea of creating such a mechanism for securing this Black Plebiscite and the consensus of the mass of our people to affirm our leadership legitimacy should be such to excite our vanguard toward this achievement. One can only imagine the great set of follow up actions that would proceed from such a moment forward.

Every one of our members deserves to have their vote count toward the great decisions which will determine our historical fate. It is time that we commit to this process so that we can advance on toward even more important group achievements. We most certainly have a lot of challenging work before us. Let's enjoy the process as we anticipate the eventual arrival at our predetermined destination of global African unification to power.

Chapter 11 – Producing for Group Consumption

"The best time to plant a tree was 20 years ago. The second best time is now." – Chinese proverb

"The most common way people give up their power is by thinking they don't have any." – Alice Walker

I trust that it has been revealed throughout this publication that there is a tremendous internal trade gap that exists within the midst of our economic situation. This gap between what we produce and what we need to consume is so great that it has become an existential threat to our sustainability over the next half-century. The more that this internal trade gap lingers on, the wider the gulf becomes. This expanding gap between production and consumption is locking us into another dangerous period of dependency, non-competitiveness, and desperation. Certainly, it becomes apparent that we must commit to solving this particular problem for other persisting challenges to even have a chance of being positively resolved.

Where are we Afri-Amers spending our money? Searching several economic and market research agencies such as the U.S. Bureau of Labor Statistics, Reaching Black Consumers, Target Marketing News, Black Men in America, Packaged Facts, U.S. Census and the Nielsen Report, along with a vast body of news coverage of so-called "African American consumer power," we have a pretty good indication of where we've been spending the bulk of our household budget over recent decades. Categories of our consumption include (in order of highest percentage of spending): housing (37.4%), transportation (16.4%), food (16.1%), insurance and pensions (10.2%), health care (5.0%), apparel and services (2.8%), entertainment (3.8%), cash donations (3.7%), education (1.4%), personal care products (.9%), miscellaneous consumables (1.1%), gifts, personal taxes, tobacco (.7%), alcoholic beverages (.5%), and reading materials (.1%). [29]

I often focus on food as an example where we spend substantial monies as a collective wherein we could carve out significant market share towards the aim of producing for self. According to the most recently-available 2014 report from the Bureau of Labor Statistics on Black Household Consumption, black households, with an average of 2.57 persons each, spent an average of $5825 annually on food, comprising 16.1% of household expenses. If we were to add annual inflation rate in this category of 2% for the two years which have since passed, this gives us a current figure of $6060 per household (with a total of 14.1 million black non-Hispanic households per the 2010 Census, 9.9 million of which were *family* households), or $2358 per capita spent on food per year, averaging $45 per person per week. With a population base determined to be 45.7 million in the U.S., in addition to some 2 million Diaspora immigrants living among us, we could see a projected total Black/African food consumption market in this country of between $109 and $112 *billion*, of which 69% of which is spent on groceries and 31% spent at restaurants (including fast food).

In Chapter 6, we discussed how $80 billion of Afri-Amer annual spending within full-service supermarkets was not representative of our ownership of supermarket chains that could serve our group self-interest. It seems so obvious that feeding ourselves would serve the highest priority of building sustainability and economic self-sufficiency for our group. Because of the persistence of subsistence agriculture as the world's most common profession, and the legacy of Blacks within this and other western nations in developing the agricultural wealth of the hemisphere, it is even more perplexing that we have surrendered our food sovereignty to corporations representing the sustainable wealth of other ethnic groups.

---

[29] Percentages taken from the U.S. Bureau of Labor Statistics, Beyond the Numbers, Vol 3, No 24, November 2014: Income and Spending Patterns Among Black Households by Reginald A. Noel

The same could be said for other major and minor annual household expenditures for Afri-Amers: housing – $486.2 billion; transportation – $213.2 billion; insurance and pensions – $132.6 billion; out-of-pocket healthcare expenses – $65 billion; and personal care products – $11.7 billion. Who is supplying the financing, construction and maintenance of our largest family expenditure of housing? Which banks service our loans and where are black workers' pensions invested? Which rental companies serve our home occupation? Who are the contractors that build our neighborhoods? Who owns the maintenance companies that service our home repairs? Where do we purchase our personal care products from in large numbers? Who is it that is retailing and wholesaling our very economic livelihood within this country?

Behind the wall of rigid racial and economic segregation, these questions were easy to resolve because we were *forced* by exclusion and circumstance to **do for self!** As you very well likely have already come to determine, so many of our leaders and advocates have pointed out the absolute desperation of continued dependency and the lack of entrepreneurial consolidation toward resolving this enormous challenge. Within this transforming project of *The Repairing*, our task is to provide viable and tangible tactics to bring resolution to this deficit.

For multiple reasons, based upon already-available resources and assets, we should see ourselves as *advantaged* in moving toward this new vision of sustainable self-development. In defiance of persistent rumors to the contrary, we are *not* bankrupt:

- Afri-Amers comprise the richest collective of Blacks within any single nation on the planet;

- Within these areas of discretionary spending that comprise our presumed $1.3 trillion in annual spending[30], much of this consumption can be redirected/channeled into investments which support economic leveraging to further the group's self-interests;

---

[30] THE MULTICULTURAL ECONOMY 2018: Minority Markets Have $3.9 Trillion Buying Power, by Jeffrey M. Humphreys, Mar. 2019, from the University of Georgia

- One of the greatest periods of discretionary spending is the Christmas holiday shopping seasonal months of November and December and, according to my detailed calculations, we can predict that Afri-Amer spending during this year's two-month holiday shopping period will exceed our normal year-long background spending level by over a record $50 billion;

- There are numerous large black-owned businesses in this country which include auto parts manufacturers, media, real estate developers, construction companies, healthcare providers (though most of the real players are non-black corporations; we do represent many levels of service providers), farmers, agribusiness and food products manufacturers, personal care suppliers, and the likes.

- There is a respectable collection of black financial service providers, to include black-owned banks (that are unfortunately seriously under-capitalized to compete against non-black federal banks effectively), credit unions, money managers and private investment firms;

- There is a broad spectrum of media either owned by Blacks or within which black broadcasters have daily access to large audiences through which directives which target our people for mass action campaigns have been successfully projected forward;

- Among our people within this nation, we still do have somewhat of a demographic advantage despite the poor attention to population issues that our so-called leadership has shown over recent decades. We can identify an impressive youthful population which can be immediately tapped that can energize their generation along with those of their parents and grandparents. As is pointed out throughout this book, young people have always been a key determinant in what causes rapid and lasting change within any society; and

- We have a large collection of Non-Governmental Organizations that do have a measurable track record of galvanizing our group members into specific actions that address serious challenges to the group. Historically Black Colleges and Universities (HBCUs) also have a strong place within this NGO spectrum with their potential to effectuate change and transformation within the great mass of our people.

It is the identification and promotion of a **Massive Transformative Purpose** that will serve as a *singularity-generating phenomenon* that will turn on this great do-for-self production, industrialization, economic consolidation and service-providing machinery which we envision as being critical for this next phase of our revitalization. The vehicle of **social engineering** must be engaged, supported by lavish financial investment, and unleashed upon our people's destiny with full force and cooperation from key group-serving agencies.

This is where the Six-Part Partnership, which was the subject of Chapter 7, will serve as a powerful and practicable tool of organization. Towards the aim of creating powerful machinery for producing for our consumption, we will engage the grassroots, stakeholders, NGOs, public and private sector partners, institutions of higher education and those of us who are in control of mass media. A scientific futurism-directed leadership can most certainly design and manage a massive strategic program to unite our people around these specific actions for our benefit. This would serve as our own "Black Marshall Plan," referring to a similar plan by Whites to rebuild Europe as rapidly and completely as possible after the devastation of the Second World War. Chapter 5 detailed 13 other historical and replicable models for rapid self-development which can serve our strategic planning.

As you can certainly see now, I am showing how many of these programs which have been laid out in the book are to be brought together in synergistic relationships to one another, guided and directed by an effective class of leaders whose scientific capabilities have been brought to their greatest potential. One of the primary tasks of such leadership will be *capacity building* within our people at all levels of society. I can repeat a dozen times that we have the entire spectrum of skills and talents, along with potential development capital, within our vast group of 47.7 million (to include the 2 million non-American Africans living among us). Our primary task is to unleash this great potential which we all know exists.

Skills development, along with the application of our vast set of acquired crafts and talents, is the basis of doing-for-self production for consumption. This sounds so simple when explained this way, yet it appears too difficult for us to have pulled it off in recent decades under our current leadership. Hence, our recurrent call for a renewal of leadership capital becomes a central theme toward the aim of rapidly changing the direction in which our group economics is headed.

Trade guilds, unions, and professional associations could have a major role to play in providing the basis for this renewed leadership of which we speak herein. For these groups to fulfill their great potential, capital investment must be in place which is not so *risk-averse* that they fail to make timely investments in exponential-growth sectors. Our scientific futurist researchers must have the capacity to alert all such agencies within our group of the powerful trends that will affect our social, political, economic and development status. Responsible, focused and strengthened black media must be in place to disperse such information in time to generate sustainable movement; such media must be healthy and focused on those things that do matter.

Innovation hubs and regional technology clusters must be created by all the players as mentioned above, working in collaboration to create dynamic career avenues for our young college graduates and other young laborers. The most developed societies are moving firmly into *The Fourth Industrial Wave*. This movement will elevate a broad spectrum of new businesses that will *thrive* during this wave but there will similarly be a vast spectrum of enterprises that are doomed to failure and collapse because they are not prepared to rapidly adapt to macro-economic and technological disruptions.

Today, black-owned businesses in the U.S. produce $1 for every $7 that our people spend on consumption. Our first task is to double that to $2 of every $7, then double it again over a period to $4 of $7 and eventually above $8 for every $7 that we spend. When we have achieved the state where we consistently produce *more* than what we consume, we will then have the luxury of selling our surplus to others and keeping the excess to build sustainable wealth which will empower generations. I have envisioned the day, and am convinced that it is a very real possibility, when our black-owned businesses will increase their production of goods and services far above our annual consumer spending, channel the surplus into a strategic investment and sovereign wealth development fund, and once again take our place on our throne of world-class leadership.

Let me make this a simple call-to-action: Black people, discipline yourselves, get in touch with your resourcefulness and build today for the benefit of unlimited generational growth and development. Our time has arrived and the spirit of Harriet Tubman is among us urging us to run as fast as we are capable. Run!

Chapter 12 – Turning Surplus into Fair Trade

" Build your own dreams, or someone else will hire you to build theirs." – Farrah Gray

Once this deficit of producing for our group consumption is resolved or at least moving firmly in the right direction, there can come a time when we produce more than is required to satisfy our own needs. Virtually all successful ethnic groups produce *more* than they consume; China is one great example of such. The Chinese economic miracle of the past three decades has largely been that of producing for export – they have managed to gain control over major industries which used to be the foundation of the American industrial behemoth. For the 20th Century, America dominated the manufacture and export of steel, military hardware, agricultural products, appliances, electronics, cinema, music, fabrics, computer technologies, and other industrial goods. Today these sectors are either dominated by Chinese and other Asian manufacturers or face very steep competition from outside the U.S. borders. Such is the state of a newly transformed global economic order.

What happens when, instead of producing $1 of every $7 that we spend, we reach the level of producing $9 to every $7 that we spend? Part of the rebalancing of this *consumption-to-production ratio* will require strategies to reduce non-essential consumption while expanding capital investment. The idea of creating investment-grade bonds for black households to purchase would serve a great purpose toward this rebalancing. Offered as gifts, these bonds would not only have perceived value within the mind of the receiver, but they would be profitable, interest-bearing holdings that also bring greater economic prosperity to the whole group, creating a positive feedback loop that would manifest in more favorable sustainability in the long run. At a mere rate of 5% of our current 2018 annual consumption of $1.3 trillion channeled into equity funding from such **Reparations Bonds**, some 65 billion dollars would go a long way toward creating a spectrum of profitable equity investments that would rapidly change our overall economic status.

A good place to begin these investments would be to take equity stakes in the most profitable existing businesses with the largest employee bases. What we don't want to do is to throw money into risky investments from untested managers with a reduced likelihood of long term success. There are some well run black-owned businesses in the U.S., the Caribbean, South America and across the African continent. With the right synergy of business management education, engagement of trade guilds, aggregation of highly-competent and experienced executive management, along with public and private participation, a vast rebirth of Pan African economics can be generated. After such, we can reasonably expect to add our revitalized industrial competitiveness to the new global economic order, reminding the world of the impact of African empirical power.

And there should be no doubt that our grassroots stakeholders could be convinced to commit to such a scheme in large numbers. More so than any other ethnic group in America, Afri-Amers take their behavioral clues from television, movies, music, and social media. Simply making movies, music, TV shows and viral networking memes which illustrate this rebirth of a global "Black Wall Street" would serve to generate such a movement in the real world we inhabit. To be sure, success breeds and feeds success. We need just to define a starting point and get a new self-determining economic system into functioning as soon as possible.

According to research from the **BLACK ENTERPRISE TOP 100 BLACK BUSINESSES, 2015**, *of* the top ten black-owned businesses in the U.S., four of them are auto parts manufacturers ranked: #3 Bridgewater Interiors, #4 Modular Assembly Innovations, #5 Piston Automotive, and #8 Global Automotive Alliance, all of which are located in Michigan and Ohio. At present, with the offshoring of U.S. auto manufacturers production, such as Ford's mid-September 2016 announcement that it plans to move all-small car manufacturing to Mexico by 2018, these black-owned auto parts manufacturers are in danger of losing market share to cheap labor south of the border. This concentration of black industry in these two "rustbelt" states need not become a catastrophic fate for these top black industrialists.

As I pointed out earlier, there are currently six African nations who have moved into automobile manufacturing and assembly: South Africa, Nigeria, Ghana, Kenya, Ethiopia, and Uganda. With the right structure of equity partnerships, these four U.S.-based auto parts manufacturers could significantly increase their production, expand their manufacturing plants at home and abroad, hire thousands of new workers and become the primary suppliers of parts to these six African auto manufacturing nations. These four majors could also serve as the basis of technology transfer, mechanical engineering, R&D, high tech workforce training and industrial infrastructure creation within both America and African nations. All of the components needed to make this expansive deal are either in existence or reasonably accessible. All that is needed is a highly motivating vision to be communicated among all potential shareholders among such a venture.

As was also mentioned earlier, African agribusiness is set to expand by some $640 billion in annual revenue to reach $1 trillion by 2030. Because organic-certifiable farmland and water are so readily available across Sub-Saharan Africa, there is a tremendous export-import expansion that could be realized in this sector. As was pointed out in Chapter 2, it was through agricultural labor and the skills of Africans in this sector that created the *Paradigm* Shift which provided the foundational basis for the wealth of the western hemispheric economies over the past 500 years. The whole world needs to eat, needs high-quality food, and wants to know that its food supply system is secure from any number of game-changing elements that should appear over the coming decades. A renewed spirit of African-driven agriculture, agribusiness and value-chain-creation could emerge from our decision to become major global players in the areas of food and agricultural production. Only our creative imagination and commitment limit the possibilities of making the most of the advantages of nature which have been allotted to Africa and it's 1.5 billion members around the world.

Even within the larger U.S. economy, we can see that generating surplus from products and services created by our industriousness could bring great growth in income to our community. In entertainment, the arts, tourism, food industries, fashion, personal care services, healthcare, athletics, fitness and numerous other personal services growth sectors, we have the potential to unleash our creative and innovative productivity at levels far greater than we are currently manifesting. Just looking through the long list of U.S. patents of inventions by Blacks gives us great cause to imagine what would have been the outcome had we consistently created the larger enterprises which took these inventions to the marketplace. Sadly, our historical record of consolidating these inventions to industrial production is a complete strikeout – no one that I've ever asked has been able to name one black-dominated industry built upon a patented invention by one of our innovators. Toward repairing ourselves, we must do better than that.

There comes the point when the momentum of our turnaround starts to create a positive feedback loop and thus can be expected to increase the rate by which we are gaining in a new and positive direction. The creation of so many new jobs for our young men and women will lessen the terrible economic burden that the prison industrial complex is still inflicting upon our households and our community development capital base. According to the most recent published figures from the NAACP, nearly 1 million of the 2.3 million currently incarcerated in the U.S. are Blacks. This population of mostly men is imprisoned at an expense to the state of about $35,000 each per year. Conversely, the average productivity per U.S. worker is very close to $70,000 annually; twice that of what it costs to turn a would-be worker into a caged captive. Rather than being a valued contributor to the business productivity and wealth of the nation, these imprisoned bodies are themselves the product of the vast, state-subsidized prison industrial complex. What a tragedy.

It is no great task of mathematics to witness the terrible burden which incarceration is placing upon our economic viability. Where is the breakthrough master blueprint to seize control over our human labor resources, put an end to this mass jailing of our much-needed workforce and unleash this great army of nearly a million laborers with their $70 billion of productive potential into this new global economic order? I intend for this book to be the spark which unleashes this dynamic potential for our stated purpose of *The Repairing*.

Of course, we are speaking in hypotheticals here; putting such plans into practical action will require effective and complex machinery for social engineering. Yet, could you imagine what would be the impact of having an additional $70 billion of productivity added to the current $182 billion that 2.584 million U.S. black-owned businesses currently produce annually? This addition would represent an increase of 38% to our productive output and would represent a major step toward closing the huge gap between what we consume and what we produce. Keep in mind that incarcerated Afri-Amers still consume while producing virtually nothing of value to our group. Still, getting them out of prison and into the right environment that would convert them to long term industrial contributors would require a vast set of enterprising accomplishments.

This conversion of our underemployed urban workforce to worker productivity was much the center of the research which went into my previous book **KUJICHAGULIA VILLAGES: A PRACTICAL PLAN FOR SELF-DETERMINATION**. It is highly recommended that readers of this book also access and read the Kujichagulia Villages strategic research as well. (*Go to* www.KujichaguliaVillages.com *for more information*)

Our primary and immediate task is to precisely determine just how, where, when, and which of these new enterprises would be developed. Some of these newly developed initiatives would encompass resource extraction, refining and smelting of raw materials, industrial manufacturing, retail and distribution hubs, transportation of goods, harbor facilities, international commercial banking and insurance, as well as training our new workforce to handle every one of these sectors and so many other specialized careers within our future of fair trade.

Because so much of the world's manufacturing output is dependent upon raw industrial commodities, it also serves our best self-interest to make moves to compete in and dominate extractive mining and smelting as well.

Last year, due to a major downturn in the prices of commodities in world markets, the South Africa-based mining conglomerate Anglo American was so beset by financial woes that they moved to liquidate 60% of their assets and layoff as many as 85,000 employees, some 2/3rds of their workforce, half of which was South African workers. The value of their stock and market capitalization declined precipitously. Anglo American specializes in mining commodities such as gold, platinum, diamonds, iron ore, copper, phosphates, niobium, coal, and nickel. By December of 2015, its market value had declined over the previous year from a high of $27 billion to $6.7 billion. With the price so low, we could have made a bid to conduct a takeover of Africa's largest mining company which would have cost but slightly more than one-half of 1% of our 2015 so-called "consumer power" of $1.3 trillion annual activity.

I railed about Anglo American's situation on my daily webcast, briefly expanding my program into a 1-hour evening broadcast to highlight this and other global business news that I was intensely monitoring. When their stock value hit rock bottom, I warned that the time to make an investment move to gain control of the conglomerate would not last much longer because some bottom-feeding investors such as Warren Buffet would soon come along and scoop up this valuable asset at a bargain rate of 24 cents-on-the-dollar and wait out the inevitable return of industrial mining commodities to their previous values within the global market.

Well, I was right that the moment to move aggressively would soon slip away. Anglo American's market capitalization has since rebounded quite dramatically, and the last time I checked, its stock value had increased some 400% since it bottomed out. Too bad that our Afri-Amer economic leaders didn't see that one coming or going. Too bad that the chance of black economic leadership getting such information from a black-owned Internet webcast was virtually non-existent. Not to worry though; I've got plenty of other powerful insights from where this new economic miracle can spring.

Another area wherein we may not even be considering producing surplus for trade is the number of empty spaces for students within Historically Black Colleges and Universities (HBCUs). Our research has shown that the spectrum of HBCUs is in dire straits for financial support as well as keeping enrollment up to a sustainable standard. With a renewed strategy for survival, an outreach between these institutions and large numbers of university-age students in rapidly-developing nations could provide an ideal basis for a renewal of energy and income for these HBCUs. After all, what is to lose? Currently, 9 of the 103 existing HBCU's are near financial collapse and 11 of their lot have already shuttered their doors.

With Sub-Saharan Africa (SSA) currently enjoying the world's greatest demographic advantage, the youngest population of any region of the world, the population of the continent expected to *double* in the next 35 years, a large dearth of universities within SSA nations, and rapidly-rising middle-class status for many nations, then it might seem quite reasonable that America-based HBCU's would aggressively step in to fill this need. In case the funding for these students U.S. college experience might be problematic, then a long-term equity position in the enterprises which these grateful students would be expected to be generating when they returned home to launch their business careers might be the most prudent pathway forward. We've got to increase our ability to "think outside the box" of conventional planning.

Toward the specific aim of producing surplus for external trade, Afri-Amers can feel confident that they have a broad resource base upon which to build such a massive transformation. While we have much capital passing through our hands, the idea of capturing some 10% of it for capital investment and equity funding has remained elusive. As this chapter should clearly illustrate, ideas for enterprise expansion to the point of supplying beyond our consumables can be extracted from the spectrum of necessary engagements that occur across populations, in this country and around the world. All the elements which would go into creating a powerfully competitive Afri-Amer directed global economic enterprise are not that difficult to imagine and identify. We have merely been lacking a proper plan and the executive management to pull it together.

As you read this work, I hope that you see yourself an integral part of this **massive transformative purpose** which underlies *The Repairing*. The world will continue to change, progress and transform whether or not you and I commit to stake out a much more important leadership role in its future. This decision is ours to make and it is my sincere hope and ambition to serve as an influential agent in helping to usher this new African Global Order into existence, for our people, at this time and "by any means necessary."

Chapter 13 – Functioning within the New Global Economy

"In the post-Cold War era, where ideology has faded and peoples seek definition from the collective past, dispersed groups such as global tribes seem particularly well adapted to succeed within today's progressively more integrated worldwide economic system." – Joel Kotkin [31]

In preparation for composing this critically important chapter on the expansion of our domestic productivity into the larger world, which is an overwhelmingly dominant trend of the recent past, present, and indefinite future, I spent a day revisiting one of my favorite books, **TRIBES: HOW RACE, RELIGION AND IDENTITY DETERMINE SUCCESS IN THE NEW GLOBAL ECONOMY, BY JOEL KOTKIN**. Throughout my career in journalism, research, broadcast and community development, I have striven to incorporate into my practical knowledge base those study materials which are critical toward comprehension of how the world functions; I have never spent much time studying fiction, novels or the mendacity of celebrities. When top scholars such as John Henrik Clarke and Amos Wilson both highly recommended that students of African-centered culture, history, consciousness and development, access and read *Tribes*, I took it to heart. Over the decades, it has proven to be one of the most valuable books within my vast library.

The author Joel Kotkin wrote in the prologue to *Tribes*:

---

[31] From TRIBES: How Race, Religion and Identity Determine Success in the New Global Economy, by Joel Kotkin, Random House 1992, pg. 4

> In defining global tribalism, I have set out to examine five principal groups—the Jews, British, Japanese, Chinese, and Indians—all of whom powerfully illustrate this phenomenon. Although each of these five tribes possesses a vastly different history, they all share the following three critical characteristics:
>
> 1. A strong ethnic identity and sense of mutual dependence that helps the group essential unity.
>
> 2. A global network based on mutual trust that allows the tribe to function collectively beyond the confines of national or regional borders.
>
> 3. A passion for technical and other knowledge from all possible sources, combined with an essential open-mindedness that fosters rapid cultural and scientific development critical for success in the late-twentieth-century world economy. [32]

Throughout this chapter I will return to some of the more revealing and impressive ideas which I have garnered from Kotkin's seminal book; I trust that you will also find these references powerfully informative.

In addition, another book which brings forward the focus of expansion of our own African global tribe is Dr. Clarke's own **NOTES FOR AN AFRICAN WORLD REVOLUTION: AFRICANS AT THE CROSSROADS**. While the book focuses on aspects of African and world history that illustrate how Africa influenced the evolution of civilizations, I will share the following excerpt from the introduction which fits our present mission of moving our collective group to an expansive, transnational collaborative state.

> Because African history, political or otherwise, has been seen mainly through the eyes of conquerors, missionaries, and adventurers, whose interpretation of Africa and its people in most cases is a kind of sick fantasy, it is time that Africans tell their own African story. In looking at African history from the Africancentric point of view, my honest attempt is to correct

[32] Ibid, Pgs 4-5

> some of the prevailing misconceptions about Africa and its people in order to see the global significance of Africa. If must be remembered that more than one-half of human history had occurred before the people now referred to as Europeans played any significant part in the shaping of world history. [33]

Functional Pan Africanism

Throughout *The Repairing* I have strived to create within the minds of the readers and the larger community a more practical, reliable, precise and transforming interpretation of *functional* **Pan Africanism**. Without going into the long and detailed history of Pan Africanism as it has evolved within the past two centuries the term refers to our ability to function as African-heritage people across borders, within multiple languages, sharing cultural commonalities, with cohesive political, social and economic ties. Pan Africanism, while never mentioned in Kotkin's book *Tribes*, is the tangible formation of his central concept of "global tribes." He wrote:

> In this process, global tribes represent a critical dynamic element—the historical protagonist—on the world economic stage. Where they appear, new combinations of technology, industry and culture flourish. When they leave, by choice or through compulsion, the commercial lifeblood, more often than not, runs dry; to the countries that subsequently receive them come the blessings of new ideas, technologies and intelligence. "Every advance of culture," noted economist Carl Bucher, "commences with a new period of wandering." [34]

Unfortunately, the idea of Pan Africanism as "a critical dynamic element—the historical protagonist" has been all-too-often absent, overlooked or otherwise displaced within the strategic leadership (or that which purports to be so) available to Afri-Amers. I have too often heard one of these so-called "economic leaders" proclaim in public

---

[33] NOTES FOR AN AFRICAN WORLD REVOLUTION: Africans at the Crossroads, by Dr. John Henrik Clarke, African World Press, 1991, pg. *xi*

[34] Tribes, pg. 17

forums statements such as "I ain't no African" or "we are *not* Africans." For myself and others of this level of political development, such statements condemn the speaker to irrelevance; from that point onward I become extremely skeptical of anything else they promote.

For Pan Africanism to truly have value in transforming our *transnational* status, it must be functional across a spectrum of group activities, strategies, programs and interactivity. There must be forms of education, trade, security, governance, economics, infrastructure development, cultural values and traditions that are essentially Pan African. Groups of Blacks, be they in Trinidad & Tobago, Nigeria, California, CARICOM, Nairobi or Philadelphia, must have common values which their constant and expanding interactivity reinforces toward creation of even more productive functioning among partnerships within the global tribe.

The future of Pan African media and communications

To inform members of the group, promote the most progressive ideas and strategies, and to unify the grassroots stakeholders toward their greatest potential, it is *unquestionably* necessary to have a powerful internal communications system that serves the global tribe. Thus, the future development of comprehensive Pan African media and communications must become a much greater priority for our collective investment. Among the man critical functions that such a global media network must provide is to clarify the extent to which our members, along with the collective group, are propelled by *internally or externally-directed motives*. As it stands today and over recent decades, our behaviors reflect our tendency to be reactive to provocations from mainstream corporate press's provocations and anti-black propaganda. This will not serve our best future of self-determination and sovereign development.

In September 2016, I was one of the featured presenters at the *Sixth Annual Pan African Global Trade & Investment Conference* in the Los Angeles suburb of Carson, California. My presentation entitled **PAN AFRICAN MEDIA AND COMMUNICATIONS: A Futurist Perspective** focused on this critical need for our leadership to organize a vast new structure of communication to serve our rapid expansion as a global power. Within this highly-received presentation were several critical points, most of which you should now recognize as important points of reference throughout *The Repairing*:

- How do we best coordinate our global population of 1.5 billion, expected to expand to 2.25 billion by 2050?
- The Tale of the Lion and the Hunter – Taking responsibility for propagating our own narrative;
- Raising awareness of the reality and viability of the "Africa Rising" narrative;
- Overcoming reactive obsession with distractions, disinformation and distortions;
- Our business enterprises must expand to match our group needs – We must produce that which we consume, to include media and communications;
- 1.5 Billion Africans on the planet remain overly-dependent upon unreliable partners. Who will be serving up the bulk of communications, news and information about the global African family in 2050 when more than 2 of every 9 people on Earth are Africans?
- Who will guarantee the integrity of Pan African media?

People won't invest in that which they are afraid of or don't understand. A convincing barrage of data-based information has convinced us that Africa Rising is a real phenomenon that has the potential to change the world for the 22nd Century and beyond. Yet, most black people in America and around the world have yet to be informed of this new reality. The persistence of such ignorance puts us in danger of what W.E.B. DuBois warned of as "race suicide." He wrote:

> It is doubtful if there is another group of twelve million people in the midst of a modern cultured land who are so widely inhibited and mentally confined as the American Negro. Within the colored race the philosophy of salvation has by the pressure of caste been curiously twisted and distorted.

> Shall they use the torch and dynamite? Shall they go North or fight it out in the South? Shall they segregate themselves even more than they are now, in states, towns, cities or sections? Shall they leave the country? Are they Americans or foreigners? Shall they stand and sing 'My Country 'Tis of Thee'? Shall they marry and rear children and save and buy homes, or deliberately commit race suicide?" [35]

A highly functioning global media and communications network will be one of the core elements of our vision of *socially engineering* a dynamic, productive, cohesive and highly-functioning global tribe, to rival that of the Jews, British, Japanese, Chinese, Indians or any others which were cited in Joel Kotkin's useful book. He wrote:

> The transition of the Indians, Chinese and Japanese from the status of "natives" to that of global tribes stems largely from the fact that, like the Jews and Anglo-Saxons of earlier times, they have developed a strong, ethnically based, morally anchored form of capitalism. Today, the rationalistic capitalism developed by the Anglo-American diaspora has lost its grip on its ethical moorings, in particular, its intrinsic belief in family and self-help and the need for continuous self-improvement. Instead those virtues seem more evident today among the Asiatic global tribes. [36]

Developing global trade infrastructure

Throughout this book, we have consistently referred to our need to utilize cutting-edge technologies toward creation of such critical, group-serving infrastructure as global media and communications. Similar facilities must be extended into means of trade-related transportation, export-import finance banking, governing bodies to regulate trade policies and institutions for sovereign development.

The World Trade Organization (WTO) reported in April 2016 that "growth in the volume of world trade is expected to remain sluggish in

---

[35] Black Reconstruction in America, 1860-1880, by W.E.B. DuBois.

[36] Tribes, pg. 24

2016 at 2.88%... [and that] Global trade growth should rise to 3.6% in 2017, WTO economists reported on 7 April." According to the report "**Trade growth to remain subdued in 2016 as uncertainties weigh on global demand**", the dollar value of global trade peaked in 2014 at $19 trillion, but declined 13% to $16.5 trillion the next year. It had been predicted that trade growth would increase from 2015-16, but those predictions have fallen short of forecasts.

Meanwhile, per the International Trade Administration of the U.S. Commerce Department, rates of most Sub-Saharan African (SSA) nations' GDP growth have surpassed World GDP growth for the past 6 years from 2010-2015 with the latest figures for Sub-Saharan GDP growth for 2015 at 5.5% compared to 3.8% for the world. We have earlier pointed out spectacular performance of rapidly expanding African economies such as Ethiopia, Cote D'Ivoire, Tanzania, Dem. Republic of the Congo, Rwanda, Mozambique, Senegal and others. As these SSA nations continue to expand their economies, this growth combines with their rapidly growing middle class populations to make for great opportunity to expand import/export market opportunities and subsequent return on investment. Increasingly, African continental exports will expand into the global economy.

By creating avenues by which Afri-Amer and other Diaspora businesses build capacity for collaboration with African partners, we will see ourselves becoming more vital to the global economy, just as have other ethnic groups pointed out in Joel Kotkin's *Tribes*. One of our advantages for building a robust global trade system in tandem with these rapidly-developing SSA nations should be our ability to relate more closely with the cultural values of these African nations. Kotkin cites the following quote from Kimondo Kusaka, adviser to Japan's Long-Term Credit Bank:

> I think Japan's role is to make certain concepts prevalent in the world [like] the custom of long-term cultivation of human relationships as the most import aspect of business. We want to be a teacher of concepts that can contribute to the prosperity of

the world. We can move beyond hardware, instructing people in such things as basic business relationship. [37]

Global citizenship

The most productive people of involved in global commerce are increasingly identifying beyond the limitations of mere citizenship of the nation within which they are domiciled. The pace of growth of personal communication, travel, transnational commerce, media exposure and cross-cultural exchange continues to bring many of the world's inhabitants closer to realization of the concept of *global citizenship.* Certainly worth repetition, of the world's current population of 7.35 billion persons, those of direct African heritage number some 1.5 billion, or slightly *more* than 1 of every 5 people living. By 2050 this will increase to nearly 1 of every 4 people. To the contrary, with fertility rates trending negative within many of the most industrialized nations, including black and white populations within the United States, we risk the danger of running out of demographic momentum within the next 2½ generations as the Afri-Amer fertility rate continues its steady decline since the most recent peak of 2.55 childbirths-per-woman in 1990, to its current rate of 1.85 TFR – replacement rate is 2.1 TFR.

As Africa's *demographic advantage* is the highest in the world and promises to deliver the continent to its greatest level of development potential in over 500 years, Afri-Amers will "run out of juice" if we do not link our population sustainability to that of our global family of African genetic heritage. Be very careful of anyone so foolish as to state "I ain't no African" because with such a valuation they have doomed themselves and posterity to ethnic annihilation over the course of the next 50 to 60 years per the rate of *African American* fertility decline.

Another very important aspect of this concept of global citizenship is that of world governance. In too many ways, our people have abrogated our responsibility to serve as wise, experienced, empathetic and benevolent leadership for the world. From our midst, we have brought forward world class leadership, innovative genius, strategies for empowering the

---

[37] Ibid, pg. 120, citing the author's interview with Kimindo Kusaka

grass roots communities, and our passion for peace, justice and economic parity within societies that we inhabit. From my own direct observation and personal experience, African-centered wisdom has proven itself capable to lead societies forward to prosperity and the equitable distribution of the wealth of the nation. We have produced wonderfully compassionate "People Power" when allowed the chance to have our contributions fully appreciated and integrated into national leadership.

Yet, because of racism, xenophobia, class-based hierarchical stratification and other shortcomings of the human character, we find ourselves consistently on the short end of political, social, economic and judicial fairness. From the position of power of a potentially highly-organized global population of our current 1.5 billion (expected to expand to 2.55 billion over the next 35 years), we should stand in an opportune position to restore ourselves to powerful empirical status. This is a reasonable and achievable goal which could place our group in position of righting many historical wrongs, protecting the Earth environment and providing security to vulnerable populations around the globe who have too long been subject to malicious and even genocidal treatment at the hands of less-charitable colonial powers. Just as Nigeria should currently serve as the African "Big Brother" state to all Africans in the world today, in the future a united Global Africa should be the benevolent partner to all oppressed people of the world and Nature herself.

Africa Rising and the world beyond 2050

By the time you've read thus far in this book, *The Repairing*, you are undeniably well-informed about the practical reality of this global paradigm shift that we now know as **Africa Rising**. As I built up evidence of this historic phenomenon over the past 3 years, I have become one of its principle ambassadors and champions for the futurist vision. The data-based evidence to affirm the veracity of Africa Rising has become my specialty. I can easily cite statistical data across a spectrum of critical engagements from demographics, to economic growth, technology trends, the growth of good governance as well as per-country specifics which will sustain this world-changing trend for the next 150 years and beyond.

Africa Rising is evidenced by middle class growth rates, industrialization, infrastructure creation, the great potential for energy generation, continental leap-frogging over previous slow rates of technology utilization, expansion of higher education, and the shift in global economic dominance away from the former colonial powers toward those who were formerly colonized. Africa Rising is in the exuberance of the youth who are coming into a world wherein which their early life is not burdened by poverty, hunger, conflict, exclusion and lack of opportunity. This is also evident in the newly-expanding acceptance of African cultural values, art, style, music, tourism, culinary influences and a renewed appreciation of beauty standards of our natural features.

Africa Rising is like the infectious rhythms of our music which permeate the emerging soundtrack of life, forcing one to begin to tap their foot in sync with these Afro-beats, gradually pulling one in further and further until the whole body wants to completely submit to the liberation of our dancing and singing. Africa Rising is increasingly impacting international financial markets causing national economies to soar in accordance with our commodities, consumer markets, creative trends and pulsing demographic expansion. Africa Rising is increasingly filling various media and communications channels with the sights, sounds, narrative and colorful brilliance of our distinct contributions to the progress of human civilization. Africa Rising is... Yes, it is and every one of our members needs to know this!

Africa Rising will continue to ascend as boldly as the rising sun on the Serengeti horizon for decades to come until we reach the fulfillment of the vision we know as **Agenda 2063**. This is the title of a *framework document* for African unity and sustainable development. African Union leaders gathered to compose this document on the 50th anniversary of the 1963 founding of the Organization of African Unity (precursor to the current African Union, formed in Addis Ababa, Ethiopia in 2001). Agenda 2063 spells out a 50-year agenda for continental unity, sustainable development, security, trade and the eradication of poverty, comprising some 71 specific initiatives for cooperative organizing. It builds upon an earlier program called the **New Partnership for Africa's Development (NEPAD)** which was adopted the same year as the founding of the African Union at the 37th session of the Assembly of Heads of State and Government in Lusaka, Zambia.

THE AGENDA 2063 FRAMEWORK DOCUMENT: THE AFRICA WE WANT is a lengthy and densely-complex constitutional agreement. It centers upon 7 African Aspirations for sustainable development which are:

- ASPIRATION 1: A prosperous Africa based on inclusive growth and sustainable development.
- ASPIRATION 2: An integrated continent, politically united, based on the ideals of Pan-Africanism and the vision of Africa's Renaissance.
- ASPIRATION 3: An Africa of good governance, democracy, respect for human rights, justice, and the rule of law.
- ASPIRATION 4: A peaceful and secure Africa.
- ASPIRATION 5: An Africa with a strong cultural identity, common heritage, values, and ethics.
- ASPIRATION 6: An Africa whose development is people-driven, relying on the potential of African people, especially its women and youth, and caring for children.
- ASPIRATION 7: Africa as a strong, united, resilient, and influential global player and partner.

In June 2015 in the Egyptian resort city of Sharm El Sheikh, 26 member states from the three largest regional economic communities (RECs) in Africa: the Common Market for Eastern and Southern Africa (COMESA), the East African Community (EAC), and the Southern African Development Community (SADC) launched the **Tripartite Free Trade Area**. This free trade agreement is one of the most important early steps which will lead to eventual full integration of all AU member states into the predicted Confederation of African States envisioned for the year

2051 and beyond. Pending ratification of 2/3rds of the 26 TFTA member states, this will the most significant development in Pan African economics to take place in history. It is imperative that Afri-Amers and others within the global Diaspora stake out a prime trade position with this TFTA partnership. The future possibilities are unlimited.

In conclusion, as this chapter clearly illustrates, we stand at the crossroads for the world of colonial exploitation, enslavement, genocide and cruel exploitation of our global African family of the past 500 years and the dawning of a new era of Africa Rising with unlimited potential. According to every measure of the critical importance of this moment, I am *urging* everyone who reads this research to spring immediately into the greatest level of proactive engagement that your individualized circumstance can bring to bear.

We don't have unlimited time to put our global plays into action. We don't have time for inattention or indecision. We most certainly don't have time to endlessly question these facts as they have been presented herein while holding on to the debilitating lamentations over our inadequacies, which have become so widespread among our collective consciousness. In too many ways, we are already a half-century late to this date with our destiny. Coming out of the period of civil rights struggles in the United States, Great Britain, Caribbean, Central and South America, as well as the period of decolonization of continental nations and the fierce struggles against imperialist warring against our liberation, we are now at a brand-new crossroads which we are very unfamiliar with since the epochs of great African empires.

We stand to witness in our lives over the next 35 years, the birth of the greatest civilization that humanity has ever known, which I have begun referring to as *The Great Swahili* Empire. This will be something quite reminiscent of the glorious age of Nile River Valley empirical rule that left an indelible imprint on world civilization history for over 5000 years (and perhaps much longer). Because this Maafa/holocaust experience has nearly broken so many of us, we are challenged to raise our sense of self-worth, group esteem, cultural valuation, moral integrity and global solidarity up to the level of receiving this empirical inheritance for what it is truly worth, as it is currently being offered up by history.

At this time, where we are domiciled, with the skills, talents and resourcefulness that Divine Providence has allotted to us as individuals within a tremendously advantaged group, we declare that **we truly are world citizens**. We have the right to be as proud, empowered, respected, and, if necessary, *feared* as any other powerful group on this planet. As our Beloved Ancestor Malcolm X stated so brilliantly and forcefully at the founding rally of the formation of the **Organization of Afro-American Unity**:

> We declare our right on this earth to be a man, to be a human being, to be respected as a human being, to be given the rights of a human being in this society, on this earth, in this day, which we intend to bring into existence by any means necessary. [38]

---

[38] Malcolm X's Speech to the Founding Rally of the Organization of Afro-American Unity, June 28, 1964 at the Audubon Ballroom, New York City

Chapter 14 – Multiple Paths to Security

"A peaceful world of today and tomorrow should be prioritized as a treasured gift that this current generation would bequeath to its posterity. Forming a society committed to the highest aspirations of humanity, progress and sustainability, must compel our duty of serving as caretakers of this world toward inheritance for our future generations. Thus, we are in great need to advance appropriate structural institutions that consolidate this inheritance." – Keidi Awadu

---

Security and Reparations

Peace and security must be regarded as a most-fundamental birthright for each of the 1.5 billion people of African heritage living on this planet, and this imperative cannot exclude the mass of Blacks that inhabit the U.S. or any other Diaspora population. While many of us may not be conscious of health as the single greatest threat to our security, the numbers expose just how great this threat has grown. In Chapter 2, we discussed just how serious this threat is as we examined health as one of the 9 Foundations of Reparations. We shared the statistical data which showed that Blacks in the U.S. were 400 times more likely to be killed prematurely by medical-pharmaceutical industries than police homicide; for all Americans that ratio of *iatrogenic* deaths to killer cops is a whopping 975-to-1.

Most people are completely unaware that Death-by-Doctor (aka *Iatrogenic*, pronounced: ah-YAT-tro-GEN-ik) poses such a security threat to the average household. I have strived over the years, with an intense focus for several months during mid-2016, on the impact that our dependence on profit-motivated allopathic medicine has taken such a bad turn of recent decades. We are too often too distracted by other mundane affairs of life to focus on what it takes to remain healthy adequately. Decades of psychological manipulation by commercial advertising has embedded many seeds of our destruction deep within our individual and collective psyche. This process of turning the population into unconscious consumers was not accidental or happenstance—it was a deliberate process, as exposed in Vance Packard's insightful 1957 book **THE HIDDEN PERSUADERS**, on page 16 he wrote:

> By the mid-fifties merchandisers of many different products were being urged by psychological counselors to become "merchants of discontent." One ad executive exclaimed with fervor: "What makes this country great is the creation of wants and desires, the creation of dissatisfaction with the old and outmoded."

Poor food choices and malnutrition have created great disturbances within the brain chemistry for most of the U.S. population. The high fat and sugar-loaded base of the Standard American Diet (S.A.D.) has disrupted the critical functioning of the hippocampus, the part of the brain which is responsible for memory and learning. The more "stupid food" that one consumes results in the lessened ability for that person to make judgments regarding just what constitutes proper nutrition—it becomes a self-generating downward intellectual spiral. As was pointed out in Mike Judge's 2006 satirical comedy movie *Idiocracy*, eventually the population becomes too stupid to survive. It appears that we are closer to Judge's black-humor vision than what our national leadership is prepared to admit. The way that Americans eat is a threat to national security which is producing a plague of unnecessary medically-caused deaths that my research shows have reached as high as 1,069,000 premature deaths per year in this country, some 170,000 of them to Blacks.

Thus, our most important pathway to security for ourselves and family members is to *stop killing ourselves by eating like Americans*.

Peace within the family

Many of the greater disruptions which impact the larger community have their foundation within male-female relations and the ties that create healthy families. For all Americans, the stress of maintaining a healthy family structure and parental integrity has become a serious threat to culture and community. As is the case in so many other areas, "when America has a cold, then Blacks have pneumonia." The metrics which expose the degrading state of relations between black women and men have been firmly moving the wrong way for over a half a century; it might seem as if there is no possibility that these degenerating relations might turn around over the coming decades. Ultimately, because black women and men can't seem to resolve this problem, our children suffer, their children inherit this disturbance of family tradition, and the subsequent generations are too-often born into communities now depleted of institutional family strength.

There can be no denial that we suffer from a terrible problem of "drive-by daddies" and single women raising males. There is sufficient blame to put on both the men and the women within this dilemma, and thus pointing fingers and "playing the blame game" produces nothing of substance that has interrupted this devolution of the family. The fact that this crisis is being passed from generation to generation indicates that it will take intergenerational planning and organization to either reverse this degeneration of the family or seek to create another model by which we can create the optimal environment within which to give birth to and raise healthy, productive children. Very few people may be consciously aware of the extent to which maladaptive male-female relations constitute a *real* security threat to our communities. Yet, when the question arises as to where these so-called "superpredator" males come from, we have to look at their family upbringing to be able to identify certain commonalities and points where these youths were psychologically traumatized and emotionally vulnerable.

One of the many avenues that have long proven to produce positive long term outcomes is early childhood development. For nearly all of our history, from the dawn of civilization to even beyond the post-enslavement reconstruction, Blacks have taken responsibility for raising our children from infancy until their entry into social institutions and adult living. The rise of corporate dominance within the larger society as well as within our families has forced new priorities on our households. My mother was our preschool and kindergarten teacher and she prepared her sons to excel from the first day that we entered public school. Today young mothers are most often forced too quickly back into the working grind after giving birth, thus requiring either expensive childcare, government-subsidized (and inadequate) child development centers, or childrearing duties thrust upon relatives who, despite their most noble efforts, are increasingly releasing these children into society ill-prepared to achieve their highest potential. These children then grow up to disrupt the family, pose an economic burden, delay maturing to self-sufficiency, and bring anything but prosperity to the families that gave them existence.

Securing the community

Multiple crises of black boys as "superpredators," so-called "black-on-black crime," urban youth angst, police killings of black and brown youth, and the social-economic exclusion of these youth have combined to pose a significant security threat to our communities. While searching for statistics on the number of annual murders wherein Blacks are the *victim* of homicide, my Internet search results were frustrated by a blitz of anti-black propaganda from right-wing sources obsessed with "black-on-black crime" and pushing the idea that there is a national security threat due to the presence of Blacks in America's cities in high concentration. While we cannot ignore the disproportionate impact of such *internecine conflict* (brother-fighting-brother), the intense focus of white xenophobia has posed no viable solution that would advance our societal interests along with those of the nation.

"Superpredators" – One could make the argument that they do exist, but such an argument must account for the foundation of their emergence as well as the fact that such a designation encompasses far more types than the propaganda machine would have us believe. While this current political cycle attributes this slander to candidate Clinton's past, in many ways, she has shown herself to be a political, social and economic "superpredator" herself, along with her husband Bill Clinton. While those in the black geographic zones have concerns about the high level of violent crime that plagues such neighborhoods, there is another arena where the violence of criminality is perpetuated by fighter jets, cruise missiles, predator drones, covert arms proliferation and the wholesale destruction of once-great nations.

Then what happens when ex-soldiers who have been pawns in the international game of state-sponsored violence return to neighborhood communities? On the one hand, the opportunity to advance one's economic fate is extremely limited, while on the other hand, these veterans are pushed into the lowest strata of socio-economic hierarchy and thus cast into a fatalistic life. This is happening while they watch the ones who ordered them to war greedily suck up the greatest portion of the national wealth. Is this justice or "just us?" In the situation which I just described, which is producing a suicide rate among these recent war vets of an average of 22 deaths a day—isn't this an indicator that the "superpredators" are the elite themselves who have assigned a generation of American youth to such a fate?

Why aren't these returning vets being invited to secure their own communities? These young men and women are being trusted to travel across the globe and serve up "security" within nations that they likely couldn't even have previously located on a map. Would it not have been better that they remain within their communities and become part of a community-based security system or service corp? Ultimately, for us to develop autonomous and sustainable procedures for securing our communities, we need to keep these young people close to home, create viable service corps platforms for their behalf, compensate them for their commitment, honor them for their duty and encourage them to rise within the hierarchy of community-based leadership.

According to a report of government spending for 2015 compiled by the *National Priorities Project*, 54% of the U.S. federal budget, some $598.5 billion on-the-record, was spent on armed forces. U.S. military forces personnel, both active and reserve, number 2.5 million. IF it were possible to divert just half of this annual budget of on-the-record military spending into peacetime salaries of $25,000 per youth service corps worker, then it would support nearly 12 million jobs for the civilian sector. This level of increased employment would have a great impact on the destiny of the 43.6 million American youth between the ages of 15-24. One can reasonably presume that such an influx of respectable employment among urban youth would go a long way to keep them from becoming a threat to their communities.

Another situation that is becoming more apparent, and could be regarded as a security challenge, is the appearance of *Autism Spectrum Disorder (ASD)* as an increasing challenge to families and communities. Recent reports have brought to national attention the suppressed scandal of the link between MMR vaccines and the high incidence of autism within the population, disproportionately affecting black boys. There should be no doubt that there is a strong connection between the high number of vaccine injections to which American youth are subjected and a range of immune system and brain function disorders which are appearing in this population. I have pointed out in my research that the vaccines are most likely not the only source of disruption causing this condition. We must also consider the impact of pregnancy ultrasounds, chemical-based food additives, in-utero exposure to endocrine-disrupting chemicals, electromagnetic radiation, heavy metal toxicity in the environment, as well as the high use of pesticides and other toxic household chemicals which can be found in the homes of these affected children.

The ultimate outcome of such toxic exposures has presented the nation with another man-made health crisis. While autism diagnoses in this country during the 1970s and 1980s were estimated at one out of every 2000 children, more recent estimates have ranged from one out of every 168 to as high as 1 of 6. For children living in poverty, the impact of autism spectrum disorder is significantly higher than those of more affluent communities, though there can be no denying that this pandemic is affecting families across the spectrum of wealth and income. My extensive research on this and a broad spectrum of detailed studies of health and environmental topics leads me to understand that this pandemic of autism is largely a consequence of controllable factors. Word needs to get out to the medical establishment serving our group that we can alter our behaviors and reverse this devolution of intelligence. We have got to 1) stop eating like Americans, 2) put an end to unnecessary ultrasounds during pregnancy, 3) reduce or eliminate exposure to *DNA-damaging* sources such as smoking, alcohol and drugs (legal and illegal), and 4) accept that the evidence linking autism to America's overwhelming vaccine schedule is credible, thus requiring parents to take the bold decision to *not* acquiesce to injecting their children with toxic chemicals.

Several other environmental exposures are damaging our children and increasing security risks to the community; chief among these are corrupting media influences. I recently hosted the sponsors of the "Turn off Killer Radio" campaign on my daily talk show. The strategy which they were promoting was to target the sponsors of commercial advertising on radio stations that feature offensive rap and hip hop music specifically targeted at urban youth audiences. While I had questions about the efficacy of their preferred tactics of calls to boycott and protest marching, nonetheless, for more than 23 years I have similarly raised alarm that the proliferation of degenerate behavior that is propagated within popular music and videos can logically be expected to increase maladaptive behaviors among those who are most exposed to this degenerative programming.

I have always contended that the best way to combat negative propaganda is to overwhelm the negative campaign with *positive media programming* featuring, directed at, and produced by the very audience which had been negatively targeted. The youth learn best when instructed by their peers and we can most certainly find a large cadre of impressive, focused, talented and disciplined young people to carry more progressive messages forward. To accomplish this, they will need lavish funding from the larger community and every pathway needed for such a broad-based communications initiative must be made available to them without hesitation.

Ultimately securing our communities will require widespread adoption of purpose and self-worth across all segments of the population. When one travels across commercial avenues that dissect our communities, you cannot help but notice an excess of negative messages which saturate these environments. Overt and subliminal advertisements insult our members. We are continually reminded that we are broken, deficient, clownish or diseased; even berated that we are underserving sinners in the eyes of The Almighty. Black community blocks have been too long neglected and too many buildings are shuttered or otherwise derelict. It is not hard to understand that when youth grow up within such a depressing "habitat," they don't see themselves with the same sense of high self-esteem that is afforded children of more affluent neighborhoods. Yet we do have sufficient finances passing through our collective hands to invest in a new ideological paradigm for our communities. We can and we must act with haste toward instigating another pathway for our children's future.

Security for the cities

In early October 2016, *USA Today* reported "The Most Dangerous Cities in America," using statistics just released from the Federal Bureau of Investigation (FBI). Using violent crimes per 100,000 of the population as the measurement of ranking, the ten worst cities were listed as: #1 St. Louis – 1,817; #2 Detroit – 1,760; #3 Birmingham, Ala. – 1,746; #4 Memphis – 1,740; #5 Milwaukee – 1,596; #6 Rockford, Ill – 1,585; #7 Baltimore – 1,535; #8 Little Rock, Ark – 1,485; #9 Oakland – 1,443; and #10 Kansas City – 1,417 violent crimes per 100,000 people. Of these dangerous cities, those who also were listed as having either the highest percentage of Blacks or the highest total number of Blacks were listed in order of ranking: Detroit, Birmingham, Memphis and Baltimore, but it generally follows that American cities with large, low-income communities are where the highest risk of violent crime also coincides. Our task is to remove this stigma of black urban geography as too dangerous a location within which to raise a family or invest in business enterprises.

As people of African heritage, not only are we living within the most dangerous of the world's most developed (OECD) nations, but we are further burdened by the disproportion of racial injustice and poverty-associated crime. **We are in a state of emergency** and it is time that our leadership adjusts whatever operational program that they have been utilizing for the past half-century. Acknowledging the reality that such an important and complex subject of how to reduce the burden of insecurity for those living within America's cities, we can highlight several practical solutions that can be implemented within the short-term that can be expected to yield a positive outcome.

- **Gainful employment for our young labor force** – It is a known fact all over the world that when young men are excluded from the economic mainstream of any geographical region, then the likelihood of them engaging in criminal, anti-social, or warring activities is substantially increased. This link between poverty and violent crime is true in Somalia, Afghanistan, Columbia and Yemen, as it is also true in Detroit, Memphis, Kingston and New Orleans. As the world is moving into the *Fourth Industrial Wave*, with its likelihood of displacing blue-collar workers due to increased use of robotics and artificial intelligence, it is even more imperative that we create the right pathways for not only engaging our youth within gainful employment but also lowering the cost of living to alleviate some of the economic pressures that youth are increasingly experiencing. We had earlier mentioned 15 Critical Careers of the Future wherein STEM education of youth needs to be focused on the road ahead. As well, the *Kujichagulia Villages Projects* are an excellent vehicle for incorporating a spectrum of solutions aimed at providing youth and community members of all ages with the right environment to create long-term solutions.

- **Beating back the illicit economy** – The single greatest source of metropolitan violent crime is due to the presence of the drug-based illicit economy. Since the early 1970s, U.S. media has overtly and covertly promoted the drug distribution networks as viable, seductive and accessible alternatives to those youths who haven't been able to secure a pathway to a better life through education and gainful employment. We also cannot ignore the fact that multiple instances have been reported of the collaboration between urban drug distribution, organized crime, law enforcement agencies, and the national security establishment to further this drug economy which is plaguing many cities. Thus, toward long term solution we must 1) create less-risky but attractive employment and entrepreneurial opportunities for our youth; 2) stiffen the backbones of elected officials and force them to challenge government agencies caught supporting the illicit economy; 3) set up our own private investigatory agencies that can track and expose the trail of drugs coming into our communities; 4) support programs which facilitate recovery from drug and alcohol abuse; 5) promote early childhood education and literacy programs which lead to better life options to youth of all ages; 6) create communications initiatives and positive propaganda with the young people, their peers, celebrities and other personalities which these youth have come to admire—emphasizing the messages that things are getting better and that there is great reason for them to be hopeful and productive.

- **Urban Youth Service Corps** – Another tactic that has proven itself to be productive is the creation of an urban youth service corps. Such a vehicle will not only steer young people into collective associations whose activities center around optimal behavior, but it also allows these youths a great sense of esteem in that they know they are making a difference in their community and to their parent's generation. Each of us needs to experience first-hand the value of authentic and selfless service to the community. As well, this brings greater value and appreciation to the geography we call our community, thus increasing the likelihood that investment capital will migrate into the area.

- **Turning urban killing zones into innovation hubs** – Frequently throughout this book, I have returned to the topic of creating shared spaces where young professionals can access the tools and office space wherein which to launch their entrepreneurial visions. Technology-centered, creative and collaborative hubs can be set amid fading commercial districts or dilapidated housing blocks. Co-working office spaces have sprung up across American cities. These spaces save money on accessing the facilities of modern business as they also bring together like-minded people in a creative environment. While there has been a long track record of putting up recreational facilities in black communities, and this has not been without merit or success, we need to comprehend that it is *innovation zones* that will create the right environment to turn things around. With more than 400 school closings in black neighborhoods since 2009 in just seven cities (Detroit, Chicago, New York, Philadelphia, Baltimore, Washington DC, and

Kansas City), we are in dire need to capture as many of these valuable-but-neglected facilities, renovate them and energize them with the talents of young college graduates and entrepreneurs. Tech hubs and innovation zones are the new faces of urban entrepreneurship and we have been too late to discover their value.

- **Supporting and expanding NGOs with the right focus** – There can be no denial that there are many non-governmental organizations that exist within our extended community that have proven themselves to be of great value, insightful, creative and led by effective leadership. While the largest such NGOs may garner a disproportionate amount of press attention (as some of these most well-known organizations also attract our scathing criticism for their ineffective strategies), there is a spectrum of such agencies across the land which have proven their value. What is needed is a communications vehicle that constantly spotlights the most effective NGOs and the brilliance of their leaders. When people see a winner they want to be with a winner. U.S. corporate media is quick to highlight such organizations that elevate the majority population's needs. These same media constantly put a spotlight on our worst behaviors, trifling activity or value as commodities (athletics). We have to search out and put an intense spotlight on highly-functioning groups so that more of the community can have a chance to engage with them, support their initiatives and create duplicate or similar models of those which best solve the challenges of the community.

- **Planning for self-reliance and sustainability for our urban populations** – I write within days of the long-anticipated, feared and loathed 2016 presidential election. There is just too much hand-wringing, lamenting and fearmongering among the communications regarding the inadequacies of one or both of the two major-party candidates. My response has been to emphasize that with a strong strategic plan, it really won't matter which party wins or what changes the new president will bring to the national stage. With a strong strategic plan, adjustments are always much easier. One had better believe that the strongest corporations in this nation or within other nations are not so worried about the possibility of a new blue or red tie leader. This book, *The Repairing,* is intended to be such a self-reliant plan. Africa Rising is a global vehicle big enough and with enough momentum to carry our powerful group of 47.7 million forward. No matter who wins national or local elections, we still have the same fundamental needs as a community and this is consistent across this or any other nation's cities. Our biggest challenges will *not* be the central focus of these politicians and we need not fool ourselves into considering otherwise. We are a great and mighty people who have been functioning too often without workable plans. With the publication of the book, you are presently reading from, that issue is resolved. Now we can move forward with deliberate policies, actions, investments and expectations of return on these investments.

- **Community Policing Commissions** – We cannot and will not ignore that within America's cities, the relationship between our people and law enforcement agencies has become strained to the point that segments of our population are near open revolt. Black people did not create this tense and too-often-violent relationship with metropolitan police agencies—this has been inherited since the days of slave catchers, enforcement of segregation, and the rigid rules of Jim Crow apartheid. Nonetheless, our leadership's sustained response has been ineffective at turning off the exploitation and injustice shown to our group's members, especially our young males. Across this nation, we must put together professional commissions that have the central task of elevating policies with these law enforcement agencies and municipal governments that alleviate the terrible pressure which we experience from law enforcement. Additionally, the best security for our communities will evolve from within the soul of these neighborhoods. Through community policing NGOs, we can not only monitor the activities of police agencies but also develop our resources to secure ourselves.

National security

In many ways, our group of nearly 50 million within the U.S. is, or could be regarded as, *a nation-within-a-*nation. As such, we require a **National Council of Security and Economic Affairs** to protect our group and develop our resources toward sustainability. Several black think tanks do exist, and some of these produce rather impressive policy positions. When one considers the number of agencies that serve as any country's national security, this facility cannot be taken lightly. There must be a spectrum of agencies with specific focus on topics such as crime prevention, demographic strength, financial security, relationships with external groups, auditing of group resources and assets, maintaining communications within the group, as well as monitoring media, conflicts, future trends, clandestine threats of sabotage, and industrial espionage. At present, there is a disproportion of black think tanks that focus solely on politics, social relationships, and social welfare. We need to expand our research and the ideas-projection capability of these groups further toward mastery of strategic affairs.

Across America, we must come to a much greater resolution of the multiple challenges of the prison-industrial complex. Prisons-for-profit within this capitalist society have fed masses of our youth into a machine-like operation which is initiated by policies and practices within our group which must be corrected immediately. Our national security thus includes early childhood education, the stability of the two-parent household, sustainable economics for families, strong community institutions which project and promote noble cultural traditions, a standard of excellence in the education of youth, and levels of economic engagement for youth and adults of every age.

The economic, spiritual and psychological drain which this nation's vast prison-industrial complex puts upon our group is staggering—draining our group of an estimated $70 billion annually in lost labor value, expenses, and debilitation. We have offered up solutions for getting and keeping our people out of incarceration through our Kujichagulia Villages projects. We could vastly expand on this vision of geographical zones set aside for career rehabilitation, establishing a peaceful environment, and unleashing creativity, which is the natural birthright of all humans. The need to consolidate and acquire much more rural and urban living space for our people is one of our greatest national security demands. To secure a nation first requires us to become nation-like in all our engagements. Land-based development is key and critical toward this self-determination and sovereignty that we envision.

For some families, we are seeing multiple generations following the life pathways which lead to long term imprisonment. The "genetics" of the incarceration inheritance are numerous and complex. When the curse of prison becomes passed from one generation to the next and then another, we must consider that we need to reconfigure the family structure to cut off this devolutionary pathway. This ongoing degeneration is mostly due to substance abuse, lack of attention to prenatal integrity, exposure of pregnant women to environmental toxins, lack of proper childhood nutrition, inadequate early education, exposure to an excess of toxic media, stressful home and community environments, as well as a failure to create the spectrum of institutions which excite our children to their highest level of creative engagement with the larger world.

The solutions to these challenges will all serve as a foundation for our transformative vision of *national security* which does much more than prevent crime but builds the whole human character of each of our members. We have a huge number of Afri-Amers with which to compete against any other national group or whole nations. What we can do to unleash this dynamic toward the aim of creating an entity capable of shaping the entire world's destiny is among our highest priorities and thus the central focus of *The Repairing*.

Regional communities

As we work to engage these strategies over the coming seasons and measure the positive return on our collective investments, then we will increasingly be driven toward working with Africans across the western hemisphere. Fortunately, the structure for such cooperation is already in place and merely needs us to consolidate our mechanisms for transnational cooperation, collaboration, and mutual development. We have within our population high numbers of African people from Jamaica, Haiti, Cuba, Trinidad and Tobago (T&T), Panama, Honduras, Belize, Puerto Rico, the Dominican Republic and the Virgin Islands. As well there is a large number of African heritage domiciled in Brazil, Columbia, Haiti, T&T, Cuba and Jamaica.

These nations belong to *regional economic communities (RECs)* such as the Caribbean Community (CARICOM), Association of Caribbean States (ACS), La Alianza Bolivariana (ALBA – The Bolivarian Alliance), Community of Latin American and Caribbean States (CELAC), Organization of American States (OAS), the Rio Group, SELA, SICA, UNASUR, and others. We must ask ourselves as to which organizations operating from within the Afri-Amer spectrum of development agencies have established working relationships with this vast set of western hemispheric organizations? What could be the possible value of us having representation among this mass of functional organizations?

One area of recent and ongoing collaboration is with organizations within CARICOM who have been working on various Reparations initiatives. Impressive efforts are emerging from St. Vincent and the Grenadines, Jamaica, and Barbados with which our mass of African people can synchronize our efforts. In 2013 Caribbean heads of state inaugurated the CARICOM Reparations Commission, which has published a **Ten-Point Action Plan** [39] that can be shared with U.S. based Reparations organizing groups as well as proliferated across the African Diaspora:

The CARICOM Ten Point Plan for Reparatory Justice

The Plan outlines "the path to reconciliation and justice for victims of crimes against humanity and their descendants." It calls for:

1. A full **formal apology**, as opposed to "statements of regrets" that some nations have issued.
2. **Repatriation**, pointing out the legal right of the descendants of more than 10 million Africans, who were stolen from their homes and forcefully transported to the Caribbean as the enslaved chattel and property, to return to their homeland.
3. An **Indigenous Peoples Development Program** to rehabilitate survivors.

---

[39] CARICOM Ten Point Plan for Reparatory Justice, from Reparations for Native Genocide And Slavery, October 2015, CARICOM Caribbean Community website

4. **Cultural Institutions** through which the stories of victims and their descendants can be told.
5. Attention to be paid to the "**Public Health Crisis**" in the Caribbean. The Caribbean has the "highest incidence of chronic diseases which stems from the nutritional experience, emotional brutality, and overall stress profiles associated with slavery, genocide and apartheid."
6. **Eradicating illiteracy**, as the Black and Indigenous communities were left in a state of illiteracy, particularly by the British.
7. An **African Knowledge Program** to teach people of African descent about their roots;
8. **Psychological Rehabilitation** for healing and repair of African descendants' populations.
9. **Technology Transfer** for greater access to the world's science and technology culture.
10. **Debt Cancellation** to address the "fiscal entrapment" that faces Caribbean governments that emerged from slavery and colonialism.

Black-owned businesses and investors can look beyond U.S. shores and find a spectrum of such programs, ideas, opportunities, and collaborations across the Diaspora. New developments can be engaged in agribusiness, ocean resources management, infrastructure creation, cultural and art exchanges, media and communications, alternative energy development, tourism, finance and other lucrative industries. We can find new consumers of our products and services as well as import partners to supply critical needs currently not supplied by our domestic industries.

The whole world is moving rapidly into a new global economic order. When regions such as CARICOM, South and Central America are showing themselves to make major strides forward in the development of global commerce, then it certainly demonstrates a critical necessity for us to get our act together and join these fellow nations on the world stage. Once this all comes into motion, we must instigate needed structures of maintenance and security. We can move immediately to open academies whereby we can train our leadership to move our transnational commerce and security-promoting partnerships forward along these emerging pathways.

As we consider the sheer numbers of Blacks in the western hemisphere, those self-identifying as "Afro-Latinos" outnumber Afri-Amers by a ratio of more than 4-to-1. There are large populations in Brazil, Haiti, Dominican Republic, Cuba, Columbia, Puerto Rico, Nicaragua, Honduras, Guatemala, Belize and beyond. While most of the time, we regard Afro-Latinos as Spanish speaking, technically French is a Latin language derivative as well. Nonetheless, the failure of Afri-Amers to be functional in more than just the language of their enslavement and oppression is a terrible curse upon our mission to rise to our greatest potential. It is critically necessary that we overcome this language deficit within the next generation.

The world is becoming closer because of radical breakthroughs in communication and travel. Our leadership has allowed us to be locked within a limiting identity, which too often begins our narrative with enslavement and emancipation. It is up to us to bring forward a more capable and expansive leadership that can facilitate building the right bridges into the new global economic order. Just like national governments, we must be able to relate to our partners in multiple languages. Continuing to fail in this obligation is not an option for our primary aim of establishing sustainable development.

As we expand within these new capacities and relationships, our abilities toward systematically monitoring hemispheric security issues and lobbying for policy shifts will advance correspondingly. As I speak to groups about my futurist projections, I am frequently praised for the broad base of my working knowledge and mastery of detailed data. This is because I constantly study within the spectrum of 14 disciplines that comprise *scientific futurism*. I highly encourage every audience to similarly challenge themselves to be walking encyclopedias of information that is relevant to sustainable development. There is just so much to know about our family of Africans throughout and across the Diaspora. We are a wonderfully rich and resourceful people. What we don't know about each other only serves as barriers to our cooperation toward mutual empowerment. We have no excuses for this persistence of ignorance in this age of instant information and inexpensive communication. We can, and thus, we will do much better to close the gap between ourselves and partners within our regional economic communities. It should reasonably follow that closer alliances among communities of Africans within the U.S. along with our ethnic partners throughout these regional communities will strengthen our collective security.

African continental security

Contrary to widespread belief, security across the African continent is better than it has been during the period since the decolonization movements from 1957 forward. The number of African nations that are engaged in conflict has decreased steadily over the decades. As well, among those regions that are still experiencing conflict, the number of casualties of warfare has been decreasing. Yet, when I engage in conversations with people about our possibilities of building sustainable futures on African continental soils, too often, I am met with resistance because of the lingering fear of conflict and warfare. There is a serious information gap that has heaped an excess of negative propaganda on our continental family and it has become one of my primary tasks in recent decades to dispel these persisting misunderstandings about African nations' transforming security possibilities and present actualities.

Closing the gap between what we have come to *believe* about Africa versus what we actually *know* (and can readily verify) can be a daunting task but it is being made all the more feasible because of the Internet and net-based independent broadcast media. Monitoring U.S. national security affairs in Africa is thus more accessible to any of us who have more than superficial interest. Net accessible research institutions such as the Africa Center for Strategic Studies, Center for Strategic and International Studies, Strategic Studies Institute, World Bank, International Monetary Fund, World Economic Forum, Institute for Security Studies, Global Risk Insights, African Development Bank and other net-accessible destinations are readily available for our investigation, each having specific focuses which include African security issues.

Toward the aim of closing the gap which exists among Pan Africans as to the current reality and future projections for continental progress, I highly recommend that you, the reader, take a full day or more exploring each of these strategic research networks I have listed. I take the most interesting articles and save them in PDF form into designated folders which are focused on specific categories of sustainable development. Over weeks, months and seasons, as insights within these folders deepen, I find myself in a better position to see these trends occurring much closer to real-time analysis. This is undoubtedly one of the critical functions which help to define my engagement and mastery in the vast field of *scientific futurism*.

From a cursory examination of these types of strategic research policy institutes, we can comprise a list of some of the top issues on African security trends upon which we should be focusing. These include (but are most definitely *not* confined to) the following **seven trends shaping the future of peace and security in Africa**, extracted from an article from the World Economic Forum [40]:

1. **Poverty vs. inclusive growth.** "Poverty and social injustice have long been drivers of insecurity in sub-Saharan Africa... Putting into place policies for inclusive growth, investments in education and health, and providing public services to the poorest, would improve social cohesion and harmony in African societies and ensure the economic allure of Africa as an area of investment for regional as well as external partners."

2. **Sustainable management of resources.** "Africa is blessed with abundant natural resources and land, but they have often been exploited irresponsibly... Increasingly serious problems with water distribution and population growth will put greater pressure on the need to modernize subsistence agriculture, while climate change effects will aggravate the problems: drought, floods or poor harvests may create new refugee populations and increase strains over shared

---

[40] 7 trends shaping the future of peace and security in Africa, Anton du Plessis (Executive Director, Institute for Security Studies) and Anja Kaspersen (Former Head of Geopolitics and International Security, World Economic Forum), June 2016, World Economic Forum

resources."

3. **Closing the "grey zones" in governance.** "Perhaps the most important driver of violence and conflict in Africa today is weak and unconsolidated governance... Indeed, the African Union (AU) recognizes that national and regional governance institutions need to be strengthened. The African Peer Review Mechanism (APRM) is seeing somewhat of a revitalization, and the AU's African Governance Architecture (AGA) is increasingly part of mainstream discussions on the need for more integrated responses to Africa's security and development challenges."

4. **Addressing the "democratic deficit."** "The (growing) imbalance between levels of human development and economic growth and political and social inclusion remains a key threat to stability. In settings where democracy has not been entrenched, there is a lack of transparency and trust in the process, or where the government has been actively factional in benefiting one ethnic group above others, election-related violence often occurs... The increasing connectedness of the population should also be viewed as an opportunity to address the deficit, including better civil education programs and election monitoring and the quality of civic processes."

5. **Regionalism that delivers on regional solutions.** "African regional organizations are finally starting to provide solutions to African problems. These institutions must further improve their ability to positively influence national politics, monitor internal behaviors of member states and prevent human rights violations. Over time, more robust regional and national conflict resolution structures and mechanisms are being developed but still struggle to raise necessary funds and mobilize sufficient political support to become fully operational. These need in turn to be given space and support by non-African actors who are accustomed to intervening in African affairs."

6. **Youth, as a stabilizing or destabilizing factor.** "Africa is a young continent, with the median age at just 19 years. The protruding youth population could become an important economic boost to the region.

Alternatively, it could further increase the risk of instability and violence if young people are deprived of a quality education, stable employment and a political voice. It is also critical to promote an education system "fit for purpose" with a strong focus on entrepreneurship and technology to optimize opportunities and re-frame narratives... It is critical to harness the potential of the continent's youthful population and meet their expectations for education, opportunities and jobs to create long-term security."

7. **Technology as a game-changer.** "Technological changes are raising the security stakes and enabling self-organization of individuals for both negative (terrorism/extremism) and positive (social change/transparency). The potential for technology to do good in Africa is however staggering, as has been demonstrated in areas ranging from improving education quality and quantity, to mobile money reaching the unbanked, data being used to improve public health, and connectivity improving transparency. However, protecting millions of newly connected Africans from cyber security threats is a major concern, as is the usefulness of the internet as a recruitment tool for extremist groups operating in the region."

As I frequently engage in attempts to update our working information on security issues on the African continent, the topic often jumps right to AFRICOM, the U.S. Department of Defense African Command. AFRICOM is described on its web page as: "United States Africa Command, (U.S. AFRICOM) is one of six of the U.S. Defense Department's geographic combatant commands and is responsible to the Secretary of Defense for military relations with African nations, the African Union, and African regional security organizations." So many of our most enlightened Pan African members have become convinced that AFRICOM is the primary thrust, and hence threat, by western powers into the security affairs of African nations, and as such have come to perceive it as somewhat a takeover of African national security interests by the U.S. government. I spend a lot of time trying to dispel or expand upon these partial truths. While I could utilize the remainder of this chapter or an entire book putting the whole of these security concerns into context, in brief, I want you, the reader, to understand that so much of what we think we know about AFRICOM is obsolete.

Initiated under the George W. Bush administration in February 2007, with the initiative pushed by then-Defense Secretary Robert Gates, AFRICOM was established by presidential authority. Over the decade that has since passed, the initiative has had a few successes but also generated a lot of resistance from African nations who perceived it as another recolonizing attempt. With its headquarters in Stuttgart-Moehringen, Germany, at present AFRICOM has operational programs spanning 18 African nations, including conflict zones in the Central African Republic, Niger, Mali, Somalia and South Sudan. Toward the aim of our being in a better position to exert influence over U.S. military interests across Africa, it does require us to have expertise in this area of comprehending AFRICOM operations.

Yet as much as we purport to know about AFRICOM and its implied threats to the sovereignty of African nations, very few are aware of the newer and lesser-known *Security Governance Initiative (SGI)*. The SGI emerges from the August 2014 U.S.-Africa Summit which took place in Washington, DC. This gathering was the largest meeting between the U.S. government and some 50 African national leaders, at the invitation of President Barack Obama. At present, the SGI has become the lead agency to engage with African nations regarding present and future security issues. Because the SGI is coordinated *not* through the Defense Department but through the office of the Secretary of State, then it serves more as an asset of the Central Intelligence Agency than DOD, thus making it much less transparent for those of us who are curious about its activities.

To close out this discussion of AFRICOM and the SGI, I cite the following from a *Foreign Policy in Focus* publication:

> Among them is the August 6, 2014 announcement of a new Obama Administration "initiative" for Africa. Actually there are two: the so-called "Security Governance Initiative for Africa" (SGI) on the one hand and "the African Peacekeeping Rapid Response Partnership, called A-PREP for short, on the other. Old wine in new bottles?...or old wine in old bottles slightly polished up?

> SGI involves providing aid – with strings attached as usual – to Ghana, Kenya, Mali Niger, Nigeria and Tunisia. On one level SGI is a response to the threat to African development posed by Islamic radical groups Al Qaeda of the Maghreb (AQIM), Al Shabbab, and Boko Haram. But its ulterior motive – actually quite openly stated – is to make the targeted African countries more secure for foreign investment, thus, as the old cliché goes, killing two birds with one stone. The stated goal of the program is to ensure the security environment of these countries as a way of encouraging future U.S. investment, and as Tunisian commentator Yassine Bellamine notes in a recent article at the Tunisian website *Nawaat.org* "as a way to play a more active role in what is shaping up to be a new investor Eldorado in the near future, Africa." [41]

The specific focus of *The* Repairing is on how we of African heritage can take firm control over our destiny, at home on the continent and around the world. It has often been declared that "Africa needs trade, not aid." – to which I will add a slight derivation, Africa needs trade, not *military* aid. The long-term resolution to the continent's security challenges lies down the road of sustainable development, equitable wealth distribution, strengthening the base of good governance, raising quality-of-life to each citizen, educating youth to sustainable power and global competitiveness along with strengthening all the institutions which serve family and community.

Toward our contributions which further resistance to the expansion of Africa-based CIA drone bases, AFRICOM's militarization of political conflicts, "making Africa safe" for western economic infiltration, and increased use of African territories for field testing the future of robotic warfare, we have got to put forward serious efforts into propagating a spectrum of transformative policy initiatives and political lobbying which will ultimately promote peaceful development.

---

[41] AFRICOM-Lite: The Obama Administration's Security Governance Initiative for Africa, by Rob Prince, September 2, 2014, Foreign Policy In Focus / FPIF.org

Thus, we extend our national outcry to also apply to Africa: **All Black Lives Matter**. To the foreign usurpers of peace and prosperity on the continent, we exhort: "Hands off Somalia, South Sudan, Haiti, Zimbabwe, Mali, Niger, Libya, Nigeria and the Sahel." Hands off African coastal waters, fertility, sovereign governance and military independence. The old security deals which have come to rule over the lives of the more than 1 billion inhabitants of the African continent are due for a major upgrade. Because so many of these detrimental policies have come through intervention and manipulation by the United States, United Kingdom, France, NATO, Arab and Israeli outsiders, we must take it upon ourselves to exert political pressure on the governments of these intervening nations, striving to create better relationships that do not center upon conflict, covert intervention, strong-arm tactics against African leadership, and clandestine manipulation of facts and circumstances in ways that hinder African progress.

If we are searching for the best contributor toward *sovereign* African security advancement, the African Union is the most fitting agency to address this spectrum of challenges. While the organization is not without its flaws (for one, it is still far too dependent on financial aid and input from non-continental sources), for the immediate future, we should look to the AU for best solutions to problems the continent faces. From the African Diaspora, we need to raise political *and* financial support for African Union policy initiatives. A small fraction of wasted consumer spending which can be attributed to Afri-Amers would go a long way toward strengthening the annual budget of $150.5 million going into AU administrative operations and $266.3 million for programs.

Before his October 2011 assassination at the hands of U.S.-NATO rebel allies, alongside Egypt, the government of Libyan leader Muammar Gaddafi was the top financial contributor to the AU budget. The U.S., under Secretary of State Hillary Clinton, instigated a cascade of lies that led to the NATO-U.S. destruction of the Libyan state regime. Therefore, it might seem fitting and proper that Africans in America take responsibility for filling in this resultant gap in much-needed funding for operations and programs of this 54-nation African Union governance body.

Returning to the projected $50 billion spending spree that Afri-Amers will drop on holiday shopping this year, redirecting a mere 1% of this increased Christmas season indulgence would more than double this year's African Union budget – a drop in the bucket for our people but a *massive* investment in peace, prosperity and governance for continental unity. To create this redirection of consumption, some tangible means of commoditizing this investment should be created. African nations could make certain products available that would be appropriate for Diaspora family purchases. Toward this vision, a specific investment bond could be developed. A campaign of communications initiatives promoting seasonal peace and goodwill could suggest our people's support for benevolent donations for African developmental support. Even tourism during the holiday season to African destinations could be promoted as a means of connecting with our deeper spiritual values and cultural ties. By multiple means, some 300 million Africans living outside the continent could raise this substantial contribution of $500 million toward doubling the African Union's annual budget.

Another of our priorities should be toward setting up commissions to investigate and expose the assassinations of important black leaders from around the world, to include Patrice Lumumba, Malcolm X, Dr. Martin L. King Jr., Murtala Muhammed, Steven Biko, Chris Thembisile Hani, Samora Marcel, Muammar Gaddafi, Walter Rodney, and others. Much of the research to expose state-sponsored conspiracies behind these assassination plots has already been produced yet the findings of these commissions and individual researchers remain largely inaccessible or unknown to the masses of our people.

I would be remiss if I didn't include the security challenge of clandestine population control activities directed at women and girls within developing nations. Nowhere is this more a threat than to the women of Sub-Saharan Africa. I've been writing about this for more than 20 years, much of which was exposed in the third book on the topic, my 1996 book **POPULATION WAR: REPORT FROM THE FRONTLINE**. Over these decades we've detailed such sterilization conspiracies as use of mass vaccination campaigns to cause childbearing-age women to be allergic to their own pregnancy hormones; the deliberate creation *of anti-sperm antibodies*, again through mass vaccinations; the secret insertion into women's wombs of IUD's and the sterilizing chemicals quinacrine and chloroquine, both of which are failed malaria drugs; the development of a genetically-modified corn called *Epicyte*, which is deliberately designed to generate anti-sperm antibodies in women and men who consume products which contain the GMO corn or its components. It should be expected that our awareness and alarm about covert sterilization should be sufficient to compel us to organize to resist this anti-life activity, especially since most such population reduction schemes are directed against females of African heritage, along with other women-of-color.

As more African nations denounce the Eurocentric *International Criminal Courts* commission because of its anti-African bias, we require the creation of a parallel organization in collaboration with partner nations which can be relied upon to be fair in our investigation of international criminal activity and genocide. For many reasons, Afri-Amers would be best to take a leading role in such investigative research toward bringing those responsible for these terrible offenses to justice and exposure before the eyes of the world. The lives that could be saved by exposing these international criminals could very well likely be those of our children and others who we need for our future development.

Global peace development

Throughout this book, we have advanced a spectrum of transforming visions, short-term and long-term goals, policy proposals, strategic initiatives, tactics, and structural reforms, along with the creation of numerous agencies and institutions that are expected to generate great changes across all levels of our global African civilization. As we successfully implement these initiatives, we should reasonably expect an outcome of increased influence in world affairs. As such, we envision a future wherein a united African bloc will be taking a firmer stance on global security affairs. A Confederation of African States (CAS) must have a permanent seat on the United Nations Security Council if the UN is to remain a credible organization within a rapidly changing global environment.

In the world of 2050, white-majority nations will have been significantly transformed by nearly a century of below-replacement fertility, population aging, and the "browning" of traditionally European-dominated populations due to immigration and high fertility within its immigrant communities. This will contrast against a world wherein Eastern and Southern Asians, Africans, Latin Americans and Muslims will constitute the overwhelming majority of the world's population. As we progress toward a world beyond 2050 when more than two of every nine people on the planet will be of African ancestry, Blacks should at present be forging a primary role in promoting and supplying leadership for initiatives which advance peace and sustainable prosperity for all of humanity, as well as protecting Earth's diversity of species.

Multiple necessary and immediate steps must be engaged toward this vision of world peace and benevolence. From the African Diaspora, we must build agencies to advocate non-intervention in the domestic affairs of countries which pose no real and direct threat to Anglo-American alliance nations. To too great an extent, questionable declarations of security threats from poor African nations have led to mass disruption and destruction in places like Angola, South Africa, the Dem. Rep. of the Congo, Liberia, Sierra Leone, Mali, Libya, Egypt, Sudan, Nigeria, Cote d'Ivoire, the Central African Republic, Columbia, Haiti, Honduras and others. The impact of these *often-spurious* claims of threats must be neutralized by unified political lobbying from well-informed and appropriately resourced Diaspora advocacy organizations and political lobbies.

Our organizing of peace advocacy institutions could go a long way toward exposure and opposition to many of these so-called "color revolutions" which have arisen in the last two decades and resulted in destructive policies toward sovereign nations such as Yugoslavia, Georgia, Ukraine, Iraq, Kyrgyzstan, Lebanon, Myanmar, Iran, Tunisia, Egypt, China, Venezuela, Brazil and others. Viewpoints of these "color revolutions" from outside the sphere of western ideology differ from that which is promoted by the U.S. corporate media establishment. Note these Wikipedia citations:

> **Russian assessment** – According to Anthony Cordesman of the Center for Strategic and International Studies, Russian military leaders view the color revolutions as a "new US and European

approach to warfare that focuses on creating destabilizing revolutions in other states as a means of serving their security interests at low cost and with minimal casualties." [42]

Chinese view – Articles published by the Global Times, a state-run nationalist newspaper, indicate that Chinese leaders also anticipate the Western powers, such as the United States, using 'color revolutions' as a means to undermine the one-party state. An article published in 2016-5-8 claims: A variation of containment seeks to press China on human rights and democracy with the hope of creating a "color revolution. [43]

A peaceful world of today and tomorrow must be prioritized as the most treasured gift which this current generation would bequeath to its posterity. Forming a society committed to the highest aspirations of humanity, progress and sustainability, must compel our duty to serve as caretakers of this world toward creating an inheritance for future generations. Thus, we are in great need to advance appropriate structural institutions that consolidate this inheritance.

A global population of 1.5 billion Africans requires creating a group-serving transnational structure for advancing a large and influential *Youth Peace Exchange*. Such a non-governmental organization could serve as a bridge into a future wherein our young people are invited to correspond as well as study in countries other than that of their birth. They would be encouraged to communicate with their peers as well as older generations through mechanisms of music, dance, art, radio, television, social media as well as a vast collective of Pan African conferences.

Our young people are expected to bring fresh perspectives to issues and challenges which have long been primary concerns of progress among nations and thus should be encouraged to develop powerful vehicles to make their ideas a part of the structure for governing the larger society. We must be very careful to include generations of young leadership in

---

[4242] Anthony Cordesman, Russia and the "Color Revolution", Center for Strategic and International Studies, May 2014

[43] US split on future relations with China, By Robert A. Manning, Global Times, 2016-5-8

all our affairs that will impact prolonged changes within our social, political, economic, and cultural development. We claim to believe in our youth truly and there is a great reason to assume such a valuing position. Now we are in need to expand upon these beliefs with long-standing structure and institutions which embody this valuation of such transforming agency within younger generations.

Too many man-made problems threaten the world of today. Great thinkers throughout history have consistently envisioned future worlds wherein the dystopian and degenerative forces within society will eventually yield to the nearly universal drive toward peace, prosperity and a sustainable environment. Today the "Lords of Capital" have driven much of the world close to the brink of wholesale destruction. They have created vast secret networks for perpetuating their disproportionate usurpation of wealth, power and the governance of nations. But these selfish manipulators of history are but a fraction of the world's people. It is one of the primary goals of our global Reparation that we use our collective resources, People Power and cooperative initiatives toward building upon the future wherein legitimate *democratization* puts the power back into the hands of the masses.

Our traditional concept of Mother Earth as a living, spiritual entity, which has been a principle foundation of all African societies from the beginning of our history, should allow us to rise to our once-held pinnacle of world leadership. We have come a long way on this often unbearable 500-year journey of the *Maafa*, the great holocaust of African enslavement, colonization and inhumane exploitation. **The End of Maafa** is upon us and it is rising, just as the morning sun, in the east. With this dawn of a new global order, we can reasonably expect that we will assume more authority and responsibility for the achievement and preservation of global peace and prosperity. For us to provide such a stabilizing function for the whole of Earth's inhabitants, it serves our best pathway forward to firmly establish peace and prosperity within our communities as well as for our global African family. This serves as a major priority as well as a measurement of the progress of our mission toward *The Repairing*.

Chapter 15 – Passing the Baton

"For Africa to me ... is more than a glamorous fact. It is a historical truth. No man can know where he is going unless he knows exactly where he has been and exactly how he arrived at his present place." – Maya Angelou

Generations build upon legacies of those before them

A statement that I frequently use when speaking to audiences, which you no doubt have read several times already within this book, is "As we reach for the stars we must remember that we stand upon the shoulders of Giants." There is a widely-used Zulu term called *Ubuntu*, which translates to "I AM because WE are." These ideas center upon the critical need to appreciate the contributions to an individual's or society's progress which have emerged from activities within previous generations or among our national peers. It does serve us best to appreciate that we truly have a great debt of obligation to respect, uphold and build upon that for which previous generations have sacrificed. Most of our great scholars and leaders of the present and the past have themselves given such appreciation to the foundation upon which their enlightenment stemmed.

Toward the furtherance of this valuation, progressive social development demands that we expand on the traditions which uphold our ancestral inheritance. While we do celebrate Mother's Day and Father's Day, we would be best to follow our pre-enslavement tradition of ancestral veneration by adding Ancestor's Day to our annual traditions. In the U.S., we have come to commemorate a Memorial Day which, unfortunately, has been conscripted by military hawks and, as such, become more of a celebration of the drafting of the citizenry to engage in America's seemingly endless militancy against the world. Surely, those of our family whose lives were cut short before they had time to create a lasting family legacy, beyond serving in the national armed forces, must be acknowledged as they have passed on into the realm of the ancestors.

What about those grandfathers and grandmothers, as well as many generations before them, whose life's work contributed directly to our family's, community's and nation's well-being? How most of us within this nation, commemorate Memorial Day doesn't keep their memory and spirit alive beyond one or two generations. This is in direct contradiction to numerous African traditions that uphold the memories of each family's ancestors and remember just how valuable they were to the progress of the larger community. Certainly, we can move beyond the commercialization of such a Memorial Day as a day to plant flags at a military burial ground, lay a few flowers and then go straight to the barbecue grill and beer keg for the bulk of our celebration. This is one area of cultural traditions wherein America has supremely betrayed our African identity and way of being.

"A people without a knowledge of their history is like a tree with no roots." – Marcus Garvey

---

Afri-Amers are wonderful people, full of love, creativity, hopes, and aspirations. We are a gentle and loving ethnicity that consistently displays empathy, compassion and a strong sense of fairness to others who share the societies within which we live. Yet, the fact is that our Noble Race is too-often handicapped because of a lack of true and in-depth knowledge of self. We are governed and communicate within an imposed language, a language that can't even carry the depth of our West African traditions, values and conceptualization of how Nature has organized life. This linguistic shortcoming is very real and I've experienced it from the standpoint of learning African languages as well as deep conversations with African scholars, sisters and brothers who have frequently struggled to explain deep concepts from their cultural traditions in English translation.

Culture is such a powerful vehicle to impact behaviors on both individual and group levels. As such, toward our goal of *The Repairing*, the achievement and maintenance of true cultural authenticity and integrity must remain of the absolute *highest* priority. Culture is language, religion, historical perspective, traditions, moral values and group-thinking (logic). As I have explained, the problem which emerges as differing cultures' language is translated, it so follows with the other five axioms of culture as they become relevant in the arena of civilization contrast. The history of "white America" is the same, in many ways, as the history of "black America." Yet, the *perspective* of this shared history is quite often 180-degrees the opposite. Both black and white America together shared the experience of enslavement. Yet it is always obvious that the benefits which most Whites accrued from enslaving our ancestors stands in the harshest contrast and contradiction to that of the enslaved Blacks and their posterity.

The same is true for our spiritual tradition, values, morality, way of thinking, and other avenues of cultural being. Africans in the American experience have adopted too many cultural values which contradict that which will greatly assist us to traverse the complicated pathway which we must take to secure a sustainable future as a sovereign global tribe. My name is an example of the way that cultural transformation results in such a life transformation. At birth, my parents gave me the name of Keith, a traditional Scottish name. My surname, Howard, was that of an Englishman who had possession of some of my ancestors at the time of emancipation which they retained. While I grew up with this name (although my blessed mother had altered my name of identity to where I could use it later once I had found my pathway) and performed rather well during that phase of my life where I was a model young American. Unlike my three brothers, as I moved out into the world and discovered the extent to which an *African identity* would so much better suite my life's mission, I discovered a pathway that led to what I now know and refer to as my "true name." I AM Keidi Obi Awadu, a name that binds me to ethnic traditions of the Ibo of West Africa as well as the original Black Fellows of the Australian continent. My name translates to "one who has discovered self on the pathway to becoming the king of the land."

More and more people of African heritage have similarly come to see how the common "Christian names" which our parents loving bestowed upon us, have left us short of a life direction, a critically-needed transformative mission that can guide our lives in a deeply psychic and spiritual fashion.

Hence, we see this fire spreading through generations as conscious parents who have changed their names then bestow upon their children great names from birth. In our household, we bestowed upon our three daughters such transforming names which convey a deeper meaning, honor our ancestors and complement a global cultural identity as African citizens within a world to which they are expected to contribute greatly.

An almost desperate search for genetic identity

It has become quite popular over recent decades for people to purchase these *so-called* DNA ancestry tests as a means of connecting themselves with a distant past, which has, in the case of Blacks, been cut off from its traditional roots. While one can certainly appreciate the value of such a quest for connection, I have the often-upsetting task of informing my friends that these ancestry DNA tests are being fraudulently represented as capable of pinpointing our African tribal roots when they are not. The complex genetic makeup of our bloodlines does connect us to Africa, easily seen in our physical features. We are an amalgamation of many different bloodlines that have, for most of us domiciled in America, the Caribbean, Central and South America, blended for up to 20 generations.

We have many, many grandfathers and grandmothers on African soils. But these DNA ancestry tests can only find two of them *at best*. Through the paternal Y-chromosome test, a person can only find their father's, father's, father's genetic imprint. Thus your father's mother and everyone connected to her lineage do not exist in the Y-chromosome imprint. Correspondingly, through the maternal test for mitochondrial DNA, these tests find only your mother's, mother's, mother's genetic pattern, and your mother's father is absent as well as every one of his ancestors. I hope you have seen that any search for your ancestral roots which, over the course of 20 generations, locates a genetic *match* for two great-grandparents while it *exempts* 1,048,574 other great-grandparents, is quite inadequate toward the recovery of our complete African heritage.

To make matters worse, using the paternal genetic testing, if there is any interruption in your backward search for your father's fathers, such as a *rapist* entering the bloodline (which was quite extensive during enslavement) then from that point backward in your Y-chromosome genetic line, all further fathers will be of the genetic lineage of such an intruder. As one can see in the variances in skin color among many Afri-Amers, myself included within this group, the likelihood that such a rape occurred against our African grandmothers is very likely. Hence, from that point of rape, many of us become descendants of Englishmen, French, Spanish, Portuguese, Dutch or some other European deviation. For some African-Americans this paternal link to Europe is desirable...but *it ain't necessarily so* for all of us who fundamentally identify as Africans as our essential ethnicity!

Yet, when informed about the shortcomings of these so-called DNA ancestry tests, some people are going to continue to believe in their intrinsic value anyway. I have no problem with such default to *partial truth* other than the fact that, for some of our members, when told that something is of such limited value, too many are just going to go ahead and do it anyway. This contradiction remains consistent in other critical areas of life such as health and nutrition. Therefore, whatever it takes for one to find their pathway toward an authentic ethnic identity and then to build functional solidarity upon such discovery – this should only produce a more beneficial outcome. "By any means necessary," we must find our cultural roots and gain the mental and spiritual advantages of such a profound reconnection with ethnic centricity. To be clear, there is no need for the expense of DNA ancestry testing when all one need to do is to open their heart and mind up to reconnecting spiritually and culturally to our tribal roots. Once this pathway is opened, then serious study must naturally follow.

Recovering our flame from before the Black Holocaust

We have talked about the profound impact of historical perspective on our cultural identity. One of the most persisting problems that handicap many African Americans is that they have very little, if any, deep knowledge of their people's history before enslavement. One can distinguish this pattern of *cultural adolescence* across the spectrum of ways that Blacks relate politically, socially, economically and otherwise to the larger societies within which we are domiciled. What African-centered historians have been clarifying is that this chronological period within which this new identity of *Europeanized* Africans has taken place is but a tiny slice of the entire chronology of civilization; particularly since humanity's first established record of civilization occurred on the geography which the world now refers to as Africa. While the period of enslavement, which forced upon many of us this current identity, is only a mere 400-600 years long, depending on one's location, there are an additional 5000-plus years of well-documented world heritage to consider. Within that additional stretch of recorded time, we can examine many epochs, lasting much longer than 600 years, wherein African-based societies rose to mighty empirical status.

Earlier in the book we pointed out that some fifteen of these African empires stand tall within the complete history of human progress. Names such as Nubia, Kemet, Kongo, Songhai, Mali, and Ghana should inspire immense pride within our youth as they matriculate along their educational and existential pathways. Within the detailed history of each of these empires, there are thousands of records of high-accomplishment, detailed facts, as well as notable biographies which have all contributed to the rise and prominence of these great nations.

Marcus Garvey said, "A People without the knowledge of their history is like a tree with no roots." – that tree will be easily toppled and ruined in the presence of the many storms of life. Malcolm X similarly told us, "Of all our studies, history is best qualified to reward our research" – such an expected reward should include our global redemption, Reparation and restoration to empirical status.

Many of us have taken our names from these pages of history far distant from the recent period of our Great Suffering, the Maafa. We need to remind ourselves as often as possible that we are *not* a people created by the vile history of captivity, brutal enslavement, and cultural displacement. We truly are a Noble Race and we do possess a glorious history and we shall, as Garvey instructed, "create another which will astonish the world." What is old and ancient can be recreated again and total resources currently available to our members are greater than have ever been before. In certain and unmistakable ways, this painful period of enslavement has added immense value and worth to our future mission as Africans rediscovering their civilization and forging a pathway forward to the pinnacle of new empirical glory and world stewardship. Thus, despite the horrible sufferings afflicted upon them, we are immensely grateful to our ancestors who suffered through the worst of the Maafa and then passed along their strength and courage to ours and future generations.

REC's making bold moves to capture our future

As well, across Sub-Saharan Africa, where our continental ancestors also suffered vile, oppressive and genocidal treatment at the hands of Arabic and European brutes, there is a tremendous and rapid recovery, Reparation, and revitalization taking place. Individual nations and, better yet, whole regions of the continent are making bold, deliberate and progressive strides toward sustainable development. The African Union recognizes several regional economic communities (RECs) and within each, we can witness measurable progress toward peace, economic growth, resource development, technical capacity building and social progress within their growing middle-class populations.

The East African Community, which consists of Kenya, Tanzania, Rwanda, Burundi, Uganda, and South Sudan (soon to include Somalia as well), is just a few years away from declaring the East African Federation of States. Tanzania itself is a fusion of two former colonized states of Tanganyika and Zanzibar. During the early post-colonial period, there were similar attempts in the Economic Community of West African States (ECOWAS) to build a single nation from another two former colonial states, Ghana and Guinea. Unfortunately, that union was interrupted by intervention from the French, American and British secret security agencies. Yet, these malevolent interventions cannot stop the progress of the history of civilization development.

Over the next 35 years, the increasing integration of African nations will continue. Transnational free trade and partnership agreements, passport sharing, regional and continental currency formation, empowering of multinational governance structures such as the African

Union—these will all contribute toward the inevitable unification of the African continent into one powerful and sustainable entity. From that point onward, the condition of the entire planet will be positively transformed for many centuries to come. We may likely see, in our lifetime, the rebirth of an African empire that can survive and thrive for more than *2000 Seasons* and beyond. I've come to refer to this vision as the "Great Swahili Empire," regarding the governing language which has been designated to be the unifying tongue of the future confederation.

Passing along the promise of Scientific Futurism

Governance of such a vast, complex and interwoven continental society will remain challenging. It demands a broad spectrum of highly qualified specialists to handle every aspect of a modern technical society. Just as the U.S. government maintains some 15 cabinet-level positions, each of which is further compartmentalized into numerous levels and divisions; just as each of the 50 states of the American union have similar parallel divisions of agency; just as America and its European allies have created equally sophisticated structures to govern their unified world affairs – Africa too will be governed by a vast, interwoven complex of agencies and non-governmental organizations.

The task of educating our people toward complete self-governance demands that we prepare the highest order of *scientifically-organized leadership* that the world has ever known. These were important instructions directed upon us by the Honorable Marcus Garvey, the greatest black leader the world has known since the beginning of the Maafa. While many of the nations within which we find ourselves are adamant on the need to train their youth in science and technology, this Pan African vision of *The Repairing* and ascendance to an empowered Africa global order demands a greater intensity of leadership formation to excel above the "best and brightest" that are produced within today's most advanced societies.

We earlier pointed out the tremendous recovery, revitalization and economic ascendancy of China and Singapore in the post-World War Two period. Within both of those societies, centralized and authoritarian governance set standards for educating the populace at a level of discipline significantly greater than their former colonial masters with whom they had become major competitors. The tremendous rise of these two nations in the half-century which followed is a clear demonstration of the *return on investment* which an intensity of scientifically-based education can produce when it is directed at serving as the foundation for future achievement. Because both Asian nations were handicapped in ways which are not a similar burden for Africans – China because of its large and crowded population and Singapore which had no substantial natural resource base – we Africans can learn much of how they applied their scientific mastery, along with national discipline and focused leadership, on overcoming centuries of subjugation and developmental backwardness.

Scientific futurism is undoubtedly a daunting task for leadership authorization. The 14 interrelated disciplines which we have herein identified as forming the broad curriculum of scientific futurism take decades to master completely. We must identify students capable of such a broad range of mastery and commit substantial resources to assure that their education to such will be complete, lavishly funded and that they will not be burdened with having to secure a proper place within our group-serving economic governance.

As one of this extremely rare breed called scientific futurists, I am constantly on the lookout for that spark within young people, which indicates that they are on the pathway of mastery. It is right and fitting that we all make the presumption that every child born has great potential to be a powerful agent for change and transformation within their generation. To cultivate and to activate this mastery will itself be a consequence of a masterful class of educators to serve our long-term group self-interests. I am quite confident that we are at this crossroads along our extended journey through and beyond the centuries of suffering and dependence that we have experienced. Our visions of massive transformation and purposefulness for the immediate and distant future motivate us to the *greatest good* that can be accomplished within our lifetime.

We are standing upon the shoulders of giants

I am brilliant. I am competent. I am the best of the best that have emerged from the millennia-long experiences of our Great and Noble Race. I can make such claims without embarrassment because I know that my capacities emerge from the greatness which proceeded my generation. I frequently remind all who would listen that "As we reach for the stars, we must always remember that we are standing upon the shoulders of giants." The character which I have presented to this generation, and for our collective future, is in great part based upon my intimate knowledge of the lives of Greats from the dawn of civilization. For my being, those who receive my ancestral libations include Imhotep, the ancient Kemetic priesthood, Sojourner Truth, Frederick Douglass, Harriet Tubman, Booker T. Washington, W.E.B. DuBois, Ida Wells-Barnett, George Washington Carver, Marcus Garvey, Mary McLeod Bethune, Malcolm X, Martin L. King Jr., and Bob Marley as well as a spectrum of African leaders such as Mansa Musa, Patrice Lumumba, Kwame Nkrumah, Sekou Touré, Thomas Sankara, Amilcar Cabral, Steven Biko, Chris Hani, Murtala Muhammad, Samora Marcel and Nelson Mandela. Also, my parents George and Delores Howard, along with my maternal grandfather Robert F. Williams, are very much a part of my life mission as they also contributed fundamental values, morality and base of logical reasoning of what I have become.

We are standing upon the shoulders of giants, and our children are thus expected to be even greater than ourselves. We are setting higher standards for their behavior and capability than ever before. Our literacy achievements of the current generation should be expected to rise even higher in those to follow. Our mastery of self, health and prosperity within this generation should be amplified in our children and those who follow. The world is experiencing great change and transformation and our African people, currently over 1.5 billion strong and expected to add another billion in the next 35 years, will be prime beneficiaries of a spectrum of advantages that serves their empowerment. These advantages include, and as you most certainly have read throughout *The Repairing*, will not be limited to demographics, natural resources, geography, marine resources, technology leapfrogging, peace and prosperity, as well as enjoying the world's fastest rate of growth of middle class households.

As we reach for this new global African order, we are always cognizant that we are building upon what countless generations of our ancestors worked and sacrificed to bequeath to us. As such, we are forever grateful for their commitments and we recommit in this generation to continue their pathway of self-determination, group sacrifice, and investment for the benefit of future generations.

Look for inspiration in the whirlwind or the storm...

We are passing the baton of this powerful united African future onto our children and to countless generations to follow. We are acting with absolute responsibility and duty to the group's well-being. We are moving unshakably in the direction which our Great Ancestors and Wise Elders have committed our group. We have their tremendous examples accessible within many thousands of biographies of those of high accomplishment.

Africans have known many great leaders throughout 5,000 years of accessible civilization history. Names such as Imhotep, Ramses II, Taharqa, Mansa Musa, Nzinga, Hannibal, Queen Yaa Asantewaa, and many more great heroes from our scattered populations leap off the pages of history and into the hearts and minds of students of this glorious history. Throughout our Maafa journey, we have similarly produced more and more of these great and noble leaders. We can be expected to continue this natural elevation of powerful leaders throughout every phase of our existence as an identifiable ethnic group.

Within this period of the great suffering, there can be no contesting that the most impressive of these group-serving leaders stands as Marcus Mosiah Garvey. There are many volumes of study on the life and times, "Philosophy and Opinions" of this great leader that are available to educate, inspire, inform and excite our members to their own magnificence. Garvey's words are timeless and always appropriate to challenging circumstances that present problems to the group for which solutions must be formulated.

I love to quote the words of Mr. Garvey and have done so many times during the publication of more than two dozen books that preceded this book, *The Repairing*. Garvey himself instructed us to keep his counsel close as we trod along our pathway to redemption and revitalization. As such, it is quite fitting and appropriate for this chapter to close with his instruction to keep his counsel and powerful vision close when we are engaging in battles wherein complete victory is of absolute necessity. Marcus Garvey anticipated such moments which would occur even long after his passing.

Marcus Garvey's enduring spirit lives on as he and the souls of countless millions of our ancestors accompany us on our long journey to global redemption. From the realm of the ancestral world, from behind the veil which separates the living from those who have ascended, he told us to call upon his spirit during our moments of struggle:

"Look for me in the whirlwind or the storm, look for me all around you, for, with God's grace, I shall come and bring with me countless millions of black slaves who have died in America and the West Indies and the millions in Africa to aid you in the fight for Liberty, Freedom and Life." [44]

---

[44] From the Philosophy and Opinions of Marcus Garvey, edited by Amy Jacques

Chapter 16 – The Repairing Life – Pulling it All Together

"Never underestimate the power of dreams and the influence of the human spirit. We are all the same in this notion: The potential for greatness lives within each of us." – Wilma Rudolph

The journey of a thousand miles...

It has often been stated that "A journey of a thousand miles begins with one step." While this cliché has some merit, it is far from complete enough to be practical. Obviously, by the time you are reading these words, you have taken many steps over the long course of your life that have led you to this stage. Unfortunately, the "one step" admonition strands too many people far short of their necessary destination – there are those among us who will not do much more than take one step on this fabled thousand-mile journey. We can do better than that.

I have altered this cliché to say, "A journey of a thousand miles proceeds from that first step by stepping, stepping, stepping in rhythm; constantly in motion towards guaranteeing that we will reach our journey in predictable time." Rhythm is important for African people to keep in mind because we have always done our best work, as well as the most difficult work, to the heartbeat of our African drums and chants. More so than other ethnic groups in the world, we have a natural tack for *complex polyrhythms*. This serves as a wonderful analogy to the multiple and complex pathways which are required for us to put together this cumulative-solutions-based planning that is advocated throughout *The Repairing*.

We return to this idea of **cumulative causation** as was developed in Chapter 2 and later revisited in Chapter 6. Because our depressing situation has been a consequence of inopportune outcome within a spectrum of societal influences, then our solutions will also demand complex and interrelated strategies. As I have grown to comprehend this "Theory of Cumulative Causation," an important stage of my development was to generate a broad-based study model encompassing: culture, consciousness, historical perspective, entertainment, economics, education, health, labor, law, politics, spirituality, family, conflict and future studies.

As my studies have advanced, I've created (or adapted) several other complex models which are shared throughout this book: the 9 Foundations of Reparations; 6 Axioms of Culture; 6 Pillars of Empire; 14 Interrelated Disciplines of Scientific Futurism; 26 Points for Social Engineering; and 15 Critical Careers for the Future. I hope that you will agree that each one of these complex models has a strong potential to generate substantive progress when diligently applied to our mission of group transformation and sustainable development. Therefore, each of these complex models calls for numerous steps, large and small. Each has beginning steps yet should, like our "journey of a thousand miles," compel us to keep on stepping along the pathway in regular, predictable and impactful rhythm. As well, since these various complex models are very much interrelated, we should thus be functioning in *polyrhythms*, just like the sophisticated African musical styles and the jazz which we have masterfully projected globally.

This is not a moment or a movement – This is a paradigm shift

I'm sure that all of us have observed those who take African identity as a somewhat faddish engagement. Yes, it can be very satisfying to dance to our music, sample our culinary exquisiteness, dress fashionably in African garb, "Hotep" each other and recite commonly heard clichés such as "Africa for the Africans, those at home and those abroad," or "One God, one aim and one destiny." Those are all wonderful, and we encourage the expansion of such cultural engagements with the deep inheritance that is Pan Africanism. In time, as one increases such cultural associations and adopts them authentically, a deeply empowering persona stirs from deep within our souls that compels us more and more toward the completeness of this cultural lifestyle.

Being African in a holistic manner is exciting, inspiring, satisfying, and extremely cool. At the same time, being whole within our African identity demands personal commitment, draws ire from those who are not able to relate to the experience, can often isolate us economically, politically and socially, and as well, frequently requires one to make uncomfortable sacrifices toward the benefit of others and to the larger group. For too many of our members, these often-straining ties to our African identity appear not to be worth the effort. There is one criticism that most ardent black power supporters have heard on multiple occasions: "Oh...There you go with that Black Stuff again." When we examine the deep structure of that particular curse, we can understand why so few people want to put in the work necessary for group elevation to sustainable power.

Yet, YOU persist through the criticism, discomfort, self-sacrifice, inconveniences, frustrations, bad relationships, missed opportunities, and times of abandonment by loved ones. YOU persist because for you, this is not a moment or a movement—this is the lifestyle to which you are unshakably committed – this reflects a *Paradigm Shift*. Therefore, you seek out and associate with others who share your perspectives on living within an empowered African global reality. Being an African on this planet is one of the first thoughts to arise in your mind each day. When you look in the mirror, you are so happy that a black face is staring you right in the eye. You love it when you encounter people in their cultural garb, wearing their natural hair, sporting symbols of African traditions, as well as those you see randomly throughout your day who LOOK like they are from your beloved mother continent.

We who are living this culturally-centered, Pan African lifestyle need never feel shame for what we have become committed. We should never have to apologize for loving our black skin and the inheritance which it symbolizes. We have come a long way in the past half-century because there was a time, even within my lifetime, that it was regarded as an insult to be called out as "you black African," even when spoken by family and friends. I will assure everyone who will listen to me, in the 22nd Century, the greatest compliment that a human could ever be paid will be to be referred to as "you ancient African."

Deliberate steps to sustainable development

I will return just briefly to the **9 Foundations for Reparations,** which were the detailed subject of Chapter 2. We must be clear that this is the prime terrain wherein our tactical engagements must be concentrated. I do recommend that each of us (myself especially) return to that critical section of the book to keep a tight focus on the details which absolutely *must* be accomplished toward achieving the goals stated throughout *The Repairing.* These fundamentals of our restoration include:

1. **Compensation for stolen labor** – Now that we have a clear determination of just this one aspect of our people's abuse, exploitation and lack of compensation, we can be much more precise when we are called to speak before others regarding the grand theft resulting from the criminal enterprise of enslavement. As well, we can be very specific regarding a dollar value for the unpaid debt for this stolen labor. We need all guilty parties and those who benefitted from stolen wealth to take responsibility for this $24.57 trillion wealth transfer, and to straighten things out regarding what is our rightful inheritance. We have also concluded that it is unrealistic under the current circumstances for us to make claims on a deeply-indebted federal government to serve up Reparations compensation. As well, numerous culpable parties are identified as having profited from our pain.

2. **Land Recovery & Development** – Coming out of enslavement and through the period referred to as the Reconstruction, Blacks worked so hard to recover those things they knew were vital to sustainable development. These highest priorities included the need for land upon which to engage the subsistence agriculture and economic development which is fundamental to any population. From a peak of some 19 million acres under the control of Afri-Amers at the end of the 19th Century, today we suffer from the loss of as much as 85% of the land our great-grandparents controlled. As we are now seeing our members being pushed further away from zones of urban prosperity, our sustainability

demands that we instigate policies which stop the yet-ongoing land loss, stabilize our presence within the urban landscape, expand land holdings, and generate robust enterprise zones across these lands which we intend to pass on to future generations.

3. **Family and Community** – We can no longer tolerate the steady downward spiral of the very core of society as relationships between husbands and wives, parents and children, youth and elders, citizens with one other, all continue to degenerate. The debilitation from enslavement devastated our families' unity and structure. Yet, despite all the deprivations of slavery, the retreat from the Reconstruction, decades of Jim Crow apartheid and the long entrenchment of poverty affecting our masses, during all of those social, political and economic offenses, we still held onto the family. Yet, at some point during our increasing urban sophistication, things fell apart. Beginning within the most vulnerable neighborhoods, multiple policies were initiated which undermined relations between men and women. Mass media offered up a spectrum of new models for living which contradicted traditional values. A vast spectrum of influences separated the father from the family and then economic policies forced the mother out of the household and into the corporate grind. Our children are now farmed out to profit-driven daycare which often leaves them unfit for proper integration into their communities. Revised strategies for rebuilding family and community must, therefore, assume the highest priority and must be acted upon lavishly and with haste.

4. **Economic Development** – Our proscription for developing a progressive pathway toward sustainable growth, begins with a holistic definition of just what comprises economics. Now that we do have this understanding of, and the *importance* of comprehending, the Theory of Cumulative Causation, we can now consider 360 degrees of economic engagement and conclude that opportunity lies in every direction we face. We are presented with detailed and viable strategies and tactics that create new enterprises, as well as expand on existing ones that capitalize on already-established consumer trends. We have exposed the impact of this problem by which our businesses currently produce only $1 for every $7 that we spend. This debilitating ratio explains why

calls to "boycott" and "buy black" campaigns consistently fall short. Therefore, our immediate focus is to develop equity investments in the best currently-operating black businesses, expand industrial output of goods and services, and expand transnationally into the new global economy as serious competitors.

5. **Education** – By now, you most certainly have come to determine just how critical it is that we revitalize processes by which we educate all members of our group, everywhere in the world, toward the mission of this massive transforming purpose of global Reparation. I have consistently expressed the need to expand the spectrum of disciplines that are critical towards increased competitiveness in the world of today and for the future. Particularly mission-critical are imperatives to enhance learning during the earliest years of life, which should also include specialized education for young parents; before conceptualization, if possible. From preschool, through to advanced graduate degrees, the approaches by which Afri-Amers might raise standards of educational excellence are in dire need of major upgrading. As well, elevating a leadership vanguard capable of managing complex affairs for our 1.5 billion-strong global family, which is expected to expand by another billion over the coming 35 years, can best be accomplished with an aggressive push into the field of **scientific futurism**. Further facilitating this education imperative, we can utilize many of the same exponential technologies which are empowering the most advanced societies and thriving private-sector competitors. Models for educating national populations to world-class competitiveness which have empowered the "Asian Tigers" (Japan, China, Singapore and South Korea), should be studied, adopted and adapted when necessary toward the education of a global African population striving for sustainable empirical power.

6. **Revising our Historical Perspective** – Although people of differing ethnicities within a nation can share common historical experiences, their perspectives of that history can be diametrically opposed. This polarization of analytical viewpoints is one of the key hallmarks of cultural identity and civilization distinction. Afri-Amers have become immensely disadvantaged because for too long, far too many have

accepted that the group's identity emerged from the trauma of enslavement. This history presents several paradoxical challenges for members of the group. On the one hand, we are domiciled citizens of the United States of America, yet we have never consistently been accorded all the rights and privileges of full and equal citizenship. As well, our identification as products of the creation of the Americas disregards very important chapters of the complete history of world civilizations, some 15 of which rose to the status of powerful empires on the African continent emerging as far back as 5000 years and more. Even today the history of the earliest humans living in the western hemisphere is being rewritten, with African migrants into South America dating back to some 18,000 to 90,000 years before Asians crossed the Bering Strait and migrated southward from Alaska. In nearly all aspects of coexistence within the borders of aggressive nations where we are an ethnic minority, an accurate assessment of history would present our group with a distinct perspective to contradict that which has been taught or propagandized by the dominant group. For us to ascend to preeminence over our developmental affairs, we must take primary responsibility for setting these records straight and communicating our distinct narrative of history. Fortunately, breakthroughs in education, media and communications favor enhanced capacity to accomplish this vital mission.

7. **Transnational Relations** – Afri-Amers exist like children who have been ripped from the bosom of their mothers, separated from siblings and, thus, handicapped, and thrown into a highly competitive arena with others who are not similarly disadvantaged. Being disconnected from our mother continent as well as large contingents of our people living throughout the African Diaspora has bred sickness within our culture as well as deprived us of valuable relationships with our genetic peers. This disorder affects each of the critical aspects of societal function which must engage our greater group interests. This presents us with a dilemma wherein we don't have access to natural allies with which to collaborate and collectively compete in this yet-emerging global political, economic and cultural contest. Too often Afri-Amers find themselves looking in the mirror with half an expectation to find a white standard reflecting back at them. Searching for such an outcome can only leave

one disappointed or, worse yet, schizophrenic. By upgrading our partnerships with African communities around the globe, there is a strong likelihood that we will find much greater satisfaction with and appreciation for our distinct collective. We are not sable-skinned clones of Euro-Americans—we are among the most resource-blessed Africans within a vast and expanding global population.

8. **Repairing our Health Status** – At this stage of our national development, health should be elevated to the top of our priorities for restoring, revitalizing, and repairing our population. We suffer disproportionately within whatever countries we find ourselves from a spectrum of communicable and non-communicable diseases and disorders. For all the assets, resources and advantages which Afri-Amers can point to with immense pride, when it comes to the collective health status of the group our smiles turn upside down. Where we have access to the greatest information base ever available to any group of Africans in recorded history, far too many of our members display gross incompetence when confronted by self-determining policies that are disease prevention. Because of the devastating impact of lifestyle-related diseases and the financial burden which they place upon each household, much of the needed capital that should energize our enterprises and transfer wealth to younger family members is instead sucked up by a massive medical-pharmaceutical complex along with their comrades in insurance. We can make substantial progress with what we already know about how to stay healthy in the face of such a stress-filled, toxin-ridden and glutinous society like the U.S.

9. **Crime and justice** – As has been detailed in earlier chapters, the debilitating effect of nearly a million incarcerated within U.S. jail facilities has put strains on the psyche of those imprisoned, their families, the economics of the community, and the larger society. For-profit prisons suck from the lifeblood of our potential labor capital base. Rather than being stuck in a cage at a major yearly cost to society, these same individuals need to be returned to their place as productive workers, parents and holistic contributors. The extensive set of circumstances that results in such a large mass of discarded citizenry is complex and needs to be addressed at a dozen insertion points from pre-conception

through to adult maturation. It should be regarded as undeniable fact that the same set of societal transformations that produce sustainable economic progress for the group also lessen the risk that our youth will go down the road of crime and punishment. There is a great need for us to all contribute toward agencies and actions which guarantee that members of our race are given all the benefits of society and that must certainly include judicial fairness, equal access to justice and lack of abuse at the hands of law enforcement agencies.

Summary – Pulling it all together

It might seem a daunting task to pull together such a broad set of strategic and tactical actions such as those presented throughout this book. During 2015 as part of my daily webcast programming, I took an entire month to focus on the topic of *exponential organizations*. These ExO's are businesses that "are ten times bigger, faster and better" than their corporate competitors. In Chapter 5, we earlier referred to a group of these new business competitors which is known as the "PayPal Mafia." A Wikipedia posting lists 24 individuals whom the technology news media consider as members of this association and describes their collective as such:

> "PayPal Mafia" is a term used to indicate a group of former PayPal employees and founders who have since founded and developed additional technology companies such as Tesla Motors, LinkedIn, Palantir Technologies, SpaceX, YouTube, Yelp, and Yammer. Most of the members attended Stanford University or University of Illinois at Urbana–Champaign at some point in their studies. Three members, Peter Thiel, Elon Musk, and Reid Hoffman, have become billionaires.

To see this vision of *The* Repairing as viable, I have strongly recommended that each of us, especially those in leadership position, study books by and about this group of high-impact young executives. Looking through the vast spectrum of corporations they have created, which, in addition to those mentioned above, also include dozens more familiar names, one should be able to grasp that our ambitious ideas also have merit as viable and doable within this ExO environment.

Let us return to the social engineering formula that we had earlier culled from Vance Packard's book **THE HIDDEN PERSUADERS**, wherein he is citing the work of Prof. Philip J. Allen. The sociologist's formula for social engineering contained 26 points for focused action which include: lavish funding, consistency, mass media, persistence, predetermined goal sets, target groups, establishing new values, policy-setting structure, communications initiatives, cultural adoption, individual and group strategies, centralized orchestration, accessing the most influential social institutions, involving schools, leisure time, engaging religion and spirituality, accessing the top leadership of communications companies, the scientific method, advertising and marketing approaches, crafted messages, timed and sequenced campaigns, mutually supportive messages from a broad base of voices, a master blueprint ("grand design"), an unlimited number of individuals working together, and a superb base of financial backing.

Each of these various points needs coordination. For national governments, centralized planning and governance can readily pull this together. We showed clear examples of this with the rapid rise to economic power witnessed in the cases of China and Singapore, which can be similarly modeled in others of the "Asian Tigers," along with African nations such as Rwanda and Ethiopia, as well as other fast-growing economies around the world. Afri-Amers have demographic and economic potential greater than most nations of the world. We exist within the midst of a technologically advanced nation wherein we have had access to every level of societal organization, industry, urban planning, national defense planning, higher education, research, and development.

We have exhausted our time for delay, making excuses, and passing off responsibility. Where we have come up short in our duties toward sovereign advancement, we have seen others whose circumstances are quite like our own overcome their handicaps and turn challenges into opportunities. Where we are strong – and we are most certainly strong in many areas – we can further extend our strengths into transnational partnerships which will compound our returns on investment in these collaborative efforts.

There is virtually nothing that China is currently doing regarding its development partnerships across sub-Saharan Africa, which brings substantial returns on investment, that 45.7 million Afri-Amers couldn't be similarly engaging. Logic would dictate that we would have a greater advantage in leading African development since we do have the deep binding ties of ethnicity which Kotkin's **TRIBES** points out as the foundation of new global economic success. More than two million African-born members living among us already send more money annually to the mother continent than the total of U.S. government aid to Africa. The same is true for Haitian migrants living in the U.S. who show the highest rate for remittances returned to their homeland each year.

We have examples of what we could be, should be, and shall be doing everywhere we look. Our vision of this *massively transforming purpose* is so powerful that everywhere we look, we see opportunity. Problems serve as challenges, each of which is another arena wherein we can display our immense creativity, resourcefulness and discipline. The very course of history is serving us up a great opportunity to enjoy our appointment with destiny which will transform the world for centuries to come—this crossroads is less than 35 years away.

Learning all that we have learned during this course of study, each of us should, at this point, be *fired up and ready to go!* If I have engaged this intellectual exercise correctly, your special talents, skills, life mission and commitment to purposeful engagement should have kicked into high gear by now. With all sincerity, I can declare with absolute authenticity that I was born to produce this book as a tour-de-force ("an impressive performance or achievement that has been accomplished or managed with great skill"); *The Repairing* is my masterpiece – my Magnum Opus.

Our magnificent journey upward, rising from the humiliation of the Maafa, has commenced. This is going to be a truly historic and awesome voyage. Let us sail on, sail on, sail on as our Great Ancestors have instructed us. Africa Rising is the wind that fills our sails and an African global empire is the only thing that can satisfy such desires.

Chapter 17 – The End of Maafa – A Futurist Projection

There is in this world no such force as the force of a person determined to rise. The human soul cannot be permanently chained. – W.E.B. DuBois

---

Close your eyes and still the mind for a moment in dedication to the enduring spirit of our Great African Ancestors. Within our very Being, They and We are One. As such, we can still feel much pain and suffering from the past. Our DNA has been bathed in an ocean of blood, sweat and tears shed as we were torn from our mothers' breasts, our native villages, loved ones and everything that we held dear. Our libations bind us together across the trans-Atlantic journey and to countless generations of lives whose dreams were crushed and nearly erased by the terror of *The Maafa – The Great Suffering* of enslavement. Here, today, we can now raise our heads with pride, self-esteem and dignity. Yet, we will forever remember the Ancestors' great sacrifices on our behalf as we offer them *Ashé* – **May your hearts have been judged as light as a feather in the great Hall of Ma'at.**

Today we turn toward and step firmly into a corrective future. The term **futurist** applies to visionary leaders, innovators, thinkers, writers, consultants, presenters and others who "look to the future" and just as frequently to those who "provide analysis of the future" via such methods as visioning, intuition, analogy, argument, logic, planning, policy analysis, cultural criticism, strategy development, marketing, road mapping, goal setting, forecasting, modeling, statistics, trend analysis, operations research, investment, surveys, horizon scanning, scenario development, prediction, prediction analysis, prediction market development, risk analysis and management, along with other future-oriented activities.

Scientific futurism includes formal disciplines involving demographics, science and technology trends, economic patterns, geology and planetary resources, sociology and culture, politics, environment and climate change, the humanities, alternative futures analysis, health and biology, as well as trends in education and industry. Scientific futurism requires the intellectual organizing of data patterns across this spectrum of disciplines toward the aim of creating processes for traversing the future.

There is a serious identity crisis occurring among most so-called "African-Americans" where they have gotten themselves caught, trapped between historically hostile cultures, intoxicated by the illusion that this "clash of civilizations" has been settled and that all that is left to do is to negotiate accommodation and assimilation peacefully. As so many have clumsily articulated this dilemma in rhyme – Folks are "caught up in the illusion of inclusion." Too many of us have misunderstood the profoundly transformational reality that we are African people, 1.5 billion strong on this Earth.

Yet, the overwhelming majority of the 1.5 billion Africans on the planet remain overly-dependent upon unreliable partnerships. Toward the idea of transforming the image and mind state of Africa along with her scattered sons and daughters, who will be responsible for serving up the bulk of communications, news, and information about our global ethnic family in the years ahead and by 2050 when more than two of every nine people on the planet are of direct African ancestry? Least we should not take into consideration our captive condition:

> "I mean, they call it Stockholm Syndrome and post-traumatic stress disorder. And, you know, I had no free will. I had virtually no free will until I was separated from them for about two weeks." – *Patty Hurst* [the *allegedly* kidnapped heiress to the Hurst family fortune]

Who among our group will commit their lives and fortunes toward guaranteeing the integrity of Pan African media and communications to project the truth about our history and culture?

The tale of the Lion and the Hunter states: **"Until the Lion learns to write, the tale of the hunt will always reflect the glory of the Hunter."** We have either allowed or tolerated outsiders and aggressors to largely shape the public image of our people, communities, African homeland, and our global identity. During a far more stressful era than our present time, the Garvey Movement showed us the power of organized people to move in the direction of self-development when inspired to cooperate within a highly motivating and transformative vision rapidly.

Why did we ever retreat from that empowering initiative? We need to set this record straight as quickly as possible!

We have strived to convince our people to invest in our redemption; we are a noble race with a long and glorious history. Yet, when we listen closely to our people's lamentations, it can be difficult to remain convinced that they share our optimism. Even among so-called "culturally awakened" members, neutralizing this *Afro-pessimism* mindset can be a frustrating task. People will not invest in that which they are afraid of or don't understand.

A convincing barrage of data-based information has shown us that **Africa Rising** is a real phenomenon that has the potential to transform the world for the 22nd Century and beyond. Currently, most Blacks in America and around the world are not yet aware of this transforming new reality. The persistence of such ignorance puts us in danger of what W.E.B. DuBois warned of as "race suicide." [45] He wrote:

> It is doubtful if there is another group of twelve million people in the midst of a modern cultured land who are so widely inhibited and mentally confined as the American Negro. Within the colored race the philosophy of salvation has by the pressure of caste been curiously twisted and distorted.
>
> Shall they use the torch and dynamite? Shall they go North or fight it out in the South? Shall they segregate themselves even more than they are now, in states, towns, cities or sections? Shall

---

[45] W.E.B. duBois, from Black Reconstruction, cited in AN AMERICAN DILEMMA: The Negro Problem and Modern Democracy by Gunnar Myrdal, Harper Books, 1944

> they leave the country? Are they Americans or foreigners? Shall they stand and sing 'My Country 'Tis of Thee'?
>
> Shall they marry and rear children and save and buy homes, or deliberately commit race suicide?

Our primary task during this time, where we currently inhabit and with readily-available resources, is to commence building up our own and other Diaspora communities. For too long, we have allowed *The Other* to direct our living arrangements, condition our intelligence, educate our youth, control our economic affairs and to determine our fate. Our breakout moment has arrived. We know that we can, therefore we *must* strike out on a course of self-determination, sovereign and sustainable development. As a powerful global demographic, we Africans have suffered in the shadows of human progress for far too long.

The undefeatable spirit of Harriet Tubman has returned to issue us one simple instruction – **RUN!**

The evolution of world civilizations is to our advantage. Traditionally, great empires have risen upon these common pillars of accomplishment:

1. A strong base of demographic strength;
2. The ability to convert natural resources and our labor into finished products and services;
3. The growth of a robust internal commerce system;
4. Production of a surplus beyond the group's needs for foreign trade and wealth accumulation;
5. Capacity for providing security for the group and its industrial assets as well as expansion of empire;
6. Training its youth to manage and sustain the economic affairs of the group for generations.

During the greatest period of European imperial expansion, from 1600-1880, Europe's population grew by 427% while Africa's population grew by a mere 150% due to the drainage of the continent's childbearing-age population. This cumulatively denied the African continent of some 600 million humans who would have contributed to the development of

Africa for more than 400 years; *to include the current 45.7 million Afri-Amers*. Scattered throughout the globe, African labor served as the foundation for the biggest economic expansion in history.

Today the world's greatest population growth is in Sub-Saharan Africa. Combining this labor potential with immense living space and an immeasurable abundance of natural resources, Africa has now achieved the world's *greatest demographic advantage*. The largest wealth deficit in the history of the modern world is being corrected as Africans are repopulating the continent as we are simultaneously expanding means of achieving our own sustainable global empirical preeminence.

The world's economic order is rapidly shifting for the benefit of our group. Because U.S.-domiciled Africans have amassed such a broad range of acquired skills, industrial experience, and access to cutting edge technological advance, we can thus play a major role in assisting African nations in rising to their fully-developed potential. Our range of experiences includes STEM sciences, governance, security, ICT, media production, capital investing, urban planning and virtually every sector of activity within the world's most technologically-advanced industrial society.

Our immediate challenge is to conduct an accurate accounting of our range of assets and to assure that they are practically applied to the great task at hand, which we've come to know as **Africa Rising**.

We truly have advanced immensely through the eras of enslavement, through Reconstruction, Jim Crow apartheid, migration from southern lands, urbanization, civil rights struggles, domestic upheavals, and disruption. We now face **rebirth**, **revitalization** and a **renaissance** based upon a **reawakening** of a new **relationship** with an eternal African identity and **renewal** of Spirit – It appears that these **Six R's** *are* favoring *our* self-determining future.

The prolonged struggles of our Ancestors, combined with brilliant direction from our most enlightened academics, have restored to members of this Noble Race a sense of identity, group self-esteem, and purposeful meaning to uplift our confidence in our Blackness. Charged with the task of recovering a sustainable future for our posterity, we are now consolidating solid plans for growth and development.

In the years that followed the emancipation from colonial status beginning in Ghana in 1957, a steep upward trajectory of African economic growth was thwarted by the intervention of western institutions like the International Monetary Fund (IMF) and the World Bank. Seduced by their lending practices and the lure of easy money from the sale of raw commodities, many fast-growing African nations fell victim to *Structural Adjustment Programs (SAPs)*, imposed upon them by the so-called "Washington Consensus."

In more recent decades, new partnerships and technological trends have put African industries on a new course. In agribusiness, renewable energy production, growth of the consumer sector, high tech education and technology "leap-frogging," African nations are witnessing a new era of sustainable growth and investment. Across the African continent, the future looks very bright for sovereign growth.

Of the 55 nations on the African continent, Ethiopia's history is unique and remarkable for numerous reasons. As the only African nation never to have been conquered and colonized by Arabs or Europeans, today, it has become an impressive model for indigenous, self-determined industrial growth.

For more than a decade now, Ethiopia's national economy has grown at a rate ranging between 8% and 11% annually, placing it currently as the second fastest-growing nation in the world in Gross Domestic Product (GDP) per U.S. State Department data. Ethiopian Airlines is now acknowledged to be on par with competitors from the world's wealthiest nations.

More recently, Ethiopia is now manufacturing automobiles due in part to a contribution from Chinese investment. Their ambition is to become the chief supplier of autos to a rapidly-growing African population of middle-class consumers. This year a railway link will open connecting landlocked Ethiopia to a Djibouti seaport on the Red Sea accessing the Indian Ocean, further expanding Ethiopia's export capacity.

The Sixth Pillar of Empire is the ability to educate youth to receive, manage, and sustain power for the nation.

As the world is moving firmly into the *Fourth Industrial Wave*, structures which educate the populace to fit into this major paradigm shift must also need to adapt radically. Futurists are producing waves of studies and forecasts which envision how education will transform over the coming decades. What we do know is that the cutting edge of innovation will not be restricted to how public education currently serves the masses. Key questions constantly appear, for which answers are sought that have a tremendous potential impact on the world of tomorrow.

Our youth, along with older generations, must be educated, informed, enlightened, and excited about being active partners and collaborators within a broad spectrum of rapidly growing sectors within the new **Africa Rising** economic environment:

- Strategic infrastructure investment;
- Energy expansion and renewable energy development;
- Agribusiness;
- Industrial manufacturing;
- Natural resources management & tourism;
- Combating the impact of climate change;
- Import / Export;
- Culture, arts & the humanities;
- Urbanization;
- Ocean resources management for Africa's Exclusive Economic Zone.

In preparation for a heightened level of economic engagement for the centuries to come, one of the first challenges is to replace transportation facilities that were installed as part of the European colonial incursion. Much of Africa's current transportation system is decades old and more. A vast spectrum of new facilities is being planned or currently under construction:

- Modern high-speed railway lines;
- Superhighways capable of moving people and cargo across national borders at a fraction of the time it requires today;

- Seaports which can handle the immense size of modern cargo container ships;
- Airports that are sufficient to handle today's jumbo jets and the rapid expansion of airline passengers per year expected for the African population growth;
- Hospitals and universities to serve the newly-growing cities which will spring up all along the new transportation corridors;
- Urban infrastructure such as water and sewage systems, communications, office buildings, and commercial space, housing for the rapid growth of urban dwellers, and facilities to educate the world's fastest-growing youth populations.

Energy expansion across the African continent needs to grow to serve 70% of the continental population currently not connected or underserved. This is forecast to require some $3 trillion of investment over the next 35 years. Fully electrifying Africa presents another chance to leapfrog a century of slow development. Sustainable and forward-looking energy generation is highlighting Africa's advantage, to include:

- Solar power generation to supply remote communities;
- The world's greatest hydroelectric generating potential;
- Geothermal energy;
- Wind and wave power generation;
- Generating biomass energy from waste management;
- Creating alternative fuels from agricultural products;
- Cutting edge, clean and safe energy production for the future.

Agribusiness is another area for a *tremendous* expansion of our production base, Sub-Saharan economic growth, as well as one of the most important global sectors which are in transformation. There are a few areas where I strive to inform my audience to get involved:

- There is much rapid change going on in the world of "agricultural innovation systems," and African nations are well poised to be prime field laboratories for the successful implementation of these new techniques;

- The combination of large pools of youthful labor and newly emerging education systems are producing a human capacity dynamic that shows immense potential for consolidating sustainable development;

- Throughout the African world, transnational, state and local governance is in great need to adapt to the style of leadership that will properly manage this paradigm shift in global agricultural policies and market expansion; and

- The role of multi-nation participation in Regional Economic Communities (RECs) is among the key factors which will help disadvantaged nations to overcome the crippling legacy of colonial exploitation quickly.

I recently showcased data from a report from April 2016 published by the Overseas Development Institute (ODI.org) entitled **Manufacturing more than doubles in sub-Saharan Africa, despite fall in share of GDP**, which read in part:

> Manufacturing production in sub-Saharan Africa has more than doubled during the last decade, dispelling the myth the sector is in long-term decline, a new report by the Overseas Development Institute has found.
>
> The report 'Developing export-based manufacturing in sub-Saharan Africa' found while the share of manufacturing in GDP had fallen from 19% in 1975 to 11% in 2014, it had still grown faster than the global average at a rate of 3.5% annually, from $73 billion in 2005 to $157 billion in 2014.
>
> At the same time, manufacturing exports doubled from $50 billion in 2005 to more than $100 billion in 2014, while many countries have also seen an increase in Foreign Direct Investment (FDI).

The spectrum of resources that span the African continent, as well as within nations with large black populations, is immense, almost beyond belief for many of our group's members. Yet, we do face numerous development challenges for the future, some of which stem from resource abundance. Here I cite the perspective of the World Wildlife Fund's Jonathan Hobbs, who wrote:

> I do not really need to start with repeating the problems we are trying to help address. The *"paradox of plenty"* / *"resource curse"* hypothesis is now the stuff of popular science and become a cliché headline in the press whenever an article is written about the current resources boom – especially articles on Africa.
>
> From an environmental perspective one would expect that countries endowed with mineral wealth would be the leaders – not only in economic growth and poverty reduction – but also sustainable development – including environmental protection.
>
> We, of course, often observe the opposite. It is not only conflict, corruption, civil strife and poverty that characterize failing (but resource endowed) states but also environmental degradation.

Another key area within which Africans need not deceive ourselves as have others is the reality of the impact of global warming. On the contrary, we should assume a major leadership position in this critical area which will determine how the entire world cooperates to protect the integrity of Mother Nature. As one such leader stated our responsibility:

> "The African voice is there," Edith Ofwona-Adera, a senior program specialist at Canada's International Development Research Center, who manages climate change projects in Africa and attended the conference, said during a telephone interview. "But the voice of Africans needs to be at the table of the higher-level global talks in terms of scientific evidence that's being produced. Developing country researchers, including those from Africa, need to be at the forefront."
>
> The impacts of global warming vary for different regions around the world, underscoring the dire need for Africa to play a larger role in framing policies on climate change -- especially when the

> continent is the second-largest and second-most-populous in the world, Ofwona-Adera said. [46]

Due in large part to enhanced communications and transportation, as well as expanded relations with Asian partners, Africa's trade relationships are rapidly changing.

The International Monetary Fund has determined that the value of India's exports to Africa (now largely high-end consumer goods) increased by over 100 percent from 2008 to 2013 — signaling that India has now surged ahead of the United States in African trade markets. However, although they benefited from Africa's robust economic growth, India's gains do not quite compare to China's astronomical increase in exports to Africa.

The value of India's imports from Africa also grew substantially between 2008-2013—by over 80 percent—compared to the sharp decline in the value of imports from sub-Saharan Africa into the United States. The decrease in U.S. imports from Africa can be largely attributed to the development of American hydraulic oil-extraction technology (so-called *fracking*), which lessened U.S. dependence on African oil and natural gas that comprised its major imports from the continent.

Further contributing to Africa's trade potential, since the dawn of human civilization, Africa has always been a major contributor to every aspect of arts and humanities. Our pioneering work in social organization, governance, trade, mobilizing human resources, and building great public works ushered in the world's earliest development of civilization and empire. Africans have made great contributions to the advance of religion, art, sculpture, dance, theater and pageantry, fashion, jewelry-making, coinage, architecture, storytelling and music.

There is no aspect of human cultural advance that has not been touched by the creative, pioneering contributions of African civilizations.

---

[46] Climate Change In Africa: African Global Warming Role Small But Crucial To Crisis Solution, Experts Say, by Morgan Winsor, International Business Times, Jul 16, 2015

Both a benefit and challenge of rapid population growth, urbanization across the African continent, as well as throughout the Diaspora, will demand a spectrum of new solutions and management processes.

How will people live within the large number of megacities which will be emerging in the world of the future? How do we solve the challenges of electrification, living space, housing the poor, managing urban transportation systems, feeding large municipal populations, providing a spectrum of utility services and providing adequate healthcare for these burgeoning populations?

What is the role of highly-educated and skilled Afri-Amers in resolving the many urban challenges of the future? How well are we solving these problems at home?

It is forecast that the 54 members of the African Union will form a **Confederation of African States** by the year 2051, giving this proposed federation the largest offshore *Exclusive Economic Zone (EEZ)* of all nations on Earth. Management of these vast sea-based resources will demand a new generation of leadership which would be best-developed from within the African population itself.

How many families are raising their children to master sciences related to marine resource management? – these to include energy extraction, energy production, fisheries, combatting pollution, waste management, constructing shipping facilities, security, food production, and protection of fragile species. Who within our group is competent to train the next generation of African coastal resources management? Are these studies currently taking place on *any* of the 103 U.S.-based HBCU campuses?

We have many critical challenges and problems which must be seriously addressed by the global African population, to include:

- How do we best coordinate leadership for our global population of 1.5 billion, expected to expand to 2.5 billion by 2050?;
- The Tale of the Lion and the Hunter – our assuming responsibility for propagating our accurate narrative of our place in the world;

- Raising awareness of the reality and viability of the "Africa Rising" phenomenon;
- Overcoming our debilitating habit of reactive obsession with distractions, disinformation, and distortions;
- Diaspora-born Africans are on a seriously *failing* health and wellness trajectory;
- Our business enterprises must expand to match our group needs – Like other successful groups, we must produce what we consume.

A major challenge to Pan Africans of today is to maintain both an acute and sustainable awareness of our need to think, act, invest and enhance our status as a united race, 1.5 billion strong on this planet. Too many of our people, including academics and leaders, have become fixated on the horrors of the past, locked within perpetual victim status.

For some of us, the promise of the future for global African growth and development has become a primary focal point. We understand that those places where we invest most of our passions, time, intellectual engagement, and financial resources will determine in large part the return on investment (ROI) we may expect within one, two, five or more decades of committed focus.

Are we a people of a bright future or a painful past?

While most of us have by now certainly become aware of the 54-member African Union, far too few have remained up to date and aware of what is being planned to transform this affiliation over the decades ahead. **AGENDA 2063** is a bright vision for Africa's future. Let me share from the Africa Union web site, which describes this strategic blueprint to traverse Africa's future toward unification. They stated that Agenda 2063 is:

> A global strategy to optimize the use of Africa's resources for the benefits of all Africans.
>
> Aiming to encourage discussion among all stakeholders, AGENDA 2063 is an approach to how the continent should effectively learn from the lessons of the past, build on the progress now underway

and strategically exploit all possible opportunities available in the short, medium and long term, so as to ensure positive socioeconomic transformation within the next 50 years.

Imagine what the world will look like in another 40 to 100 years if current trends continue along the same trajectory.

For far too many of us, the imagined vision is that of continued domination by oppressive forces whose sole intention is to keep their boots upon our necks.

For others of us with a *futurist* outlook, the vision is of a powerful and influential **Global African Empire**, inspired by its greatest historical models, charged with the energy of the world's greatest human and natural resource base, and fixated upon a future where the current trend of **Africa Rising** will have been consolidated to the point of declaring the achievement of **The African Century** for the benefit of our posterity.

We have solutions that have been explored in detail within the four previous books on Pan African economic development that I've authored since 2000. In composing these offerings, I have built a vast library of books, research reports and other material on topics of future studies, exponential technologies, global trade, infrastructure investment, transnational issues, politics, sustainability and Pan African economics.

I hope that these materials will best serve an emerging leadership toward equipping them with the right knowledge and information to become better competitors for our future global positioning. I encourage people to go to one of my web sites to see what we are doing – go to AfricaDestiny.com and look for such solutions.

As part of a spectrum of immediate calls-to-action, I offer the following short but critical reading list, specific to Pan African development, which highlights the following seven must-read books:

1. BLACK AFRICA: The Economic and Cultural Basis for a Federated State – Cheikh Anta Diop;

2. EBOLA, AMERICA & THE NEW SCRAMBLE FOR AFRICA – Keidi Awadu;
3. THE ROAD TO POWER: Seven Steps to an African Global Order – Keidi Awadu;
4. THE CLASH OF CIVILIZATIONS: and the Remaking of World Order – Samuel P. Huntington;
5. THE NEW HARVEST: Innovation in African Agriculture – Calestous Juma;
6. CHINA'S SECOND CONTINENT: How a Million Migrants are Building a New Empire in Africa – Howard French;
7. THE NEXT AFRICA: An Emerging Continent Becomes a Global Powerhouse – Jake Bright and Aubrey Hruby.
8. THE FASTEST BILLION: The Story Behind Africa's Economic Revolution – Charles Robertson.
9. THE BLACKEST SOIL: Africa Can Feed the World – Keidi Awadu (March 2020 publication date)

As well, PLEASE start listening to my daily broadcast on our Internet radio and IPTV network. Check out LIBRadio.com or LIBTV.com for daily programming featuring transformative strategies and cutting-edge research to serve an emerging leadership.

I'll close this book with an excerpt from my visionary book from 2000, **THE ROAD TO POWER – SEVEN STEPS TO AN AFRICAN GLOBAL ORDER**. In the final chapter, entitled *The World is Mine*, I shared an extended manifesto which included the following:

> Great people build and do not destroy. Great people project their youth into the future as empowered, bound to the traditions of their community, and valuing of those things which please the elders. Great people educate their own young people in their culture, their spirituality, their language, their traditions, their

history, their values, and the inherent logic which is common among the group.

Great people do not allow themselves to degrade into decadence and self-destruction. Great people realize that history is a continuum and thus do not waste years pursuing those things that mean nothing to their posterity. Great people are not easily distracted by trivial and non-productive affairs or activities.

We are a Great People.

Afterword

I composed this brief addendum one week after the completion of the 2016 national elections with the stunning upset of the "dark horse" candidate Donald Trump over the media favorite Hillary Clinton. While I did my best to stay aloof from the election as it had deteriorated past the point of what many of us maintain as the standard of civilized engagement, there are some significant impacts on the national psyche that have become evident in the days that have passed. Post-election stresses have exposed cracks in the foundation of American society in many areas. Large protest rallies against President-elect Trump have taken place in cities across the country. The corporate media led the nation astray in not being able to detect that the level of grievance felt across the populace was as close to revolt as the Trump victory indicates. Now those same media outlets are wringing their hands in endless post-race analysis about what this means to the nation – why should we pay attention to them this week when they got it so wrong the weeks and months before the election?

Leading up to this divisive election, I consistently pointed out our need to have a strong strategic plan and to stick to the plan despite any outcome. Toward the aim of reinforcing this instruction, my daily radio broadcasts have focused upon such planning as well as refining the leadership which will be needed to orchestrate such a master blueprint. I created and shared the following 10 points for post-election focus, each with just a few suggestions for specifics that will contribute to each focal point. I trust you will find this practical and easy to engage.

The "What Next" Check List (An Action Agenda)

1. **Get your health straight**
   a. Read and study daily on health improvement.
   b. Cut out that stuff that you already know is bad for you.
   c. Smoking, drinking, and eating excessive sugar for the holidays is bad.
   d. Reduce your weight with the technique known as caloric restriction.

2. **Decrease unnecessary consumer spending**
    a. Make a list of critical and non-critical holiday spending.
    b. Don't waste money with spontaneous purchases.
    c. Cut back on total spending 10% from last year's holiday budget.
    d. Buy nonfiction books, DIY kits, and other creative holiday gifts.

3. **Eliminate debt and interest payments**
    a. Do not use credit cards for gift giving.
    b. Increase paying down on existing debt.
    c. Take another look at your credit interest rates and knock out the highest ones.
    d. Learn to live without credit / Take a year-long holiday from new debt.

4. **Declutter your life**
    a. Start with your kitchen - throw out all junk and unhealthy foods.
    b. Get rid of stuff you haven't even seen or used in over a decade.
    c. Downsize your old clothing.
    d. Make sure your office is not filled with unnecessary stacks of work.

5. **Get a passport and learn a new language**
    a. Stop procrastinating and get ready for the worst inevitability that you may have to leave the country.
    b. Pick one or more countries of interest and do deep research on them.
    c. Travel outside of the country at least once every year or two.
    d. Learn to speak Spanish, French, Portuguese, Chinese, as well as at least one African language.

6. **Refocus your information flow and research**
    a. Detach your focus from the divisiveness of domestic politics.
    b. Hone your mastery in one or more critical areas of life (education, economics, health, community organizing, security, etc.).
    c. Learn to vet information for its value as true or otherwise.
    d. Look closely at the behind-the-scenes of financial markets, real estate, wealth development, industry, and sovereign development.

7. **Join or form an action coalition**
    a. Find and join a study group or community development organization.

b. Support at least one NGO that is legitimately engaged in development.
c. Bring together associates at your home once a month to focus on mutual interests.
d. Use your social media contacts to promote community-building actions.

8. Identify family-held land and development investments

a. Create a written list of telephone numbers of extended family.
b. Who in the family has responsibility for retaining inherited land?
c. How can unused farmland within the family be restored to productivity?
d. Each family should have a means of collective savings for acquiring land, paying taxes, and upkeep.

9. Become increasingly transnational

a. Pay attention to the news that affects our global population.
b. Stay aware of government plans that affect development and security within countries of our mutual heritage.
c. Celebrate national holidays and traditions that relate to our global population.
d. Tune into news, Internet broadcasts, and online news sites which focus beyond the borders of this country.

10. Make detailed plans and stick to your plans

a. What is your massive transformative purpose in life?
b. Write your short term, midterm, and long term plans down.
c. Wake up early daily and make a list of priorities for the day.
d. Keep a journal or other writings to measure your seasonal progress.

I hope and trust that you will find this checklist handy. I intend it to be a motivating stimulant to aid you in your planning for the future that you truly desire. Let's be clear about this simple rule:

"If we do not have a plan for action, and action for our plan, then we are doomed to reacting to what others do." – *Keidi Awadu*

Bibliography

1. THE PHILOSOPHY AND OPINIONS OF MARCUS GARVEY, Or, Africa for the Africans – Marcus Garvey / Edited by Amy Jacques Garvey

2. BLACK AFRICA: The Economic and Cultural Basis for a Federated State – Cheikh Anta Diop

3. Rap, Hip Hop and the New World Order – Keidi Obi Awadu

4. EXPONENTIAL ORGANIZATIONS: Why new organizations are ten times better, faster, and cheaper than yours (and what to do about it) – Salim Ismael

5. ABUNDANCE: The Future is Better Than You Think – Peter Diamandis & Steven Kotler

6. BOLD: How to Go Big, Create Wealth and Impact the World – Peter Diamandis & Steven Kotler

7. KUJICHAGULIA VILLAGES: A Practical Plan for Self-Determination – Keidi Obi Awadu

8. LIVING SUPERFOOD LONGEVITY: Mastering the Possibilities of High-Quality Life Extension – Keidi Obi Awadu

9. THE NEW HARVEST: Agricultural Innovation in Africa – Dr. Calestous Juma

10. THE NEXT AFRICA: An Emerging Continent Becomes a Global Powerhouse – Jake Bright and Aubrey Hruby

11. CHINA'S SECOND CONTINENT: How a Million Migrants Are Building a New Empire in Africa – Howard W. French

12. THE EVOLUTION OF CIVILIZATIONS: An Introduction to Historical Analysis – Carroll Quigley

13. THE CLASH OF CIVILIZATIONS AND THE REMAKING OF WORLD ORDER – Samuel P. Huntington

14. TRIBES: How Race, Religion, and Identity Determine Success in the New Global Economy – Joel Kotkin

15. MOVING BEYOND RACE-ISM: New Strategies for a New Millennium – Keidi Obi Awadu

16. NOTES FOR AN AFRICAN WORLD REVOLUTION: Africans at the Crossroads – Dr. John Henrik Clarke

17. HONORING PROFESSOR WILLIAM LEO HANSBERRY (1894-1965): An Intellectual Libation For The Architect Of America's African Studies Department – Kaba Hiawatha Kamene

18. The Hidden Persuaders – Vance Packard

19. MARKETING 3.0: From Products to Customers to the Human Spirit – Philip Kotler, Hermawan Kartajaya and Iwan Setiawan

20. TOWARD BLACK COMMUNTIY DEVELOPMENT: Moving Beyond the Limitations of the Lecture Model – Professor Manu Ampim

21. EXCESSIVE FORCE: Power, Politics and Population Control – Information Project For Africa

22. THE SMARTEST PLACES ON EARTH: Why Rustbelts Are the Emerging Hotspots of Global Innovation – Antoine van Agtmael and Fred Bakker, 2016

23. SHOULD AMERICA PAY? Slavery and the Raging Debate on Reparations – Edited by Raymond A. Winbush, PhD

Index

Made in the USA
Monee, IL
04 November 2026

67391571R00177